# SPERANZA

# SPERANZA

## HOW PAIN BECAME THE PATH TO HOPE

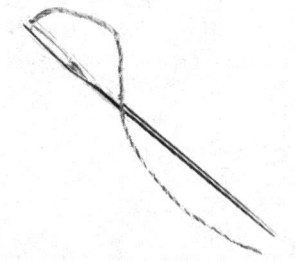

## ASHLEY ONDRICK

FOREWORD BY KELLY K. McCANN, MD, MPH

*Speranza: How Pain Became the Path to Hope*
Copyright © 2026 by Ashley Ondrick

All rights reserved. No part of this publication may be reproduced, stored in a retrieval system, or transmitted in any form by any means, electronic, mechanical, photocopy, recording, or otherwise, without the prior permission of the publisher, except as provided by USA copyright law.

No patent liability is assumed with respect to the use of the information contained herein. Although every precaution has been taken in the preparation of this book, the publisher and author assume no responsibility for errors or omissions. Neither is any liability assumed for damages resulting from the use of the information contained herein. This book is intended for informational purposes only. It is not intended to be used for the sole basis for medical or health decisions, nor should it be construed as advice designed to meet the particular needs of an individual's situation.

Some names and identifying details have been changed to protect the privacy of individuals.

Unless otherwise indicated, all Scripture quotations are taken from the Holy Bible, New Living Translation, copyright © 1996, 2004, 2015 by Tyndale House Foundation. Used by permission of Tyndale House Publishers, Carol Stream, Illinois 60188. All rights reserved.

Scripture quotations marked MSG are taken from The Message, copyright © 1993, 2002, 2018 by Eugene H. Peterson. Used by permission of NavPress. All rights reserved. Represented by Tyndale House Publishers.

Scripture quotations marked NIV are taken from The Holy Bible, New International Version® Copyright © 1973, 1978, 1984, 2011 by Biblica, Inc. Used with permission. All rights reserved worldwide.

Published by Forefront Books, Nashville, Tennessee.
Distributed by Simon & Schuster.

Library of Congress Control Number: 2025927530

Print ISBN: 978-1-63763-538-4
E-book ISBN: 978-1-63763-539-1

Cover Design by Mary Susan Oleson, Blu Design Concepts
Interior Design by Mary Susan Oleson, Blu Design Concepts

Printed in the United States of America
26 27 28 29 30 31 RR4 10 9 8 7 6 5 4 3 2 1

FOR THOSE GRASPING to find purpose in a life that hasn't gone the way you planned. For those desperately trying to fill an emptiness inside. For those who think you could disappear, and no one would notice. For those who feel broken beyond repair and wonder if you'll ever be made whole. For those who feel the weight of the world on your shoulders. For those exhausted from the fight. I see you—and this book is for you. Don't lose hope. *Speranza.*

# CONTENTS

Dedication .................................................................................. 5

Foreword .................................................................................... 9

Preface ...................................................................................... 15

One: The Kentucky Derby of Cooking ................................. 21

Two: Sowing the Seed ............................................................. 29

Three: Where Are Your Organs? ............................................ 43

Four: Fresh Ink of Agony ....................................................... 51

Five: The Depths of Grace ..................................................... 63

Six: That's *Amore* .................................................................... 71

Seven: Teach a Man to Fish ................................................... 79

Eight: The Learning Curve of Pain ...................................... 89

Nine: Waves of Grief .............................................................. 95

Ten: Kitchen Confidential ................................................... 101

Eleven: *The Stagista Chronicles* ........................................... 115

Twelve: Fingertip Salad ........................................................ 137

Thirteen: Gigs and Giggles .................................................. 145

Fourteen: Pacific Oceans ..................................................... 155

Fifteen: All the Single Ladies .............................................. 161

Sixteen: Beautifully Broken ................................................ 179

Seventeen: Thank You, Ang Babait Ninyo ........................ 193

Eighteen: Somebody Feed the Females ............................. 207

Nineteen: Summer of Spritz ............................................... 223

| | |
|---|---|
| TWENTY: Tick, Tick, Boom | 239 |
| TWENTY-ONE: Bobblehead Barbie | 251 |
| TWENTY-TWO: Stroke of Genius | 263 |
| TWENTY-THREE: Hail Mary | 275 |
| TWENTY-FOUR: Providence | 285 |
| TWENTY-FIVE: The Good Doctor | 293 |
| TWENTY-SIX: Squid Games | 307 |
| TWENTY-SEVEN: From Surgery to Savasana | 321 |
| TWENTY-EIGHT: Washing Off the War Paint | 341 |
| TWENTY-NINE: Untethered Heart | 351 |
| EPILOGUE | 371 |
| ACKNOWLEDGMENTS | 373 |
| NOTES | 377 |
| ABOUT THE AUTHOR | 379 |

# FOREWORD
## By Kelly K. McCann, MD, MPH

---

I FIRST MET Ashley Ondrick through her writing. Unlike most new patients who share a few paragraphs or pages of their story, Ashley's medical history was fifteen pages, single-spaced! As I read the intense and painful details of her many surgeries and years of unrelenting pain, my admiration for her tenacity grew. Threaded through her story were glimmers of hope and clarity. These were moments of fierce resilience that stood out amid both her suffering and the joy she found through cooking.

By the end of reading her history intake form, I felt awe and trepidation. How could I help this young woman who had endured so much, whose body had undergone so many surgeries, who had already seen dozens of other skilled practitioners, and who had spent years in excruciating pain? Wow. What an incredible human being! I couldn't wait to meet her. I took a deep breath and reminded myself that I didn't have to know all the answers, I simply needed to be present and trust that, together, we would uncover her path.

## FOREWORD

What I didn't know then was that Ashley had sought me out not only for my medical expertise, but for the soul-level work I was just beginning to bring into the world. Nor did I know that she would be as much a catalyst in my journey as I would be in hers.

In our first appointment, her trauma and pain were nearly hidden beneath the surface and I experienced an intelligent, thoughtful, and compassionate young woman. In subsequent visits to California, she would schedule week-long intensives so we could address her many questions and concerns. During those times, our conversation began to explore deeper layers of her beliefs, her inner narrative, and the stories she told herself about who she was. I encouraged her to question those accounts, to reframe the thoughts, and to release ideas that no longer served her. She approached every suggestion with openness and curiosity, diligently peeling back each layer. She listened to the podcasts I recommend and committed wholeheartedly to herself and to this deeper inquiry.

Over time, our relationship grew beyond doctor and patient into friendship. We shared a love of food and the healing power of nutrition. One occasion, we met at a local farmer's market, fawning over the vibrant and colorful produce! On another trip, she cooked dinner for my family—a beautiful gesture that spoke to her generous spirit.

When hurricanes were ravaging western Florida and she was unable to return home after another visit, she called me, slightly panicked, and told me that the Airbnb she'd rented was moldy. Guided by my intuition, I invited her to stay with me and my family. As we cooked together—well, truthfully, she cooked and I chopped vegetables—I asked her to consider being interviewed for a book I was working on. It's a collection of transformational stories from

# FOREWORD

patients at the Spring Center. That conversation led to an interview with me and my writing coach, which then became the spark that ignited this book—the story you now hold in your hands.

I have the privilege of caring for many people with complex, chronic illnesses whose symptoms bewilder their doctors, frighten their families, and bring many patients to their knees. They come to me in pain, frustrated and fearful from years of gaslighting, but with a quiet flicker of hope that maybe, finally, they've found someone who will truly listen and help guide them to a better place.

As a physician practicing functional, integrative, and environmental medicine with specialties in mast cell activation syndrome (MCAS), mold and mycotoxin illness, and Lyme disease, and with a master's in spiritual psychology, I believe that we are spiritual beings having a human experience. Our bodies, our intuition, and our connection to our purpose are intricately linked. When physical symptoms arise, they are not betrayals; they are messages. Yet many people, like Ashley once did, view their body as the enemy—something to suppress, ignore, or conquer.

Ashley's determination to live fully, despite her body's hypermobile fragility, is awe-inspiring. Where others might have succumbed to despair or victimhood, Ashley kept seeking light, led by her passion for cooking, her intellectual commitment to microfinance, her devotion to service, and her deep care for others. But sometimes, the very drive that keeps us going—the willpower to push through—can also prevent us from surrendering to what true healing requires.

In functional medicine, we search for root causes: the toxins, the infections, the exposures. For Ashley, parasites, mold, and Lyme disease all played roles in weakening her connective tissue and inflaming her system. But what made her body so vulnerable in the first place? I came to see that the deeper dysfunction lay in her disconnection from her true self, from the divine, from the quiet voice inside. Ashley's healing required not just treating the infections, removing the mold, or repairing the structure, but in her reconnection with what she calls God, and with what I might describe as Spirit, Higher Self, or Life Force. Whatever name we choose, it points to the same truth: We are part of something greater.

Every human being carries that spark of divinity inside. It's the whisper that urges us forward when we feel lost. We are born with it fully intact—just look at a toddler's joy and curiosity. Then, life's early wounds cause us to forget this spark. Experiences make us feel unsafe, unseen, or unworthy, and sever us from that innate connection. In that forgetting, we lose sight of who we really are.

The irony is that we must sometimes lose ourselves to find ourselves again. As humans, we rarely grow when things are easy, rather we learn best through adversity. Illness, pain, and crisis become the curriculum for awakening. Physical suffering forces us to listen to what we would otherwise turn away from. I often say that those with chronic conditions are on the fast track to spiritual growth, because their bodies refuse to let them ignore what wants to be healed.

There is no pill or protocol that can restore this connection. Medical treatments are crucial—they stabilize the body and create space for the deeper work—but healing ultimately unfolds when we begin to listen to the body's language.

Each symptom carries meaning. The path to healing is to discover the language of your body. For example, Ashley's struggles to speak her truth and to hold clear boundaries for herself could have manifested through her thyroid, located over her voice box. Her belief she wasn't wanted could have contributed to the collapse and

## FOREWORD

degeneration of her spine, the literal support structure of her body. The calcified, herniated "stone in her heart" is a metaphor made flesh, and its surgical removal opened her heart not just physically, but spiritually, to love—her own and God's.

Symptoms reveal where misbeliefs have taken root. As we identify and release them, the body's messages soften, and clarity emerges. We begin to remember. We remember that we are not broken. We remember that love and belonging are our birthrights.

Ashley's story is both singular and universal. Through pain, she found her way back to herself, to faith, to love, and to a life guided by Spirit rather than fear. She began to see her symptoms not as punishments but as teachers. She replaced frustration with compassion, and in doing so, transformed not only her health but her entire being.

Her journey stands as a beacon for anyone who feels lost, dismissed, or disconnected—from their body, their truth, or their purpose.

Life is a school, and each of us is given our own curriculum. The lessons differ, but the objective is the same: to remember who we are. To honor the body as a wise messenger. To cultivate curiosity, compassion, and connection. And to unforget all that no longer serves us, so that we can return to the deep, abiding connection that was never truly gone, just forgotten, and find our way home to our wholeness, love, joy, and purpose.

*Kelly K. McCann, MD, MPH*

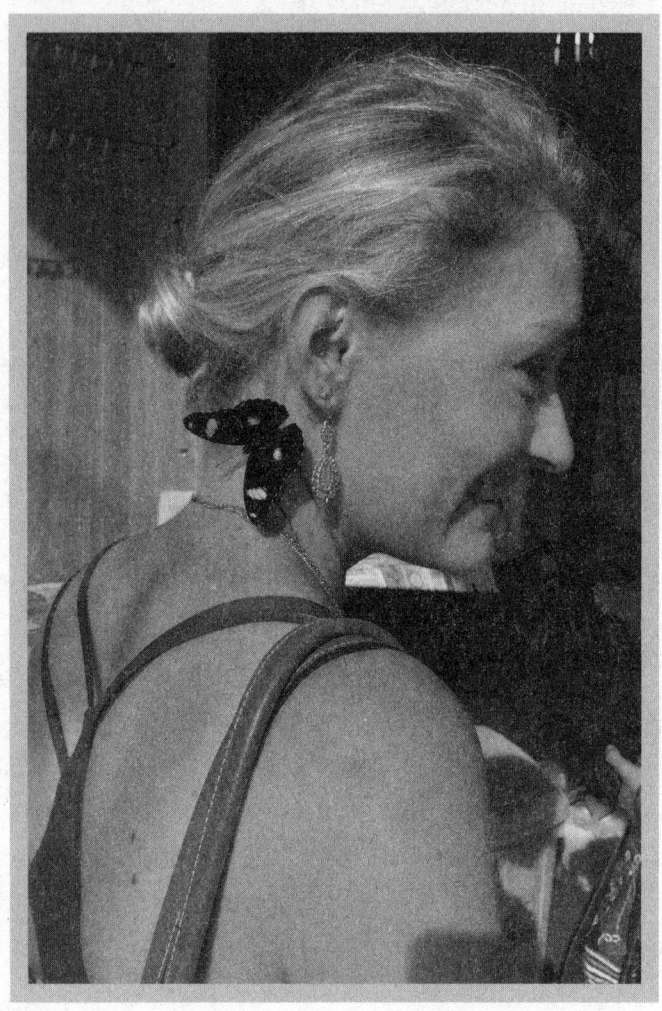
*Butterfly kisses in Davao, Phillipines*

# PREFACE

To my younger self . . .

> *There's another way—a beautiful and compassionate way—to look at yourself, at life, at the world, my sweet, sensitive soul. You're built differently than most, but that's not something to punish yourself for—it's a gift. Your ability to feel so deeply, which has at times brought profound darkness to your life, will prove to be what lights the path toward freedom for you and for others. This pain you see as a conquest is really a cry for help—your body's desperate plea to pause and rest from assault and burnout. Your pain is also a gift, because in your quest to break free from its grip, you'll expose the lies you've believed as truth. Lies that have caused you to live in bondage for far too long. At one time you used your pain to find worth, to feel seen, to grasp for control, to grapple with brokenness, and to search for love, but after unraveling its many layers, you will emerge the butterfly you were created to be.*

# PREFACE

*And you were created—not by accident or mistake—but by a God who spoke every intentional detail of this earth into being. By a God who imagined into existence resplendent skies and butterflies' wings, and who, with a breath, forged the majestic landscapes that will one day awaken your heart. By a God who made multitudes to mirror his creative image while exerting their own will—revolutionaries, inventors, artists, scholars, saints, and all those in between. By a God whose world wasn't complete without you in it. His purpose? To pour his radical love into your uniquely radiant soul until it spilled over into the world.*

*You've tried so hard to hold it all together and are fiercely tough and oh so brave, utilizing survival traits forged in a world where vulnerability didn't feel safe. You've been fighting for so long—do you even remember what life was like before the war began? In earnest, you've carried the weight of generations on your back despite the constant threat of rupture. Let it break. That exterior you've tried so hard to make impenetrable, once fractured, will let divine love seep in, and with it, new life. Supernatural peace will displace the fear that's had a chokehold on you, and it will anchor you through storm-tossed seas. It's in that chaos where you will willingly dive into the deep.*

*You've spent your life judging every need, emotion, sensation, and symptom as wrong, broken, or something to be ashamed of, slipping you further and further into*

## PREFACE

*darkness, dysregulation, and dis-ease. But the light will break through and expose the fault lines, and you'll see it clearly—the antidote, that is: radical self-love. Just as infants are helplessly dependent on their needs and desires being met before they can feel safe enough to fall asleep in a loving embrace, you have to meet your own primal needs with the utmost respect and care. Anchored in eternal love—in your own nurturing arms—you will experience safety. And only when you are safe will you finally heal.*

*It all comes down to love!*

I know that the experiences of our lives,
when we let God use them,
become the mysterious and
perfect preparation for the work
he will give us to do.

—Corrie Ten Boom

*Caprese bar at the farm in Ocala*

One

# THE KENTUCKY DERBY OF COOKING

---

I'M RUNNING ON a bumpy concrete path flanked by stall after stall of horses, who watch unapologetically as I dodge streams of urine and piles of hay mixed with God knows what, while periodically jumping over sand pits and holding on to large platters of food with a death grip. It feels more like I'm competing in *America Ninja Warrior* than completing a typical day at work. My longtime client Jen recently bought a horse farm in Ocala, Florida, about two hours north of my usual stomping grounds of Tampa Bay. The property is still being renovated, and the only functional kitchen is inside a small apartment on the back side of the stables. I hear the guests gathering in the family estate at the property's entrance—fifty equestrian enthusiasts who have come from all over the world for event season. I've set out a sprawling caprese bar on a rustic wood table, showcasing the late-summer bounty of juicy heirloom tomatoes and peaches, and a vibrant bruschetta made with cherries. Paired with fresh mozzarella and burrata, arugula and pesto, an assortment of olive oils, balsamic vinegars, and sea salts, and served with an abundance of homemade focaccia, the spread is hardy enough to act as the main course. Today it's just a part of the show. Creating beautiful, bountiful spreads of food is one of the best parts of my job as a private chef—and one of my favorite things to do in life—although the hours leading up to its completion are, without fail, a frantic race to the finish line. Not wanting the food to sit out any longer than necessary, most everything needs to be cut, plattered, and served at the very last moment, then decorated with a few perfectly positioned garnishes that make it pop. One of the first things I learned when starting out as a catering chef well over a decade ago was that people eat with their eyes before any other senses. A primary rule of catering is: Even if it doesn't taste good, make it look good (although my food always tastes as good as it looks). Another obvious rule of catering is: Don't kill anyone, and, of course, don't be late.

I've crammed two large foil pans into the oven—one containing about fifty Italian sausage links, and the other holding an equal amount of chicken piccata. Pasta is boiling in a six-gallon pot of water on the electric stove next to a vat of one hundred meatballs gently simmering in marinara. The swirling steam sweeps my thoughts back to Italy—to days spent in the kitchen with Franca and Grazia as they braised beef cheeks and blanched broccoli rabe in a similar industrial manner. I can almost smell Anna's bread coming out of the oven when my daydream is interrupted by the sound of an approaching engine. Jen's sister, Natalie, who has a knack for coming to my rescue right on cue, pulls up driving a Gator, just as I am

# THE KENTUCKY DERBY OF COOKING

*Apple spice cake at the farm in Ocala*

about to start hauling each pan of food through the equine obstacle course. She helps load the pans, then chauffeurs me to the awaiting chafing dishes. I usually display my food much more attractively than these clunky metal troughs, but today I'm grateful that their lids are shielding the food from the swarms of flies. We are on a farm, after all! I hoof it back toward the kitchen to start on dessert, and as I turn my head from side to side, admiring the horses' striking features, I think to myself, *Next time I'm here I won't be able to turn my head.*

In a matter of days, I'm having yet another life-altering surgery—the fusion of my skull base to my cervical spine—and I will lose much of my ability to move my neck. Jen has hired me to cook for a one-hundred-person engagement party three months from now, and I'm compiling mental notes on how I'm going to execute that job as seamlessly and as efficiently as possible. I'm also picturing what it's going to feel like doing it in my new body. I have some trepidation as I wonder things such as, *What if I crash the Gator because I can't look both ways at an intersection?* Mostly, though, I'm envisioning running through those horse stalls with the same vitality as their inhabitants, and without the ever-present pain, headache, blurred vision, dizziness, nausea, air hunger, racing heart, brain fog, tinnitus, and the many other symptoms I've lived with every moment for the interminable past five years.

I cut giant pans of apple spice cake into precise two-inch squares, piping a swirl of whipped cream on top, and finishing each slice with a drizzle of salted caramel and a freeze-dried apple chip. Once dessert is served, I load up my SUV with my coolers and gear, then meticulously clean the kitchen, as another rule of catering is that you should always leave a kitchen cleaner than you found it, and I start the two-hour drive home. It doesn't take long for the

# THE KENTUCKY DERBY OF COOKING

*Building a salad for a dinner party in Tampa*

adrenaline to wane and for pain and fatigue to set in, but I barely notice, lost in my excitement, awe, and gratitude.

Every day is a tug-of-war between my desire to live a full life and work to the best of my ability in a job that utilizes so many of my talents, versus the reality of what my body actually allows, which lately hasn't been much. But God and I have this arrangement, and so far he's come through every time. Always, in the days of prepping for an event, my symptoms threaten to crush me at every turn, and I collapse in agony as evening approaches. But as I keep praying for strength and endurance, God keeps on providing it. When the big day arrives, without fail, the storm clouds of pain and weariness clear, and rays of sunshine warm my skin, putting a spring in my step and joy in my heart as I go about my work.

It will take days for my body to recover to "baseline shitty," as a friend and I often joke, but I will remember the strength and stamina God gave me, and the prayer he answered so I could get through the day and feel well enough to truly enjoy it. I will remember my excitement in every sprig and flourish, every detail and garnish, and this practice of remembering will give me assurance that he will show up next time too. I remember my past—not to get stuck in it, but to learn from it; not as the victim, but as the victor.

*Family party at my grandparent's house in Cape Cod*

Two

# SOWING THE SEED

STANDING PROUD and tall in the center of our living room—the orange shag carpet tickling my feet and the sun warming my back as it streamed through the windows—I had an audience of one. My mom, with her gorgeous golden curls and trademark teal eye shadow, sat on the beige leather couch in front of me. I had always loved performing, and as a young child I held the misguided belief that school was one big show. My older brothers have ten and eleven years on me, while my sister has six, and it seemed that every time I visited their school, it was to watch them in a play or concert. I couldn't wait for the day when I stood on that stage. Soon enough, I was taking the lead in church and school performances and proudly bringing home blue ribbons from the regional school Speech Meet for the poems I recited impeccably.

My seventh-grade teacher assigned students to take turns leading the class in a morning devotional, and I chose a tearjerker from *Chicken Soup for the Soul*—arguably one of the most revealing glimpses into the human spirit ever printed. I don't remember much of the story, only that it had to do with a child being sick, family members fervently praying over her, and likely a miraculous recovery. Always the overachieving perfectionist, I stood in our living room the day before and practiced reading it aloud to my mom.

Every parent says things they wish they could take back, including my mom, who, partway through my performance, stopped me and said, "You were almost a failure-to-thrive infant, and we didn't know if you were going to make it. I wasn't supposed to get pregnant with you. Three kids was enough, and I had an IUD! Your dad's anger and frustration made my pregnancy an extremely stressful time, and you were born very sick because of it."

The shag carpet under my feet suddenly felt like quicksand, exposing the true foundation of my life. *I wasn't wanted? Dad was mad about my birth? That's why I was sick? Do they want me now? Am I a burden? And if so, will I always be one?* A storm of emotions blurred my thoughts. All I recall saying was, "Um, what's an IUD?" Had I instead asked these other questions, my mom would have quickly recovered from her fumble, assuring me that when she and my dad brought their little pink bundle home to my awaiting siblings, pure joy superseded everything else from that day forward. But because I didn't say much, my mom didn't think her comments affected me. The growing habit of stifling my voice and emotions was as damaging as any vice I'd later come to use.

One misbelief shaped my entire life.

My mom went on to explain that I was born with a zinc deficiency and, through the recommendation of a naturopathic doctor, I lived on carrot juice for a year of my young life. This explained a lot. I didn't have a carrot top or orange skin, but I recalled how often I was sick. I got frequent acidosis from eating either too much sugar or overly rich foods, and I threw up every time I ate birthday cake, pizza, or the occasional KFC when my cousin came to visit from Martha's Vineyard. In grade school, I had a cough for over a year, finally attributed to allergies. After many arm pricks, a list of food and environmental triggers to avoid was revealed.

Mold was one of the worst offenders. We had a lake house, which my dad built as a kid with his father. They used recycled materials from a school my grandfather was demolishing. I slept on the top bunk with my face about one foot from the ceiling, listening to mice scurry above the insulation and waiting for the time when one finally chewed its way through and landed on top of me. The air was dense with the smell of mildew, and I'd often wake up in the middle of the night unable to breathe, wheezing and coughing until my throat opened back up and I could suck in some air. My allergist explained that the body is like a bucket left out in the rain, and offenses build up like raindrops until the bucket overflows, causing symptoms. Much later in life, I'd come to see that repressing emotions works much the same way.

In my classroom the next morning, attempting to read the devotional I'd flawlessly read to my mom the day before, the news of my unwantedness hit me like a sucker punch. My chest felt as if an elephant was sitting on it, my heart raced, and I was so short of breath I could barely eke out each word. *What is happening to me?* I couldn't bring myself to go on, ending where my mom dropped the bombshell on me. I stopped reading before the child in the story miraculously healed or died, almost as if knowing would determine my own fate.

Especially in the young, formative years, perception is reality, and the way I interpreted many of the experiences of my childhood shaped my subconscious mind. As I grew older—and wiser—I thought my rational mind was driving my thinking, but my subconscious—and the pain and beauty that shaped it—were the real masterminds. This realization became a huge piece in my healing as an adult.

I spent my days as a free-range child, biking around our small town for hours on end without anyone knowing my whereabouts, climbing high into pine trees, catching amphibians, and building elaborate homes for them. I had a basement "laboratory" where I made Creepy Crawlers—insects I created by piping colored gel into metal molds and baking them in a small oven, all the while inhaling the melting plastic fumes. Another (less-than healthy) '90s favorite was my Easy Bake Oven, which I'd use before artistically decorating the miniature cakes and serving them to my family for dessert. I also formed detailed figurines out of clay and never went anywhere without a sketch pad and pencil. I built igloos in giant snow piles my dad formed with a bulldozer after a blizzard, and my sister and I loved pretending we were Olympic skaters on the ice rink my dad made by flooding our backyard with a garden hose. My snow-day favorite was when my mom poured boiled maple syrup over cold snow, transforming it into sweet, chewy bliss—the perks of the long, cold, Massachusetts winters. My mom arranged piano and sewing lessons, and I proudly wore my handmade Halloween costumes and recital outfits.

My absolute happiest childhood memories revolve around the holidays, summer vacations, and other occasions when my

## SOWING THE SEED

extended family gathered together. My cousins and I put on plays—usually remakes of Disney classics, orchestrated by my sister and older cousin, Lily. Picture fourteen kids lip-syncing to the *Beauty and the Beast* soundtrack while wearing clothes from my mom's giant dress-up closet. There were platform shoes, fur scarves, curly wigs, lace blouses, feather boas, and muumuus. My Auntie MJ once laughed so hard, her convulsing body broke the leg of the wooden chair she was sitting on. Our family loved spending time together and looked for any opportunity to throw a party. Everyone put on the best version of themselves, no matter what was going on below the surface or on the real-life stage, so to speak. That was one reason I liked our gatherings so much.

Another attraction was the food. Every woman in my family was an excellent cook, and good food headlined the show. I can still see my aunts, grandma, and mom standing shoulder to shoulder in the small kitchen of our otherwise spacious house, fussing over every detail. I'd often squeeze my way in, loving the contagious excitement of watching what was coming out of the oven, before I was usually ordered to help.

I loved being part of the action, especially when tasked with slicing my Auntie Linda's pumpkin bread. It was always moist, but with a slight chewiness. And its sweetness was tempered by an intense pumpkin flavor and a balance of spices. Its perfection has ruined me from ever enjoying another pumpkin bread. As I put the slices on an oval plate adorned with a purple and green lady slipper, I nibbled any crumbs that "accidentally" appeared, knowing there would be mutiny in my family if I dared take a piece before dinner was served. My cousins and siblings were equally obsessed, and we savored each bite while fighting over the leftovers, reminding ourselves that more would be coming at another holiday soon.

My dad's nickname for my mom was Martha Stewart. "Maatha," as my dad said it, often hosted forty of us for family gatherings and graciously entertained large church and school groups with finesse and ease. I helped her set the table, arranging placemats and folding matching cloth napkins into hats, or carefully putting them through ornate napkin rings. We used the fancy glassware and china, and there were always fresh flowers on the table. I'd also write our guests' names on place cards, making them feel welcomed. My mom exuded hospitality, and I dreamed of one day having a family and home of my own where I could extend this same welcoming warmth.

My mom devoted her life to caring for our family of seven and for those who didn't have much. She cooked for five picky eaters, and, to this day, she says I was the worst, but I argue that I had the makings of a chef's highly developed palate, one which wasn't being fully satisfied at the time. She shuttled hordes of kids around in her oversized van, and one year, my dad—who never went shopping on his own—bought her magnetic racing stripes, which she felt compelled to use. Thus, I was picked up from middle and high school in a large blue van with red, orange, and yellow flames tattooed down its sides. I was royally embarrassed. After that Christmas, my sister, dad, and I took an annual holiday shopping trip for my mom—a (face-saving) tradition I always looked forward to.

My mom handled the affairs of our home and the daily ins and outs of raising five kids. To say she was spread quite thin is an understatement. I rarely saw her break from her work, except to read to me and my younger brother the adventurous tales from Beatrix Potter, *Sweet Pickles*, and *Little House on the Prairie*. She'd make up voices for each character and read with enthusiasm for about half a chapter before her eyelids got heavy and we tiptoed off to play—or more likely, fight—while she snoozed.

My dad was a pioneer in the fields of portable rock crushing and recycling contaminated soils, using the finished products in asphalt production and large-scale paving. He also donated prolifically to the community, including countless parking lots, a skate park for the Boys and Girls Club, and expansive school athletic fields. He left the house at 5 a.m. and returned just in time to shower and eat dinner with the family. He was always tired, so instead of conversation, a heavy silence usually hung over our meal. My dad then retreated to his recliner in the den, where he'd work on a lap desk, crafting replicas of his crushers out of magnetized graph paper and moving them around like puzzle pieces until they fit together most efficiently. All the while, an old John Wayne Western played in the background.

Every year, we worked together making my Soap Box Derby car, which always took home a ribbon because my dad turbo-charged it by weighing down the tires with melted pewter. A handful of times we went on weekend-long father-daughter trips with church friends, and we once took a deep-woods canoe trip in Canada, spending a week paddling to different campsites before being airlifted by pontoon plane back to where we had embarked. I learned important life skills, such as how to cook over a fire, find level ground to pitch a tent (or how to make it level), and, most importantly, how to pee in the woods! I gathered kindling wood for summer cookouts at the lake, where my dad cooked kielbasa, dozens of burgers, and hot dogs on his Weber charcoal grill, never dreaming of using lighter fluid to start the fire.

We went on hikes to forage for mushrooms and fished for

*Fishing with my dad*

trout in the bubbling brook that fed into our lake. My dad taught me to filet the little fish and hang them up by their gills on a stick, cook them in a pan, and pop the cheeks out to eat the most tender little morsels. On one occasion, a passerby told us we'd never catch anything in our fishing hole. No sooner had the words come out of his mouth, I reeled in a trout, which I promptly swung around toward this naysayer, the fish flopping on the hook just inches away from his face. My dad was so proud of me, and we laughed about it the rest of the day and every time we went fishing thereafter. I felt my dad's love in his laughter and when I made him proud, but not in the more mundane moments—and certainly not in his impatience or anger.

My dad had a hair-trigger temper. The worst of it came out behind the closed doors of our home, but it wasn't solely confined there. Without fail, every birthday, we'd choose a restaurant that wouldn't sing "Happy Birthday," and my dad would make a scene, yelling at the server as I sunk lower and lower in my chair. My birthday wish as I silently blew out my candles? The superpower of invisibility. I should have heeded the saying, "Be careful what you wish for."

On the occasional Saturday morning, my dad took me to a greasy spoon for corned beef hash and blueberry pancakes, then I'd go to work with him, where fine dust danced in the air. I left a handprint on my dad's dashboard every time I got into his pickup truck, and often, as a birthday or Father's Day gift, I cleaned it for him. Breathing that congested air filled my "little bucket" even more and eventually became another allergen my body had to fight off.

On one of these take-your-daughter-to-work days, I had to jump from the bed of a rock truck down into my dad's arms. "C'mon, Ash, just jump," he said, as his patience wore thin. I had no doubt he'd catch me, yet it felt as if someone had nailed down my feet—I was paralyzed by fear. I'm not afraid of heights, but at eight years old, I learned that I am terrified of jumping from them. *How can Dad still love me when it seems like I don't trust him to catch me? When I'm too weak and scared to jump?* Weakness was not a trait I felt my dad was proud of. He was the toughest person I'd ever known—and would ever know.

> *My little soul, your structures of safety often felt like a threat, and, at such a young age, you learned to turn to yourself for protection—appeasing, pleasing, and achieving your way into safety. But when you couldn't jump, in that loss of control, the unthinkable happened—you weren't safe in yourself either. Suddenly, it seemed like your body had betrayed you, forcing a vulnerability that exposed your weakness and fear, leaving a stain of shame. You equated weakness with being unworthy of love, and your silent vow was for survival:* I'm never showing vulnerability again.

I was afraid of everything but never told a soul. I'd hear about an illness and almost instantly worry that I'd contracted it. My dad had pneumonia, and I was convinced I had it too. My chronic cough from allergies didn't help my case. I once saw a speck of red in the toilet after I peed, and for years was terrified to look before I flushed. When I was in grade school, my dad got sick with acid reflux before it was a widely known condition. He'd choke on his rising stomach acid and have to pull the car over while we sat helplessly in the back seat. Often, when my mom would tuck me into bed and take an older sibling out for the evening, I'd force myself to stay awake, listening to my dad's breathing, fearful he was going to suffocate. Only as I heard the van pull into the driveway would I finally let myself drift off to sleep.

My grandpa died when I was five, and some of my earliest memories are glimpses of his funeral. It was an evening Catholic mass, and I can still see the priest anointing the coffin in pungent incense, the fumes looking like a genie coming out of a magic lantern. I was terrified. We lived in a hippy-type area, and every time I smelled incense in a store, I'd have flashbacks to his funeral. Around the same time, my mom's youngest brother died of a cocaine overdose. Watching the many tears she shed, I swore an oath that I'd never use drugs, especially not cocaine...

In grade school, I often went on bike rides with a group of neighborhood girlfriends. One afternoon, when two of my friends were riding, the girl in the back rode too close to the other, colliding with her tire. The sudden stop threw the girl in front, Brie, over her handlebars. Her skull cracked open on the pavement, and the impact caused her brain to shift. The doctors couldn't control the swelling and bleeding. She died within hours of the accident.

My mom asked me if I wanted to go to her funeral, and I said no. She questioned why, and I had no answer that I was willing to say aloud. The thought of death and eternity gave me crushing panic. I believed in God but viewed him as a fear-inducing tyrant looking to dole out punishment, not as a loving Heavenly Father. The blood stain that remained on the asphalt in our neighborhood for weeks after Brie's accident left an indelible imprint in my mind. Death became, by far, my greatest fear.

Also high on my list was this ever-present thought: *If I choose to follow God, what if he calls me to be a missionary in the remote jungles of a third-world country, where they subsist on bugs, and I catch malaria and get bitten by deadly snakes* (my other biggest fear)?

I recently read Dr. Jill Carnahan's beautiful and riveting book, *Unexpected*, and had so many aha moments regarding the role of fear in my life. She wrote,

Much research has been done using neural scanning technology to show how fear, one of the most primal and powerful of emotions, creates ingrained neural pathways in the brain. These pathways become like deeply worn grooves that are easy to fall back into. Anytime your body feels a stressful event, your subconscious opens these well-worn pathways of fear that were created years before and have been reinforced by every stressful event that's happened since. More positive emotions, like love and hope, can also shape these pathways, but once fear has established its route, it is hard to change. But it can be done.[1]

Fear was a constant companion, but it wasn't until much later that I realized its driving force over my life. It clouded other emotions, informed my decisions, shaped my actions, and in many ways hindered me from truly living.

*Driving the roller*

## Three

# WHERE ARE YOUR ORGANS?

---

**STARTING AT TWELVE** years old, I spent my summers working at my dad's rock yard/asphalt plant and complained endlessly to my mom about the injustice of earning a paycheck while my friends spent their days floating in their pool and licking popsicles. I reluctantly traded flip-flops for work boots and hopped on my bike to my job in quality control. I ran gradation tests on rock samples to ensure the rock was the correct size for the asphalt aggregate. My older brother taught me how to collect a proper sample, dry it in the oven, pass it through a specific set of sieves, weigh out each quantity, and calculate the percentage of each mass.

"This is such riveting work," said no child, ever!

I was alone in a small trailer all day, and in addition to running gradation tests, I analyzed the asphalt coming out of the plant, which involved applying chemicals and drying a sample in the lab oven.

One time, I placed the chemical paper into the oven after removing the asphalt, and the combination of fumes caused an explosion that sent the oven door flying open. Flames darted out right next to where I stood. I went screaming around the yard until one of the welders, Gary, heard me yelling "There's a fire!" He came to my rescue with an extinguisher, protecting himself with a welding mask while I wasn't even wearing a hard hat—let alone any other PPE.

Before I had a driver's license, I sometimes drove the vibratory roller on paving jobs. Now *that* I liked—even though my body shook for the entire night afterward. My grandpa's nickname for me was "The High Roller." He'd sometimes watch me work and then take me to lunch. My favorite job was driving the pickup trucks around the rock quarry, though I later learned that my dad was subjecting me to his own driver's ed obstacle course before he'd let me take an actual driver's license test. His course entailed weaving through pylon cones and coming to a complete stop without spilling a drop of a full cup of water perched on the hood.

I always admired the excellence my family modeled in all that they did, and I am so grateful for the work ethic my parents instilled in me. But that respect didn't mean I wanted to join the family business. As soon as I turned sixteen and could legally work elsewhere, I applied to be a waitress at Friendly's—the local restaurant/ice-cream shop. I wanted out of the rock yard so badly that I asked my mom to drive me to check on my application status daily, until finally one of the senior servers noticed my persistence and told the manager, "This girl has been coming here every day. You'd better give her a job!" And he did.

Babysitting was my other specialty, including looking after kids from our church and school, and I eagerly helped with nursery duty

# WHERE ARE YOUR ORGANS?

*All smiles with my brother and nephew, Tadju*

on a Sunday morning or Vacation Bible School over the summer. It was a given that I'd get married and have a swarm of my own kids one day. At twelve years old I was the flower girl in my oldest brother's wedding—a high point in my childhood, as was becoming an aunt the following year. Tadju was born a redheaded cutie pie, whose smile lit up his big blue eyes and mine. I prided myself on knowing how to get him to stop crying. Rocking him to sleep while singing lullabies was his favorite. He gave my life purpose at a time when God knew I was going to need it—everything holding my life together was about to come crumbling down once again.

At fourteen years old, during the fall of my freshman year of high school, I started having pain in my back and stomach. Initially, I didn't tell anyone. It was my first audition for the role of "stoic poster girl." All my friends were getting their periods, and I was anxiously anticipating mine. Instead, all I got was worsening pain to the point that I almost passed out at school one day. The nurse called my mom, and we saw my doctor that afternoon. The doctor immediately sent me to the hospital for an ultrasound. The technician made me drink a bucket of water and covered me with a slimy gel before sliding the wand over my belly, when she abruptly stopped and exclaimed, "Where are your organs?" It was the first of many times that a practitioner's words would replay hauntingly in my mind.

After that, the elderly male on-call OB-GYN prodded me with a Q-tip and exclaimed, "Just what I expected, there's no opening!" I was diagnosed with a rare birth defect called "agenesis of the lower vagina," meaning that my vagina had developed but was sealed off—there was no external opening. I had started my period months before, but the blood had no exit route and was blanketing my insides. One of the foremost surgeons in adolescent gynecology was at Boston Children's Hospital, an hour and a half away from where we lived, and I was scheduled for emergency vaginoplasty surgery at 6 a.m. the next morning.

I was terrified. I didn't want to have surgery, so I quietly asked my mom if there was another option, trying not to show her my fear, and likely succeeding. The blood was pooling dramatically inside of me. By that evening, it had pinched off the opening to my bladder and I couldn't pee out the water from the ultrasound. I felt like the Goodyear blimp. My mom suggested a warm bath, only to discover that we had no hot water—our oil tank had run dry. So enters a mother's selfless love for her children—my mom heated water on the stove in the middle of the night until there was enough of a bath for me to lie down in. It was the first of many, many times my parents would be by my side during surgeries and medical procedures.

The nurse who administered my pre-anesthesia drug said, "This will feel like your first margarita except you won't be able to sip one for another seven years." (I made that one year instead.) I counted backwards from ten, ending at six before drifting off, only to wake up later to my first taste of agony. My most delicate, highly sensitive parts had been sliced open with a scalpel. My surgeon, Dr. Lauffer, told me surgery went perfectly, and that he drained three liters of blood. I'd been carting around a half-gallon jug, yet in my fear of seeming weak, I hadn't voiced a single complaint.

I was in the hospital for five days. Before I was allowed to leave—and just when I thought the ordeal couldn't get any more humiliating—a nurse set up a three-way mirror on my hospital bed. The medical team watched as I inserted and removed a vaginal dilator that looked like a particular male organ, then informed me I would need to use it for the next year. Between the pain and embarrassment, my body felt out of control—and lack of control was my nemesis. Per usual, I stuffed my discomfort deep inside and completed their challenge.

I convalesced at home for another week before returning to school. One of my brothers brought me a thoughtful care package of candy and *People* magazines. I felt like I had suddenly—albeit forcefully and traumatically—stepped into adulthood. No one asked how I felt about what I'd gone through or if I was holding up okay, and I certainly wasn't about to offer up my feelings.

The Christian school I attended had 250 students in pre-K through twelfth grade. My mom loves to recount the story of when a student at our school contracted head lice and the parent stormed into the school office exclaiming, "Why do you think I send my children to a Christian school?!" As if head lice respect religion. Turns out, the devout aren't immune to juicy gossip and putting others down to prop themselves up either. Such behavior can run rampant in all circles, and I've certainly been guilty of my share.

The rumor was that I'd had back surgery, and I let that fly. But I was on the volleyball team and during a weekend overnight tournament, I confided in my teammates about what had really transpired. Teens will be teens and some of the seniors on my team leaked my truth to the rest of their class. Soon, the entire high school knew. I was already having a difficult time clicking with most of my peers, and, making matters worse, I felt invisible at home, as several of my family members were dealing with serious illnesses, along with other issues. Due to these circumstances, and the earlier established misperception that I was unwanted, I faded into the background. I didn't think I had anything worthwhile to say, or that anyone cared to listen, even if I did. So, I stuffed my voice down into my "bucket" as well. Suddenly, my symptoms started overflowing.

As if being shoved into womanhood and experiencing the joy of surging hormones wasn't enough, I developed undiagnosed thyroid issues, culminating in sudden weight gain and other changes I couldn't understand or prevent.

## WHERE ARE YOUR ORGANS?

*Your security blanket of control has been stripped away, again and again, leaving you feeling trapped in a body you don't fully comprehend—in a body you're afraid of and are at odds with. It pains me to say this, but you'll remain its prisoner for more than two decades. Your nervous system recognizes this loss of control as a threat and stressor, and it has one goal: keeping you safe. But I know you don't feel safe. This primal self-protection has come at a great cost. I see it, even though you feel invisible. That spark of joy is gone from your eyes, replaced by constant exhaustion and nagging pain, as the boundless resources of your youth are suddenly viewed as scarce and in need of preserving. Your nervous system is defensively on high alert, constantly scanning for more perceived threats. Oh, my sweet girl, there's about to be an onslaught of them.*

*Spritz vs. Miss Piggy*

Four

# FRESH INK OF AGONY

---

I'M SITTING IN my Barbie-pink bedroom, regretting the choice of paint color I'd made as a seven-year-old, when I finally got my own room after sharing one with my sister and younger brother. I'm twelve or thirteen now and deep in the throes of a Christmas campaign. The bubblegum walls are gradually being covered by photos of puppies and signs declaring, "All I want for Christmas is a Cavalier King Charles Spaniel." On Christmas morning, I would open up a carefully wrapped fluffy beige dog—a stuffed animal, with a red bow tied around its neck.

Fast-forward twenty years to when I finally got that puppy—a red and white Papillon named Spritz. About a year into being a dog mom, I had an interesting epiphany. I was always waiting for my pup to screw up. Don't get me wrong—I loved this little fur ball to pieces. But rather than looking at her as a "good girl" who occasionally chewed all the moldings and weather stripping of my house, not to mention every carpet, throw, or pillow tassel, or who sometimes had accidents inside and randomly decided to shred one of my plants, I viewed her as an inherently naughty dog.

I realized I was raised with this same line of thinking. The environment I'd grown up in often felt punishing. I believed I was unwanted, inherently unworthy of love, and that everyone—including God—was waiting for me to screw up. I took everything my mom said to me as condescending and critical, and that feeling of judgement came as a personal assault to my sense of self—or lack thereof. I was angry and easily triggered, and our limited interactions became mostly arguments. I avoided my dad as much as possible and shriveled up inside every time he yelled or even raised his voice. I'd spent years silently begging God to quiet the tumultuous sea in and around me. Eventually, as nothing changed, I began thinking that my prayers were falling on deaf ears and my circumstances on blind eyes. Or worse, that I was praying to a God who saw this torment and didn't care.

My mom had a lot of baggage from her life before meeting my dad. When she was young, her father had a similar raging temper, and my dad was gasoline to the embers of her past. She cried a lot, which I was extremely uncomfortable with. The climate of our home was mercurial. Every display of emotion around me seemed inflated. There was no middle ground to emulate. The last thing I wanted to do was contribute more to this chaos, so, aside from occasionally screaming at my mom or brother, I kept everything bottled up.

Just because I didn't voice my emotions didn't mean I wasn't experiencing them. In fact, quite the opposite was true. I had a bottomless reservoir of fear, anger, anxiety, sadness, despair, loneliness, and unworthiness that I couldn't explain. I didn't understand why I felt so deeply, so I came to view my emotions as inherently defective, the same way I perceived my body—broken and out of my control. So began my search for coping mechanisms.

I looked to my peers to see how they were navigating the choppy waters of teenagehood, and noticed fresh scabs across the wrists of a few schoolmates. *Maybe that's it! Maybe I need a physical means to express my emotional pain. Maybe if someone sees that I'm in turmoil, it will allow me to open up about it. Maybe—just maybe—if someone knows how much agony I am in, they will love me for it.* I never did utter that sentiment to anyone, and in high school my pain didn't earn me the love I sought. But my subconscious mind sure liked the idea and tucked it away to use in the near future.

I cut deep grooves into my arms and legs, hoping to replace my fear and other emotions with a tangible sensation. It was also a cry for help. I talked to a few concerned schoolmates, but ultimately I was too scared to let them see *me*, to let them see my brokenness. I didn't know how to be vulnerable, and I started thinking that wanting to be noticed and listened to was desperate, needy behavior, and that I should toughen up instead. The belief I'd adopted as a child—that weakness was the last thing that was going to earn me love—was winning the battle in my mind.

Sometimes, the thought crossed my mind that if I cut just a little deeper into my skin and ended my earthly pain, death wasn't even going to be the end of it. Instead, I would have eternity to deal with. There was no way out, and the thought of eternity set off an instant panic attack. *God, why did you create me for this life of torment?*

During my sophomore year, I found myself at a crossroads of conviction. Path A, defined as a continued devotion to the faith I'd been raised with, led to certain death by malaria or venomous snake bites. Path B, defined as a rejection of said faith, had just as dark a fate, yet seemed to offer me at least some control, and way more fun, over how I got there. My body had betrayed me, my peers had betrayed me, and God had betrayed me. Path B it was! In the absence of any light, I spiraled even further into darkness. I felt broken, hollow, and empty. I viewed God as cruel and unloving. And I hated him.

Exposing my pain through cutting myself hadn't gone as planned, and I traded that self-harm for vices that dulled my emotions instead. I replaced my wide-legged JNCO jeans and Airwalks for Hot Topic goth from head to toe, complete with knee-high black patent leather lace-up platform boots, gauged earrings, and a black lace choker. Instead of DC Talk and Phil Wickham, death metal played on my Discman. And the puppy photos once covering my bedroom walls gave way to torn-out magazine photos of Tool, Nine Inch Nails, Rage Against the Machine, and the like. I made it pretty obvious that I was unhappy, and my dark clothing matched my mood. I never let myself smile, especially around my parents, teachers, or any adults, for that matter.

In this darkness, God didn't abandon me; he brought a best friend into my life. Kelly and I had been in school together for several years, but we bonded while in the same driver's ed class. She saw my brokenness without me having to say a word, and her glistening smile proved she loved me anyway. She always made me laugh and never once betrayed my trust. We became partners in (harmless) crime and would camp out in a liquor store parking lot for hours until we found someone to buy us Mike's Hard Lemonade, which led to the aforementioned coping mechanisms.

The vow I'd taken never to do drugs? Well, I attended my

brother's fifth-grade D.A.R.E. graduation slightly hung over and wearing a Black Dog sweatshirt that still smelled like weed from the night before. I rolled on ecstasy on a somewhat regular basis and abused painkillers, which several doctors prescribed to me. I drank alcohol, smoked cigarettes and pot, and sank so low that I rolled a joint or two from pages I tore out of a Bible at school.

Every fall brought a new school year and a new injury. Each injury was one more manifestation of my body's failure to cooperate. There was the vaginoplasty ordeal, then a broken wrist from a Rollerblade accident. I dislocated my pointer finger when an opposing teammate kicked it instead of the ball during a game at youth group. Lastly, there was the freak hot-tub accident in San Diego while I was visiting my sister and soon-to-be sister-in-law, who was engaged to my brother.

I was trying to hold a horizontal plank over the hot tub with my bent arms gripping the edge. I'd pulled off this feat on the edge of a countertop, but hadn't accounted for how slippery this surface would be, and my body fell onto my outstretched hands, tearing several ligaments in my dominant thumb. The injury didn't heal as it should have, and I spent more than a year in and out of splints and physical therapy. One physical therapist noted that my ligaments were much looser than they were supposed to be—a warning I wish I'd paid more attention to.

As so many teenage girls do, I hated how my body looked because it didn't match the picture-perfect standard I aspired to. In my family, appearance was everything. My grandmother had been a model in New York City, and even into her eighties she remained the picture of glamour and poise. I was obsessed with my aesthetic and constantly dieted, restricting my eating, but I still couldn't control the way my body changed. I compared and critiqued every inch of myself—quite literally. I had a little too much love on my handles and more curves than I cared for.

I wasn't overweight, but I wasn't thin either, and maintaining a slim physique—something that appeared so effortless for everyone I compared myself to—seemed like an impossible task. I begged my parents for a treadmill, thinking I'd start running and instantly drop my unwanted weight, but running didn't come easy either. I'd always been very strong—I was one of the few people in my grade school who could climb the sixty-foot rope to the top of our gymnasium. So, after an eleven-minute mile on the treadmill that felt like it would never end, I lifted weights in the gym my dad built in the basement room, which had once been my Creepy Crawlers laboratory. My dad frequently praised me for my diligence and muscle definition—further ingraining my perception that love was earned through maintaining my figure and my might.

I was tired all the time and dark circles swallowed my eyes, mirroring my anguished soul. Makeup, baggy clothes, lots of coffee—and Kelly—were my best friends. I often received compliments about how pretty I was and for the clothes I wore, but I feared that I was only liked for the image I portrayed. I believed that if they found out my imperfections, I'd be discarded and unloved.

I drew a lot of attention from boys, which superficially filled the gaping void in my life. I gave up far too much of myself to any guy who showed an interest in me, desperate to feel loved. My rebellious streak persisted throughout high school, and I lived on the edge—smoking joints in the school parking lot, making out with boys in their cars, and throwing parties every time my parents went out of town. I loved the endorphin rush of rebelling—one thing I did let myself feel.

There were a few life rafts during those difficult high school years that kept me grounded, engaged, and from doing more extreme self-harm. Kelly showed me the brighter side of life, even if I didn't dare admit it. Several caring teachers invested time in me, loved me as I was, and prayed for and believed in better days ahead. My nephews were the light in my dark life; and since I would never dream of doing anything to harm them, their existence made me—sometimes—think twice before getting high. I was always completely sober when I was around them and all the kids I babysat for. That was one vow I made and kept.

During our senior year, Kelly and I took a weekend trip to visit my sister in California, missing a party one of our classmates threw. A junior who attended was trying to be cool and leaked that there had been booze and pot. Kelly and I returned from California to find almost our entire class on probation. Our theme for senior year became, "We weren't there!" The fingerprints of God's grace were all over my life, even though I didn't see it and certainly didn't deserve it.

In spite of my obstinance, I aced my AP classes, played sports, starred in the school play, was on the student council, and was inducted into the National Honor Society. I was a defiant and directionless overachiever. I applied to a handful of random colleges, one being a business school outside of Boston, Bentley University, which I only did so because it shared a name with a pretty sick brand of car. When I was accepted and learned it was one of the top-ranked business schools in the US, I took a tour and was blown away by the beautiful and technologically advanced campus. It had heated steps and a live trading room. Sold!

The day I graduated high school was one of the best days of

*With Kelly, heading to our sophomore banquet*

my life—as it is for many teens, but even more so since I'd been in school with some of the same classmates for fourteen years. I longed for a fresh start, and the autonomy and freedom of college—a place with no parental supervision and the ability to party whenever I wanted.

The day after high school graduation changed my life forever. My mom threw a big party, and my Auntie Lorilee, Uncle Dan, and cousins came from Vermont for the weekend. Sparks of playful mischief glimmered in my Auntie Lor's fiery green eyes, and her laugh was wildly contagious. After hours of sitting on our living room floor in a competitive series of board games, one of my cousins tried to hoist me up, but my grip slipped, and I fell onto the frame of our beige leather couch in a seated position, breaking my tailbone. Pain exploded throughout my lower spine, but I downplayed it for several excruciating days, then visited my primary care doctor who said the bone would heal on its own in time. Sitting was unbearable, and none of the dozen different donut pillows my mom bought me helped. That was the day pain tattooed itself into my flesh, assuming permanence in my life.

I went off to college, where I endured sitting through class, and then often stood while doing my schoolwork. But even standing became painful. An orthopedic doctor ordered an X-ray that showed my tailbone was bent to a ninety-degree angle when it should have been at a fifteen-degree angle. I was sent to a physical therapist who went in rectally and pulled the bone back into place—yet another embarrassing ordeal for anyone, let alone a teenager. But the ligaments were stretched out, and my tailbone moved back into what had become its new normal. I could actually feel the bone moving around and joked that I had a wagging tail.

## SPERANZA

The pain was far from funny. I was sent for a course of traditional physical therapy to stabilize my core, and the only change I came away with was searing pain in my lower back. Finding a comfortable position was impossible. I would arch my back to relieve some pressure from my tailbone, which only made my lower back hurt even more. There seemed to be no way to relax my lower back without putting pressure on my tailbone. My mom heard about craniosacral therapy, so we flew to Toledo, Ohio, and then Bethesda, Maryland, to work with skilled therapists. Unfortunately, I had zero pain relief.

I remember one of my craniosacral therapists exclaiming, "Wow, did you feel that energy shift?!" After the session, I asked my mom if it was okay that I'd lied and said yes. I felt nothing but misery. Many years later, I recognized that because I was so desperate to no longer feel my body, I had closed off feeling my own energy—my own life force. And going one step further, the root chakra at the base of the spine is believed to be where one grounds and stabilizes oneself—where a person feels the energies of security and belonging.

Instead of feeling safe and connected, my constant pain made me weigh every decision by how much suffering I was willing to endure. A car ride, a movie with friends, or a dinner at a restaurant left me squirming in my seat while trying to mask my discomfort. In an effort to encourage me, my mom often relayed stories about people who had been in pain for five or ten years, and even longer. I remember thinking, *Ten years! I won't last that long. This pain has tainted my whole life. I can't keep living with this agony!*

As I write this book more than twenty years later, after enduring more physical pain than I knew was possible, I realize that I'd take that body and its agony in a heartbeat. It was a toothache compared to what was to come.

I saw another orthopedic surgeon at Boston Children's Hospital who prescribed more physical therapy, did extensive imaging, administered a series of cortisone injections and pain blocks, and put me on several anti-inflammatory drugs and narcotics. He also performed testing on the nerves of my lumbar spine, sacrum, tailbone, and legs, looking for referred pain. When the analysis was complete, my surgeon went to the waiting room, and with a pale face, told my mom that I had the highest pain tolerance he'd ever encountered, which my mom proudly relayed to me. I felt the sting of pain as much as everyone else, but feared that showing weakness would make me unworthy of love. I was still stubbornly resolved never to reveal it to others.

Many years later, Dr. Jill Crista said during a webinar, "The people with the highest pain tolerance have the lowest self-worth," echoing what had been my agonizing truth for decades.

Although a life of chronic pain was the last thing I expected when I graduated high school, it's been an even bigger surprise to see how God has used it in the most profound ways, including as my life's greatest teacher. But just as I had all the learning of college ahead of me, it would be some time before I learned the lessons my pain had to teach. At that point in my life, I didn't want to learn from it. I didn't even want to acknowledge it. I simply wanted to bury it.

*Morning coffee*

Five

# THE DEPTHS OF GRACE

Warning: This chapter gets intense. Take a deep breath.

---

AMBER AND I pulled into side-by-side parking spaces at freshman orientation, stuck together during those first few days, and were fast friends by September. Fall semester began with all its newness—friends and crushes, college classes, dorm life, cafeteria food, shuttle rides into Harvard Square, and meeting Amber's boyfriend, Brad. Amber told me he had assaulted a former girlfriend, and while he often spent the night in our small dorm room, I uneasily slept in the bunk bed about twelve feet away.

Brad's redeeming qualities were his car and his connections, and we made frequent trips to his brother's house to get weed and smoke blunts. I started crushing and snorting the painkillers my doctor was prescribing and sold them to classmates—a budding entrepreneur. It was the height of the OxyContin epidemic, and Amber had a friend attending Bentley who was hooked on Oxy. I was curious to know if that high would in any way dull my pain. Amber was content smoking joints with Brad and his brother, while I diversified my drug portfolio with another friend group.

During the week, I stuck to smoking pot, sometimes going to class stoned and then staying up half the night doing schoolwork. On the weekends, when I wasn't working my babysitting job, I'd go on an OxyContin bender, paid for by my prescription painkiller sales and babysitting proceeds. I sold my painkillers for $20 each, while one pill of Oxy sold for $80—the same amount I made in a whole night of babysitting. At that price, Oxy wasn't sustainable. But powdered heroin was a fraction of the cost of Oxy, so I switched to snorting that most of the time, going to shady places in South Boston and the North Shore to get my drugs of choice.

Such powerful downers needed uppers. In February of my freshman year, I got a phone call that my grandma had died, and that night was the first time I snorted cocaine—the very drug I'd sworn to never touch. That fueled my days, and I'd often go into the bathroom between classes for a bump. One night, a group of us were driving around Boston, having just scored some coke, and we were pulled over for speeding. My friend who was driving got the speeding ticket, but the rest of us were fined for not wearing our seat belts. Had the officer suspected we were high and searched us, we'd all have been arrested for possession. This was the closest I came to being caught, but the same scene minus the police officer was a regular occurrence. I was reckless.

I wish I could explain what was going through my mind as I made these decisions, but I'd succeeded at my mission of becoming numb. Numb to my surroundings, numb to fear, numb to pain,

# THE DEPTHS OF GRACE

numb to caring what happened to me, numb to acknowledging any consequences for my actions, numb to God, numb to life . . .

Until I nearly overdosed. After days of taking a cocktail of drugs and the biggest bong hit of my life, I passed out with my head on the toilet bowl of the communal dorm bathroom. My best friend spent hours debating whether or not to call an ambulance, as she listened to my strained breathing and I went in and out of consciousness. I eventually came to, went back to my room, vowed to turn my life around, and never looked back.

I don't know why God spared me that night and saved me from a life of addiction. I watched my friends go in and out of rehab, working daily at achieving sobriety. It was a long time before I even sat with the question. True to form, I pushed it all down and pressed on as if it were a mere hiccup. But God gave me an anchor that night in the middle of my sophomore year. He knew I was going to face future trials so consuming they'd threaten to undo me. For the rest of my life, when I felt broken beyond repair, doubted God's ability, or questioned his motives, I'd remember his grace, his power, and his love. But remembering his grace is not to be equated with bondage. I know for certain that God's compassionate rescue was *not* meant as a bargaining chip for a life of shame or indebtedness to him. It was God acting in the only way he knows how—with perfect love.

Savannah Guthrie's book *Mostly What God Does* poignantly gets to the heart of God, and it's no coincidence that, as I was searching for the words to explain God's grace and how he washes our slate clean, I read her chapter on guilt and shame. She wrote, "God doesn't just forgive our failings and then let the memory of them hang around, tormenting us. He takes our guilt far away and replaces it with his peace."[2]

# SPERANZA

*Manhattan skyline at sunset*

"For as high as the heavens are above the earth, so great is his love for those who fear him; as far as the east is from the west, so far has he removed our transgressions from us" (Psalm 103:11–12 NIV). Or as *The Message* translation puts that last line, "As far as sunrise is from sunset."

God took my past and covered it with his grace, but I replaced my drug use with an eating disorder. Being on that many drugs didn't leave room for much of an appetite, and I had lost a significant amount of weight. I liked my thin frame and the attention I was getting because of it. Since I was a teenager, I'd drawn my value from how I looked, and all the comments of, "Wow, you've lost so much weight, you look amazing!" only cast me deeper into the bondage of equating how thin I was with how much love I was worthy of.

I still had constant pain in the whole lower part of my body, but no matter how much pain I was in, I wouldn't let myself eat anything each day until I'd done an exercise circuit of push-ups, crunches, planks, and squats. I incessantly counted calories, set a daily limit, and avoided certain food groups entirely. I measured out my Cheerios and skim milk, and even tallied the fifteen calories of a cough drop or peppermint. I didn't want anyone to know how manic I'd become and was ashamed of my behavior, so I became reclusive and even more withdrawn. Shame's favorite sidekicks are secrecy and isolation.

> *I know you don't want to be this obsessive, but once again, my sweet girl, you've lost control, and this compulsion over your weight is consuming you. And it's terrifying! Fear has followed you like a shadow, etching its way deeper into your neural networks and physical body. That fear has kept you small, quiet, hidden, closed off, and believing its lies that your only security is control. If only asking for help felt safe, but letting people in never has been. No wonder your recourse is to pull inward even more. How I wish I could wrap my arms around you and fill you with the love you will one day know.*

I started each morning by looking at my thin frame in the mirror, making sure I could see each rib and hip bone protruding through my skin—my worth staring back at me through hollow eyes. Many times, my blood sugar got so low that I almost passed out, triggering a panic attack. I'd spent years on a desperate quest to regain some semblance of control. Instead, anorexia consumed my life.

Anorexia—and schoolwork. During my first semester at Bentley—the college, not the car—I was required to take a history class. In high school that had been my most deficient subject, so I opted for History of the World. As implied, the class covered all major world events going back centuries. I barely studied for the midterm and scored a D+, the equivalent of a jolting hotel wake-up call. I aced the term paper, and then, before the final, I locked myself in my room for three days, making and memorizing detailed flash cards on every topic we'd covered—around fifty cards in total. I got a perfect score on the exam and a B- for the semester, and I never sank that low again.

I started out at as a marketing major and wrote my acceptance essay on opening an artist collaborative one day. Bentley had a requisite general business core curriculum, and during my first semester I took microeconomics. I was instantly hooked. It attached titles to commonsense principles that transformed the way I saw our economy and world. I switched my major to economics and finance and loved every bit of what I learned, though I always felt a tug-of-war between my left, analytical brain, and its right, creative counterpart.

*A stall at Il Mercato Centrale, Florence*

Six

# THAT'S AMORE

TEASPOONFULS OF glistening *olio extravirgine di oliva*—extra virgin olive oil—are being enthusiastically offered to me as my confused thoughts scream, *Why would I waste my precious calories on a bland, greasy oil that belongs in a frying pan?* Begrudgingly, I bring one spoonful to my lips and am met with an explosion of peppery spice, tempered by the smooth butteriness of the lipid. I'm getting an education in more ways than I ever thought I'd signed up for!

It was fall semester of my junior year, and I was studying in Florence, Italy, living the kind of dream you never want to wake up from. I saved all my electives so I could take several art classes and a six-credit Italian intensive. I dove into learning the language with gusto. In Italian, you pronounce every letter, unlike with French, where those pesky silent endings caused me to struggle in high school. Nevertheless, that prior language education helped me pick up Italian quickly and easily. I lived with a host family—Silvia, Federico, and their friendly seven-year-old daughter, Alma—and

I traded my English for their Italian. My goal was to leave Italy speaking fluently enough to get by in daily life. Finito!

I always loved art but had never been in a real art class before, with an easel, professional-grade tools, and nude models. My art classes were a revelation in more ways than one, and learning so many new techniques was thrilling! I could have spent all day in the art studio, and at times I did. By far the biggest revelation of my new Italian life was falling in love—with the food! It's ironic, because I was still struggling with anorexia and restricting my eating. At times, while my friends were enjoying cheese and *salumi*, I instead munched on a seventy-calorie apple.

I was enthralled by food, and real-deal Italian was unlike anything I'd ever experienced. Clearly I never knew that olive oil had different taste profiles depending on the region, the varietal, and the method used to pick the olives. Handpicked olives are generally less ripe than those shaken from the trees and thus more peppery and astringent. I was fascinated by how Italy's history and geography shaped its food, as well as the differences in cuisine throughout its twenty regions.

Florence is in the well-known region of Tuscany, and their cuisine is called "*Cucina Povera*." Its simplistic roots make the most of sparse ingredients and local produce. Due to embargoes in the sixteenth century, salt was a scarce commodity and reserved for curing meats, so the bread was made without salt. The ancient food traditions have been preserved, telling a story of ages past, just like one of my favorite Tuscan classics, *ribollita*, a vegetable-and-bean soup thickened with leftover bread.

The simplest dishes are packed with flavors and textures I didn't know were possible. Silky fresh pasta is made with nothing more than egg and OO flour—a finely milled, low-protein wheat, the long strands then tossed in pesto or a wild boar ragu. Blistered pizza is topped with creamy *mozzarella di bufala*, prosciutto, and arugula. Focaccia is baked with sun-kissed tomatoes. I had never even liked tomatoes! All a revelation, and all finished with a generous drizzle of grassy, pungent, Tuscan olive oil. My favorite sweet was a cake only Italians would so adoringly name *"Amore Polenta,"* a.k.a. "For the Love of Polenta." Their adulation for all things culinary was exemplified as I wandered the stalls of the large Mercato Centrale with its rows of butchers, fishmongers, cheese makers, bakeries, fruits and vegetables, and so much more, all of which I'd never seen or tasted.

My other haunt was under the marble arches of Piazza della Repubblica, where I'd often walk, entranced by the electric notes of Vivaldi flying off the strings of a violin quartet, and where I'd let any tension of the day be carried away on the wings of the melody. Strangely, Italy is where I learned to sigh. My host parents, Silvia and Federico, sighed a lot, and this was as foreign a concept to me as the country I was living in. A sigh is a quick and effective tool of releasing stress and calming your nervous system. Once that concept clicked, I was tempted to join in, but, as you can imagine by now, I was so afraid of my own voice, I struggled to let out even the faintest sigh!

I don't think it's a coincidence that Italians are way more relaxed and joyous about life than much of the rest of the world. They have a phrase—*il dolce fare niente*, meaning "the sweetness of doing nothing." Doesn't that sound lovely? To be honest, it didn't sound that way to me at first. The shops closed for several hours midday for lunch and a rest. The American in me was annoyed and taken aback, thinking, *Well, this isn't good business! How inconvenient!* But soon I began to see the value of living in a culture built on slowness and patience.

## SPERANZA

The Slow Food Movement, founded by Carlo Petrini in Italy during the 1980s in reaction to a McDonald's opening in his area, highlights and preserves the age-old techniques and foods that are the hallmark of this fascinating country. This concept of safeguarding regional culinary traditions has spread to other countries as well. Spoiler alert! A few years after my semester abroad, I returned to Italy for culinary school and dove deep into the wonders of making Italian food, watching these artisans who had mastered their craft. Here's a taste of why I fell so hard for the food of Italy: *Parmiggiano Reggiano* ages for a minimum of two years and is tested for quality by inserting a horse bone into the center of the giant wheel so one can observe the aroma and density. *Cullatello*, the king of aged meats, is tied and hung from a ceiling in a cave or basement where it ages for at least three years. Chefs, as well as those in the know from all over the world, buy the young ham and tag it with their name for the duration of its aging.

Super Tuscans, the bold red wines of the region, can age for fifteen years or longer—the passion and story of the vintner reflected in every sip. *Aceto Balsamico di Modena* is aged for twenty-five years in a series of barrels until it is thicker than molasses. I saw barrels that were part of women's dowries, passed down through generations. These are processes you can't rush, and they result in delicacies that are savored, much like the culture that doesn't speed through life but relishes each moment. A chance to embrace a slower pace and a less rigorous academic load was just what my weathered body and soul needed.

In her book *Unexpected*, which I referenced earlier, Dr. Jill Carnahan described a toxin as "anything that decreases optimal vitality and function," and discussed the concept of the Highly Sensitive Person (HSP), which spurred me to read the fascinating book by that same name.[3] What I learned about HSPs is that they

# THAT'S AMORE

*Sunset over il Ponte Vecchio, Florence*

tend to "process the environment around them more deeply before acting...[and] are also more easily overwhelmed; overstimulated by things that are too intense."⁴ *That's me!* My "little bucket" gets filled up so quickly and easily! No wonder I've always been most at ease, most at peace, most at home, most myself, in these seasons and in a country of such beauty, quiet, slowness, solitude, and rest.

My school in Florence, Lorenzo de' Medici, arranged a few weekend trips for my study abroad cohort—one on a sailboat around the island of Alba and another to Capri, Sorrento, and Pompeii. I saw lemons as big as my head, the bluest water imaginable, and stunning coastal landscapes. Other weekends, I explored Italy by train— sometimes with friends and sometimes solo. I was in awe. Each place was more beautiful than the last, with rugged countrysides, magnificent cathedrals, and charming towns filled with animated and warm people. Imagine a place where it's a regular occurrence to stumble upon a spirited gathering in a town square with live music playing and kids, adults, and the elderly dancing without a care, drinking mulled wine, and eating warm roasted chestnuts. I treasured every trip, every day, every moment, every experience, as sacred time, where the stress and cares of life faded into the background, replaced by wonder and awe at my magnificent new home.

I use the word *sacred* for a reason, because something else was stirring in me. The more I saw, the less I could deny that the majesty of this country was purposefully and perfectly composed not by chance, but by the ultimate *Maestro*. Subtly, gently, God began tugging at my heartstrings through his beauty on full display. My awe of Italy became awe of God himself. I'd see him in a sunset strewn over the skies of the Tuscan countryside. But he also felt that far away and out of reach.

One Saturday, I hopped on a train alone to Bologna to sightsee, shop, and yes, eat authentic *pasta alla Bolognese*. After dinner I was walking around and got quite lost. This was nearly twenty years ago with no Google Maps to come to my rescue. I remember standing amidst ancient brick buildings, their walls feeling as if they were slowly closing in on me. As panic set in, I looked up to that faraway God and suddenly felt his presence right there in that place. The unreachable God had reached down and made himself known to me. He'd been there the whole time, waiting for me to want him to draw near.

I had a huge dilemma on my hands. God's presence was undeniable, but technically I was still mad at him for many things—the constant pain in my spine being one. What happened, though, is that when I leaned in, God met me there and eagerly showed more of himself, spurring me to seek him further, thus becoming this glorious

## THAT'S AMORE

*Gondola ride with my mom in Venice*

continuum. My brother and sister-in-law had given me the very fitting devotional *Jesus Calling* by Sarah Young when I left for Italy, and I'd been dutifully starting my days reading what seemed like platitudes. After feeling God so near, the words took on personal meaning and application, and I wanted more. The late Dr. Timothy Keller's books quickly became favorites, and a few years later, I'd spend my Sunday mornings riding the subway from Brooklyn to Upper Manhattan to listen to him candidly preach. Like so many of his poignant insights, these words hung out for quite a while in the back of my mind:

> If you have a God great enough and powerful enough to be mad at because he doesn't stop your suffering, you also have a God who's great enough and powerful enough to have reasons that you can't understand. You can't have it both ways.[5]

*Fresh pasta in the making*

## Seven

# TEACH A MAN TO FISH

*HELP! HELP!* The pasta was growing longer by the minute, and I was trying not to panic, but my parents couldn't hear my cries over Andrea Bocelli's voice blasting through the surround-sound speakers. It was my first time making fresh pasta, and I didn't know yet that I needed to cut the dough into pieces before feeding it through the pasta machine. At first, it was just fine, but as the dough got thinner, the piece grew longer. Finally, my parents rushed into the kitchen to lend a hand. I was feeding the dough through the mouth of the pasta machine and cranking the lever. It took both my mom and dad to hold the dough that was coming out, as it quickly extended the entire length of our kitchen! I tossed the homemade pasta with a simple pesto, and my mom, who had visited me twice while I was abroad, was transported right along with me back to Italy. That's the power of food!

# SPERANZA

I returned from Italy on a mission to re-create the dishes I'd eaten there and to indoctrinate anyone who would listen on the superiority of Italian food and culture.

I also returned to have surgery to remove my tailbone. All the therapies, injections, and medications I tried had failed, and the pain was worsening. The crooked bone was affecting the surrounding muscles and ligaments. I was desperate to be out of pain, and I trusted my surgeon's wisdom.

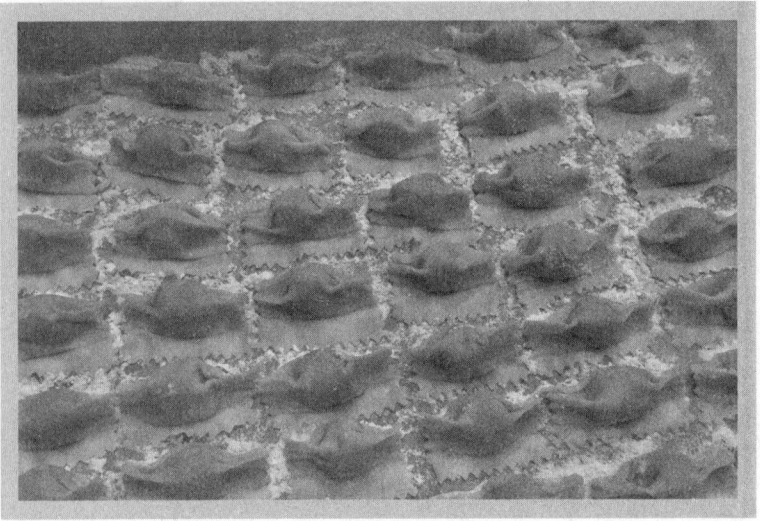

*Little bundles in a row*

I spent my short convalescence watching the Food Network, reading cookbooks and cooking magazines, and turning my parents' house into a test kitchen. I was painstakingly slow and had no sense of timing, but my mom was patient and cheerily washed my mountain of dishes. Finding purpose amid pain is paramount to being able to rise above it, and I do not doubt God's intention in choosing this

# TEACH A MAN TO FISH

*Pumpkin anglonotti*

season to ignite the flame that would later fuel my life.

Two weeks after surgery, I returned to college. Again, sitting through class was agony, but for the first time I was hopeful that the pain would go away. Instead, the only change was that I no longer felt my tailbone moving around. I returned to my surgeon for more imaging, and there appeared to be a floating bone fragment near the base of my sacrum, visible even to my untrained eye. But the surgeon said it was nothing and advised me to give it more time and have more cortisone injections. He also applauded my quick recovery, attributing it to the strength I maintained through my fastidiousness in my daily workouts. What he meant as an affirmation, I took as a mandate: *Controlling how strong you are is what's keeping this house of cards from crashing down. Don't. Ever. Stop!*

Notes of encouragement had been arriving from family friends, past teachers, church friends, and even from people I didn't know at my parents' church, saying they were praying for me and cared about me; not because of anything I'd done to deserve it, but out of the overflow of Jesus' love in them. Despite having been raised by Christian parents and attending church, youth group, and a Christian school, this message clicked with me for the first time.

Jesus took on flesh and lived on this earth to show the enormity of his love for each of us. To *see* those who felt invisible. To mend the wounds of those who felt broken. To heal the hurting. To listen to those who had lost their voice. To erase guilt and shame. To replace fear with peace. To welcome everyone to his table. To be near. And, even though he is God, to model a life of obedience and being rooted in and reliant upon his Father. And then to hearten us to live in this same way. To be Christ-like. To be Christian. This precious group who prayed for and encouraged me were the hands and feet and heart of Christ Jesus to me. As I began to rest in this love and trust that God was on my side, I wasn't so fearful about going through surgeries and all that was happening to me.

My insecurities about being unwanted and unworthy of receiving love from other people—and, as I'd see much later, from myself—had deeply ingrained themselves in me. One of the core principles in Amy B. Scher's transformative book *How to Heal Yourself When No One Else Can* is to uncover the limiting beliefs of our subconscious mind.[6] Just as I had done in my high school cutting days, I was placing my value on being in pain. I still held the limiting belief that my pain made me worthy of love, and that in pain's absence, there would be no reason for anyone to love me. My body clung to pain with a death grip, thinking it had to for survival.

After my Italian sojourn, the rest of junior and senior year were full throttle ahead. I was a live-in nanny for a sweet family in Newton, Massachusetts, and I worked my tail off—no pun intended—through demanding and complex coursework. I excitedly went deep into my analysis of the concepts I was learning, often extrapolating ideas from one subject to another. I was unabashedly the teacher's pet in every class, surely annoying my classmates with how many times my hand went up with the answer and how often my professors cited my work.

God had created me with what was an exceptional memory—note the past tense here. A decade later, one tick bite would steal my stellar recall. But for now, I'd rewrite the copious notes taken in class, read them slowly a handful of times, and have them memorized, word for word. I threw all my energy into doing the best I possibly could, spending the majority of my time on my schoolwork, except for some "wild" weekend nights with my friend Jag, either at Barnes & Noble, drinking lattes and reading magazines, or trying new restaurants in Boston.

The term *foodie* had recently been coined and fit me to a T. This was ironic because I was still held captive in the unrelenting grip of anorexia. When dining out, I'd starve myself all day to make sure I didn't go over my caloric limit, and if, in a weak moment, I did, I spent the next day mentally beating myself up while depriving myself of anything else to eat.

*One day, after letting your heart break for the bondage you were living in, you will laugh at the absurdity of it all. The way you chastised your body for being tired all the time, while you continuously drained your energy with negative self-talk, maintaining straight A's, starving yourself, and living in chronic pain!*

I was, apparently, supposed to be able to go from zero to sixty in three seconds flat, on an empty gas tank. With a broken axle!

I attended church in Lexington, and tried out the young adults' group, but it was more like group therapy, and circling up to share my feelings was still not my cup of tea, to put it mildly. Before bowing out of circle time for good, I donated baked-to-order cookies for their fundraiser. A cute guy named Tony won the bid. He'd graduated from Bentley the year before and was one of four kids in a big Italian family. He checked all the boxes according to my dad's stated criteria. My dad once (half-jokingly) said that, to win his approval, my partner needed to be Christian, drive a Beamer (Tony's car was a Lexus), and have season tickets to the Red Sox.

My three older siblings got married right out of college. Starting a family was the only expectation I felt my parents—especially my dad—ever had of me. For a first "serious" boyfriend, Tony was as good as they come. I loved his family, he bought me thoughtful gifts—one of my love languages—and he was down for trying all the new restaurants. Tony was also my first Christian boyfriend. He introduced me to books on what God had to say about dating and marriage, and we aimed to make that the foundation of our relationship. We dated through my senior year and, initially, I thought, *This is it!*

During that last year, I took an economics elective called Economics of the Developing World and learned about microfinance for the first time. The premise? Don't give a man a fish; instead, teach him how to fish and give him the resources to do so. Being at a business school, it was drilled into us that the number one goal of a business is to turn a profit. Yes, money is what makes the world go 'round, but the corporate world we were being groomed to join perpetuated a cycle in which only a few at the top continuously got richer.

Microfinance held the key to breaking the generational cycle of poverty, hunger, and homelessness, in a way that lifted up and empowered the marginalized, unseen, dismissed, and forgotten, while transforming entire families and communities. I couldn't empathize with being materially poor, but I knew the pain of feeling invisible, unworthy, and broken. The idea that I could help lift someone else out of their darkness, into the light—well, that was something I could get behind! I would have taken a microfinance job in a heartbeat, but I couldn't find any paid positions, and, while money wasn't my primary motivation, it was still important!

I'd been interning for financial advisors at A.G. Edwards in Connecticut over the summer and in Boston during the school year. Preserving one's hard-earned wealth is important work and I was drawn to their passion, but I didn't share it. I was searching for a career path that lit me up inside because I was making a difference in people's lives, but I wasn't finding that in any of my prospects. I adored economics, but my love affair with cooking had only matured over the years. I was torn.

I graduated summa cum laude and was inducted into a slew of economics, finance, and business honor societies. To say I was burnt out by then is a gross understatement. I toyed with joining the Peace Corps or going for a master's degree in economics, but I was held back by the unrelenting pain in my spine. That was the official story. However, I was also filled with a deep fear of inadequacy—a secret truth that blanketed me with a dark shadow of shame for nearly two decades. I graduated at the top of my class with a résumé that could have earned me an interview at my pick of employers, but I didn't believe in my ability to make it in the business world— or *anywhere*, for that matter. I was my harshest critic, and my pain was a convenient reason to stall figuring my life out.

My parents always valued education and had the means to provide me with every academic pursuit I wanted to follow. Most people don't have as many possibilities afforded to them in life, and I've never taken that lightly. In fact, just the opposite. This Bible verse has always been prominent in my mind:

"When someone has been given much, much will be required in return; and when someone has been entrusted with much, even more will be required" (Luke 12:48).

I would come to see that this verse applies as much to blessings as it does to pain.

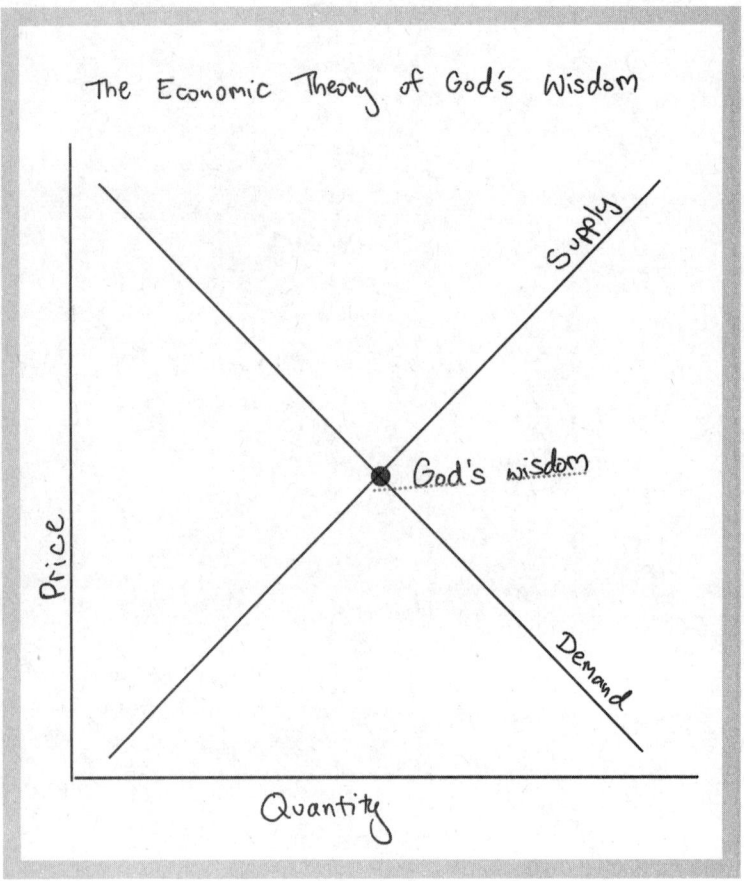

*The economic theory of God's wisdom*

Eight

# THE LEARNING CURVE OF PAIN

"MA, WHEN'S DINNER going to be ready?" I stare in disbelief at Tony, as I sit beside him in the upper level of his parents' house. *Did he really just call his mom from his cell phone while she was cooking an Italian feast for us in the kitchen below? Is this going to be my life?*

I was raised in a household with very traditional gender roles, but this display raised those expectations to a level of extreme discomfort. Tony and I were a match on paper, but eventually I saw how different our aspirations were. I was only twenty-two years old, and I didn't yet know what I wanted to do with my life, but I knew I never wanted to settle.

My immediate focus post-graduation—after making a clean break from Tony—was tending to the pain in my spine, which had continued to worsen. Even without a tailbone, the pain there was constant, and I learned that the explosive pangs I was experiencing throughout my lower back, which I'd been living with for the past four years, were from a ruptured disc. I had cortisone injections during my senior year with no relief, so the fall after graduation I had a microdiscectomy, which was supposed to clean up the broken parts of the disc. Mostly, it taught me how nauseated I get from anesthesia. I spent the night in the neurosurgical ward bent over the toilet bowl, each heave threatening to break my fragile spine.

Those first few weeks after surgery were an agony—by my standards then—but I made the choice not to wallow. I read the book *90 Minutes in Heaven* by Don Piper (not to be confused with the kissing game, Seven Minutes in Heaven) about a man who was in a horrible accident, died, and went to heaven, witnessing its perfection, beauty, and majesty before being resuscitated. He awoke to a grueling recovery process and the anguish of why God sent him back to the brokenness of earth.[7]

Reading his story put my pain into perspective. As I've come to learn, perspective is a highly effective way to fight the slippery slope toward self-pity, especially as it pertains to pain. The story also made me examine my purpose. *What are God's plans for my life? Am I walking in the path he wills for me, or merely living to satisfy my own desires? How do I even know what God's will is?*

I was looking to fit God into an equation like those I'd used in my economics classes. If the price of a commodity is determined at the intersection of supply and demand, is God's will at the intersection of his supply of wisdom and how earnestly I ask for, or (more often) demand, it? As you can see, my relationship with God was heady and transactional. I hadn't yet learned to hear that still, small voice.

The book *90 Minutes in Heaven* also shifted my view about the fleeting nature of my time on earth. Yes, some days are excruciating.

# THE LEARNING CURVE OF PAIN

But then, in the blink of an eye, eternity will begin. Every tear will be wiped away, my pain gone forever, and I'll be exactly who God created me to be, living with him forever! *Forever.* Suddenly that word wasn't quite so terrifying anymore.

At my post-op appointment, my surgeon, who spoke with a heavy yet unplaceable Southern accent, said, "The microdiscectomy went perfectly, and you'll be free of pain after this, so have a nice life. I never want to see you again." *Well, okay then!* In addition to reading, I spent my convalescence cooking, which is by far my favorite outlet. No matter how much pain I was in, as soon as I got into the kitchen and dove into the task at hand, everything else—pain included—faded into the background.

My parents didn't know why I had struggled so much in my younger years, or about the vices I'd gotten into, but they had certainly sensed the growing gap in our relationship. I felt compelled to make up for what a world-class screwup I'd been. Bringing them joy through my food was one way to show my love, as well as my bound-up emotions, without having to say a word. Cooking also made me feel worthy; it was a way to earn love.

During this convalescence, I also resumed the arduous task of sealing my fate, a.k.a. deciding what I was going to do with my life. I made up my mind to try the culinary route and applied for an internship on an agritourism farm in Tuscany. When I wasn't accepted, I was sorely disappointed. Shortly after, my mom and I got a phone call with the news that my Auntie Lorilee, who was like a second mom to me, had been diagnosed with a stage-four glioblastoma—an essentially unsurvivable brain cancer—and was being rushed into emergency surgery. This devastated our tight-knit family, and we started spending as much time together as possible.

# SPERANZA

Wanting to stay nearby, I took a job at my old high school, teaching microeconomics for a semester while they were in between full-time faculty. I made the curriculum exciting and relevant with initiatives such as Freakonomics Fridays. I was determined to make these kids fall in love with the subject matter the way I had. Instead, they behaved like teenagers: apathetic, disinterested, and mostly checked out. It gave me a whole new appreciation for high school teachers, and I realized the only way I could ever teach was if the students were there by choice.

To burn off steam—and fulfill my exercise mandate—I went to cardio kickboxing a few nights a week. I woke up one morning unable to walk and had to crawl down the hallway to get to the bathroom, then downstairs for help. My lower back pain had returned with a vengeance. The problem with the surgery I'd had was that it was the equivalent of cutting off the bulging part of a flat tire rather than reinflating it. New imaging showed I'd developed degeneration throughout my lumbar spine, as well as more herniated discs and tears around the surgical site. I'd also developed neurological issues affecting my colon and bladder function. *So much for never seeing my surgeon again.* Despite his stellar bedside manner—cue eye roll—I looked into other options, and the whole cycle of doctors, imaging, various therapies, invasive testing, and injections began yet again.

Honestly, I'm getting as depressed in telling these parts of my story as you probably are in reading them. But the stage is almost set. One more season of pain—a pivotal point in my life—and then we'll have some fun. I promise.

*American Idol concert with my mom, Uncle Dan, and Auntie Lorilee*

NINE

# WAVES OF GRIEF

MY AUNTIE LORILEE was given six months to live, but she was resolved to be present for a few more milestones and outlived all expectations by nearly a year. She lived each day with joy and vigor, carrying an unshakable peace in believing that the end of this life meant the start of a perfect eternity. One of my favorite memories during those final months truly encapsulates her spirit. She was an avid *American Idol* fan, so my uncle, mom, and I took her to their concert. Her brain tumor was so severe that her vision was limited, and she was having seizures, but my auntie was determined not to let anything stop her from being at the show. She marched into the arena sporting a neck pillow, sunglasses, and noise-minimizing headphones—an image of bravery I will never forget.

It was this same passion and excitement, not to mention how delicious her food was, that drew me into the kitchen with her. I'll never forget sitting, mesmerized, as my Auntie Lor explained to me the science behind a flaky pie crust—how the butter *must* remain chilled and in small chunks. "Since butter contains about 15 percent water, it turns to steam when it enters a hot oven, and that steam forms layers in the dough, producing a puffy, flaky, tender crust." I went home and soon after baked my first strawberry rhubarb pie with an all-butter pie crust. Before then, it was my grandma who taught me how to bake my first-ever pie—apple with a shortening crust. Both pies were memorable and delicious!

One fleeting summer weekend at my Auntie MJ and Uncle V's house in Cape Cod, I again sat in the kitchen as my Auntie Lor instructed me on how to make her famous *quattro formaggio*. As I went to chiffonade all the basil, she insisted I leave a perfect sprig untouched. I pulled the bubbling cheesy crostini from the oven and transferred them to a Polish Pottery platter, then watched as she garnished one side of the platter with a flourish of basil. That simple herb made the dish complete, and little did I know that, not too long after, I would spend countless nights that turned into years, garnishing platters in my job as a catering chef, thinking of my Auntie all the while.

When my Auntie Lor got sick, and our family started visiting frequently, it was known we would show up with food. There was no prior phone call asking, "Should I bring something for dinner?" but instead, "I was thinking of making spinach manicotti, how does that sound? Do you want to get the bread from Babalouie's?" Bringing a meal wasn't something expected in the sense that it was taken for granted; the act was an outpouring of love, an extension of oneself, and a mutually shared sentiment by all who gathered at the dinner table. My Auntie MJ—yet another one of my culinary muses—probably made enough meatballs to feed half of Rutland, not to mention clam sauce, chicken Francese, manicotti, and many more Italian delicacies that came pouring out of her kitchen with the same love and care as new olive oil flows from the press.

The weekend of my mom's birthday in late October, I left work Friday evening and drove toward Vermont as I often did. On the way, my mom called and told me that my aunt had slipped into a coma. It was highly probable she wouldn't make it through the weekend, and I was likely driving toward what was still my biggest fear—death.

Panic started setting in, identifiable by the familiar elephant sitting on my chest. But then I prayed. I prayed for strength to get through whatever lay ahead. I prayed for peace to wash over me and my family. And I prayed for courage—much like the courage I'd seen my aunt live with each day. I arrived in time to have dinner with my family, and we sang "Happy Birthday" to my mom before having slices of chocolate cake, all while my aunt lay unconscious in the next room. I'd like to think she could hear our voices, our laughter, and our singing. I know she would have wanted the party to go on. In fact, she would have insisted!

My grandparents went to their hotel, and my mom and I made our way to bed in the room next door to my aunt. But instead of sleeping, we soon found ourselves by my aunt's side while she took her final breaths. My chest tightened as anxiety encroached on the moment. But stronger than any fear was an overwhelming sense of strength, peace, and courage. My mom and I hugged and cried and cried and hugged some more. It was the first time I had let myself be vulnerable in a very long time.

## SPERANZA

There was no denying that God had heard my cries to him, as well, so I continued praying through the events of the next hours and days, each one stained by the traumatic, gut-wrenching, and heartbreaking pain that unfolds after someone dies. I had been terrified of death my whole life, but when faced with it, God gave me a strength I didn't think possible.

That's when I knew I could face anything with God by my side. I kept thinking, *I just watched life leave this earth, I experienced my biggest fear, and God was right there, seeing me through.* That day, I took the anchor God had given me years ago and threw it overboard with a newfound trust that, no matter what my future held, I would never weather it alone. I had no idea just how much the seas would rage and how strong that anchor was going to need to be.

My aunt's wake was on Halloween, and, for years after, as soon as I'd feel the chill of autumn in the air and see Halloween décor in the stores, I'd get a pit in my stomach that lasted until November. I wanted to go to a dark corner and hide until the season had passed and I could go back to burying the pain.

*I know you wanted to cry, to scream, to let someone in, to let it all out, but how could you when you'd spent your life equating the very presence of emotions with weakness, and weakness with unworthiness? When vulnerability never felt safe? But there was no containing this heaviness, and since you couldn't make a sound, your body did so for you. How I wish you could see that your body's not in rebellion. It's presenting its requests. The draining fatigue is a plea to end the war within your mind—the mind that shames*

## WAVES OF GRIEF

*you for not knowing how to grieve and rebukes you when you do. Your thyroid that won't regulate is your body's cry to let yourself shed those tears you keep fighting back. And that ache in your belly is mirroring your bereaved soul, yearning for the nourishment of being comforted.*

*With my mom in her garden*

Ten

# KITCHEN CONFIDENTIAL

SPORTING A BLACK-AND-WHITE gown I'd worn to my high school's lame excuse for a prom, I spent the evening of my twenty-third birthday at a charity gala for the Food Bank of Western Massachusetts. This was much to my dad's dismay, as he would have preferred I were on the hunt for a husband instead of networking at an event for a worthy cause. I had dated a bit since Tony, and starting a family was absolutely still on my radar, but I was going places and didn't want to put down roots in my hometown. Every Friday night I had to listen to my dad tell me that he knew the mayor, who could get me my pick of inmates at the local prison—literal jailbirds with nowhere to go. My dad often made me laugh, but this was not one of his better jokes.

A longtime friend of my parents asked me about my aspirations, and, with one introduction, I had landed an interview

# SPERANZA

*A hug from my dad*

and a job as the office manager for the Lisa Ekus Group. Lisa was renowned in the fields of literary agenting, PR, endorsement deals, and media training, with a focus on cookbook authors and chefs, and was integrally involved with charities such as the Food Bank. I was surrounded by unparalleled talent and gaining exposure to the breadth and depth of the culinary world. So many of my skills were being utilized as I crafted PR campaigns, received and paid out royalties, managed the books, spearheaded charitable events, and a few times, even prepped food for chef demos. I loved all that I was learning, but the longer I sat at my desk each day, promoting extraordinary chefs, the more I knew I had to become one.

## KITCHEN CONFIDENTIAL

That job was the push I needed.

But first, more surgery. Because the pain hadn't improved at all since the operation on my tailbone, and sitting was still quite literally a pain in the rear, I finally decided to look into what else could be done. I found a surgeon in New Jersey known as "the tailbone doctor" who confirmed that there was, despite my earlier surgeon's denial, a floating piece of bone as well as a jagged edge to the end of my remaining tailbone. To clean up the mess, the tailbone doctor removed bone at the base of my sacrum and adjusted some soft tissue to pad the area, aiming to make it more comfortable to sit.

Again, I was hopeful. And again, the surgery didn't help the pain. Unlike before, however, when surgery had bought me time to flounder in thoughts of the future, this time I finally had a purpose and a plan. I was ashamed of the way I had let pain become a crutch—a weakness, really—and decided it was no longer going to dictate my actions. I had to push my body even harder, and pain was just one more challenge to conquer.

Learning to honor my body was clearly a pursuit for another time, but I was finally standing on a solid foundation. Although I was still far from growing those deep roots, I was well beyond where I'd been. I was a broken, shell of a person during those high school and college years, and by God's amazing grace I had—quite literally—been given a second chance. And I was seizing it! I had blossomed in profound ways during those years since graduation, and, as I'd come to see many times, God was working during that season of waiting. Facing my greatest fear and watching God carry me right through the valley deepened my trust in him and emboldened me to hand over my other fears, including my archnemesis, *control*. This surrender allowed me to adopt a much healthier, less restrictive way of eating, but I was still fastidious about working out every day, no matter how much my body protested.

While I was living back home for those years, my family became my best friends, and I now had five nephews to dote on, play with, and rock to sleep. They lit up my life! My parents—especially my mom—had lovingly poured time into me while I recovered from surgeries and navigated other health challenges. Around my dad, however, I still braced for impact. Sometimes he lived up to my expectations, but more often he pleasantly surprised me. Despite his insistence that becoming a chef meant I was going to spend my life flipping burgers, he and my mom cheerily took me to tour culinary schools. I relished that time with them, as it was something I hadn't experienced when choosing a college. This go-round, I did not pick my culinary school because I liked the name!

Six weeks after my second tailbone surgery, at the ripe old age of twenty-four, I moved to New York City to start culinary school and a new chapter of life. *Woot woot!* To say I was excited is an understatement, but more than anything, I was immensely grateful. The city's endless possibilities breathed new life into my adventurous spirit.

Most culinary schools teach and build upon a foundation of French cooking. But Italian food—don't get me started again on Italian food! You know by now that's where my passion lies, and there was one culinary school in the US that had an all-Italian-based program. It was the Italian Culinary Academy (ICA), the sister school to the famed French Culinary Institute (FCI) in Manhattan. I started in the FCI's restaurant management program, where the syllabus was broken down into the parts of a business plan. Each class was taught by restaurant professionals.

# KITCHEN CONFIDENTIAL

*Coffee with a view of Midtown Manhattan*

It was fascinating learning from people who were living and breathing this work in one of the most cutthroat cities for owners and operators of restaurants. Chefs from all over the world demoed dishes in the FCI's culinary theater, and I quite literally ate up everything

I was learning. I once sampled beaver tail *chicharone*; at some point in history, the tail was categorized as fish and allowed when fasting from meat during Lent. On another occasion, I watched the cavity of a raccoon casually packed with several blocks of butter before being roasted, as part of a "roadkill" series.

A few weeks into my new life in the city, I was reading the winter edition of *Edible Manhattan* and came across a story about Chef Marco Canora, who had an Italian restaurant, Hearth, in the East Village. He had worked at my favorite restaurant in Florence, Il Cibreo, then opened a restaurant on Martha's Vineyard, where I'd spent a lot of time growing up. I shared his ingredient-driven food philosophy and cooking style and knew I wanted to learn from him. The article mentioned that his restaurant had a chef's counter with a view into the kitchen.[8] That was my in.

One night after class I scored a seat at Hearth's chef's counter, and Chef Marco was in the kitchen. While eating my way through the impressively seasonal menu, I struck up a conversation with him, making sure to include our mutual love for Florence and Martha's Vineyard, and mentioning that I'd recently moved to the city for culinary school. By the end of the night, I'd landed myself an internship!

I had never worked in a professional kitchen before, and it showed. My first day, I showed up in neon pink Nike running shoes with a canvas bag holding my knives. It's no wonder, for the first few weeks, they stuck me down in the basement prep kitchen to peel fava beans, weigh and form meatballs, and pass sauce through the food mill. Eventually, I moved up to the main kitchen, shaving paper-thin fennel using a meat slicer and prepping other *garde manger* items, such as salads, charcuterie, pâtés, and cold hors d'oeuvres. A few nights, they even let me stay after my shift to work the dinner service.

To this day, Hearth is still my favorite restaurant in Manhattan, especially when I can snag a seat at the chef's counter.

I think it's safe to say that you could live your whole life in New York City and still only scratch its surface. I had hit the pavement running, racking up tens of thousands of steps each day traversing Brooklyn, where I lived in student housing, and Manhattan, where my school was located. I started having intense pain in my feet and went to a podiatrist who diagnosed me with bunions and bone spurs. I was just a few months away from starting culinary school and about to be on my feet even more. The doctor recommended bunion surgery, and since I didn't have much time to spare, I got both feet operated on at the same time. That was my fifth surgery and I wasn't even twenty-five. I spent the next month walking all over Manhattan and Brooklyn in giant black surgical boots. I don't think I started any trends with that fashion statement, but in New York City, I wouldn't rule it out!

The day after surgery, it was back to my schoolwork. I was in the throes of my capstone project for my restaurant management program, which entailed writing a business plan for the restaurant I wanted to open one day. I'd written business plans at Bentley but never one so personal. I'd go to restaurants doing "research," making detailed notes on the likes and dislikes of the service, layout, table setting, and menu. I loved writing that business plan. The irony is that it saved me from ever wanting to open a restaurant. The hardest part of owning a business is finding reliable workers, and even the most well-intentioned employee isn't going to match your commitment and diligence. As a perfectionist, I knew I'd have a really hard time finding employees who worked to my standards; thus, I would end up trying to do everything myself and it would take over my life. But learning the business of the culinary field, especially the financial side of it, was invaluable later in my career as a catering chef, purchasing manager, and then running my own private chef business.

Culinary school started, and right away it was absolutely thrilling and terrifying. My only frame of reference was reading Anthony Bourdain's harrowing tales in *Kitchen Confidential* and watching Gordon Ramsay bring chefs to tears in *Hell's Kitchen*. The heat of our kitchen matched the stifling summer weather in New York City. There were twenty students in my class, including a handful of eighteen-year-olds, a few twenty-somethings like myself, and several fifty- to sixty-year-olds. Everyone was there for different reasons and with varying goals, but we were all about to spend the next nine months together. In New York, we learned the basics of cooking using traditional Italian recipes and had Italian language classes in preparation for our upcoming six-month culinary immersion in Italy.

Our three chefs were uber-talented and passionate, and also borderline drill sergeants. This was culinary boot camp. We spent long days in the kitchen and then, each night, had to write out the recipes for the next day's lesson plan, plus study our Italian and kitchen terminology. The fast pace pushed me far past my comfort zone. I did well on the many cooking exams they administered, but my chefs often noted that I lacked confidence and didn't believe in myself.

They were right. I'd come a long way from the angry, goth teenager, but had traded my rebellion for people-pleasing and overachieving. The weight of judgement had been a constant presence in my life—other people's and my own. That, coupled with believing I hadn't been wanted, eroded my inherent sense of worth. With no identity or intrinsic value, I constantly compared myself to others and always fell short. This tainted reality had been mine for so long, I knew no other way to exist. I continued stuffing my voice down into that "bucket," fearing that being disagreeable would make me less loveable.

> *There are so many clouds blocking you from seeing the light of truth! You feel it. I know you do. The shame that follows you, reminding you of your shortcomings. The continuous reel of self-criticism that takes captive every thought and buries the real you under the weight of judgement. So you keep pushing far past the boundaries you know you should respect, while hiding all the parts that are desperate to take up space in the world. You feel that void in both the holding in and what you fill it with—other people's opinions and beliefs that shape your view of yourself, the world, and of God. You've never experienced love you didn't think you had to earn from others, and certainly not from yourself, so how could God love you without asking something in return? It's going to be glorious when the Son breaks through and you see how recklessly loved you have always been!*

After spending eight hours a day together, every classmate became known for at least one quirky trait. Eddie liked to stuff all sorts of fowl with all sorts of random ingredients. Maggie provided witty narration of our culinary school dynamics. Courtney had a vibe that was "like, whatever, guys . . ." and I could be counted on to always have the correct answer on a pop quiz or test, and to hum while I cooked.

## SPERANZA

Nineties rock transports me to the back seat of my brothers' pickup truck en route to school—one of my earliest and happiest memories. I used to hum the songs I loved during class and was probably the only kindergartener who knew the lyrics to every Stone Temple Pilots and Smashing Pumpkins ballad. To this day, I usually have Lithium playing on my XM car radio, often singing along at the top of my lungs. I hum when I'm happy or need to calm my nerves, and cooking often induces both emotions. I don't think I realized I was humming until my culinary school friends started teasing me about it, calling me a little old lady. I certainly felt like one!

By that point, I had pain in much of my spine and many of my joints. I could tell you days before a storm that it was going to hit—I might as well have moonlighted as a weatherperson. What fascinates me, though, is that humming was a coping mechanism I'd learned at a young age. Later, I discovered that humming—like a sigh—is a way of activating the vagus nerve, the nervous system's powerful conduit connecting the mind and the gut. By activating this nerve, I shifted my body out of stress mode into a more relaxed state. Humming calmed the chaos I felt internally and in my environment.

I never knew what famed chef I was going to brush elbows with, as the likes of Jacques Pépin regularly graced our kitchen. I loved what I was learning, even though sometimes it felt like my brain couldn't contain it all! There were so many new ingredients, terms, knife skills, techniques, and methods. We came to know how to properly season a dish, reduce and mount a sauce, sear a protein, emulsify a vinaigrette, brunoise a potato, make—not break—a béchamel, and the skill that was drilled into us more than any other: how to make the perfect *risotto alla parmigiana*. It was a total sensory experience that epitomized Italian cuisine.

*Risotto ala parmiginana*

A shallot is diced to a fine brunoise and cooked in butter until softened, but not at all browned. Carnaroli rice is added and toasted until you hear it dancing in the pan. White wine deglazes it all and cooks until you no longer smell the alcohol. Stock is added by the ladle-full, and the risotto is stirred after each addition of liquid. When you hear the rice start to boil more rapidly, it's time for more stock. The rice is perfectly *al dente* when a single grain slid against a wooden spoon reveals no more raw white starch in the center. Cubes of cold butter and *Parmigiano-Reggiano* are added and left to melt ever so gently before being rigorously beaten into the risotto.

The consistency of the finished dish is to be *all'onda*—"like a wave"—as the risotto should flow in a creamy, rippling manner. Each grain of rice should be thoroughly coated in a perfectly emulsified sauce, and when scooped onto a plate should extend outward in complete harmony. After a long day in the kitchen, we'd think we were done and would start packing up our gear when one of our chefs would shout, "risotto alla parmigiana, vai!" *GO!* And we'd all rush to gather the needed ingredients and make our (sub-par) version of the dish. It is now one of my favorite things to make, and I have not only mastered it, but I find its creation completely cathartic.

Continuing a thread from the book *Unexpected*, regarding the neural pathways of fear, Dr. Jill Carnahan wrote, "flow-state activities are one of the best ways to rewire those old neural pathways. . . . Each time I choose to try something new and challenging despite the fear I feel inside, I gain courage. I begin to trust in my ability to figure things out, releasing the addiction to well-worn fear and trauma pathways that have previously been my default."[9]

Embarking on my culinary career was thrilling, yes, but absolutely terrifying at first. Dr. Carnahan got it right—at each turn, I built confidence and trust in my abilities, and that old adversary of fear held a bit less of a chokehold on me. In time, cooking led me to a flow state—that sweet spot of full immersion in an activity where movements are intuitive, focus is razor-sharp, creativity is abundant, and time and the outside world seem to stand still.

*Final exams at ALMA, Colorno, Italy*

Eleven

# THE STAGISTA CHRONICLES

ITALIANS, AS A WHOLE, exude impeccable style, flair, and an appreciation of the finer things in life. Older women don fur coats at the grocery store without eliciting a stare, and men casually go for their evening stroll in a three-piece suit, elaborate scarf, and pocket square. Italians gave us some of the world's most majestic art, music, and architecture, as well as expertly crafted food and fashion. The country's magnificently rugged landscape mirrors the nonchalant opulence of those who live there. The small town of Colorno, in the region of Emiglia-Romagna, the food capital of Italy, radiated the same alluring charm. That is, until the circus came to town.

Our rowdy American class of all ages, shapes, sizes, and levels of decorum took up residence in two apartment buildings owned by our school. I was roommates with Christine, a former Spanx consultant, planning to start a catering business back in Atlanta. We'd become fast friends in New York City, along with Maggie, who had just left a decade-long career at the TV network Lifetime, and Gregg, who was a tenured drama professor taking a sabbatical from the University of Mary Washington. There was also Eddie, an eighteen-year-old skateboarder from Mongolia, who became like a little brother to me.

Our class spent so much time together, we became like one big, dysfunctional family. We knew one another's quirks, yet loved and tolerated one another anyway. The teenage girls innocently spent their nights fishing for Italian men at the town bar, while the real troublemakers ended up being the retirees. One turned into a raging alcoholic, and after we found her one morning, passed out in the bushes outside our apartment, we were compelled to stage an intervention. Some of the women refused to age gracefully and tried way too hard to fit in with the "cool kids." And some of the men viewed every chef demo as a free pass at the Old Country Buffet. Throwing their chivalry out with the dishwater, they elbowed their way to the front of the line.

We were part of ALMA, a large Italian culinary school founded by Chef Gualtiero Marchesi, the father—or should I say Godfather?—of modern Italian cuisine. Our school building was a beautiful, ancient castle surrounded by lush gardens and fountains, a setting that, in many ways, was a 180-degree departure from New York. I welcomed the slower pace, except when we had to watch our chef, Carlo, plate a salad quite literally one piece of lettuce at a time.

The curriculum was broken into the twenty Italian regions—each week, we focused on one. Our days started out with a history, wine, or language class, then we either went into the kitchen for a day

# THE STAGISTA CHRONICLES

*A composed seafood salad at ALMA*

of cooking modern interpretations of regional cuisine or watched a chef from that region demo dishes using traditional ingredients. One of these chefs was missing a finger on his left hand (understandable), and the chef from Sicily was missing an ear (quite suspicious). Chef Carlo was mild-mannered and all about precision over speed. *Now that's what I'm talking about!*

We worked with premium ingredients, many of which I'd never seen before. Spot prawns from Sicily that tasted like the ocean. Sides of venison, which we broke down, making stock from the bones to turn into rich demi-glace. A whole guinea hen, a.k.a. a pigeon, that still had feathers and all of its organs intact. We learned to pluck and burn the feathers, detach the head to access the windpipe and innards, and remove the talons and ligaments in the legs with a twisting motion. I wouldn't even touch raw chicken as a child! On one occasion, Chef Carlo broke down a whole lamb, butterflied it, set aside the organs, removed all the bones except its hips, then placed the organs back inside, seasoned the whole lamb with salt, spices, and herbs, and rolled it up by its hip bones into a roast that conjured images of a medieval feast.

Our history teacher, Aldo, was the stereotypical animated Italian, and entertained us as we learned the ways history shaped the food of each region. Our wine teacher, Massimo, was equally spirited and obsessed with American pop culture. He'd somehow work it into almost everything he said, for instance, "This wine has some residual pulp . . . fiction," or he'd break out into song, triggered by some characteristic of the wine we were sampling: "He's a *smooth operator*." The only downside was that this class was at eight o'clock in the morning, and we had to spit each sip of exceptional wine into a bucket so we, too, wouldn't lose a finger.

We went on several field trips to watch iconic Italian products being made, arriving in a small town with cobblestone streets and Instagram-worthy vignettes, only for our bus to disgorge its Yankee passengers. I'd like to know what the villagers watching our circus had to say as they sipped Barolo, wore their Gucci loafers, and were serenaded by Puccini. On free weekends, we'd host potluck dinners and finally enjoy the wines we weren't allowed to drink at school, or we'd hop on the train to another city and use the travel time to study Italian. Our classes were in English, but Italian would soon prove critical for our restaurant internships.

In the first email I sent to everyone back home, I signed off with a sentiment that remained throughout the experience: "It's surreal that I am here amongst this beauty. I keep thanking God and

*Testing a wheel of Parmigiano Reggiano in Parma*

pinching myself!" I loved my Italian life. Christine and I started each morning at the local cafe, sipping an espresso *dopio macchiato*, then enjoyed another after lunch, served by the elderly barista/bartender, Giorgio, in his three-piece suit and colorful scarf. After class we'd go for a Campari Spritz and a complementary spread of delicious bite-sized snacks. The Italians have also mastered the art of Happy Hour. I named my dog "Spritz" after my favorite pastime! We'd often cap the day off with a run at dusk; traversing the hills that surrounded the town, watching the mighty cypresses turn to shadows as the sky faded to an ember.

Running hadn't gotten easier than in my high school days, but my willpower had been fortified. I weighed my worth by the metric of how hard I worked, how much I pushed myself, and how disciplined I was. My grit was my rubric, and each challenge set the bar that much higher. My back ached with every stride, and I was left with painful shin splints for days afterward, but my spine also hurt while sitting through demos and being on my feet cooking. I was in near-constant pain anyway, so what was a little bit more?

If only I'd leaned into my body's pleas and asked what my pain was trying to tell me, I would have heard its wisdom. This pain was protection—my body's bracing and compensating for widespread weakness as the glue that held it together was slowly losing its stickiness. Never could I have imagined that each painful stride was pushing my body toward absolute destruction. Never did I think I'd hear the words "Soon you'll struggle to walk" or "It's by God's grace you aren't paralyzed."

The climate in Colorno was similar to that of the Northeast, and as the leaves changed to shades of gold and the air turned crisp, the pit in my stomach showed its colors too. My heart ached to tell my Auntie Lorilee about my culinary adventures. Instead, I turned to fall comfort food, knowing my schoolmates were also longing for a taste of home. I set out to make my Auntie Linda's pumpkin bread, but couldn't find canned pumpkin anywhere, so I bought a fresh pumpkin and cooked it in a cryovacked bag (in sealed plastic) in the school's steam oven. I then stayed late after class, joined by two classmates, to pass the pumpkin through a sieve, yielding a creamy purée. We changed out of our uniforms and, with purée in hand, attempted to head home.

My description of the school as an old castle was no exaggeration. There were twelve-foot wrought-iron gates surrounding it, and when we tried to leave, we found that the gate was locked. We were trapped inside the school grounds! We went back into our building and looked for anyone still lingering there or a janitor cleaning up from the day. The castle was empty. Trying not to panic, we searched for a way out, periodically yelling for a rescue. Finally, we found a back entrance where the gate was only about six feet tall. We rallied our courage, threw our bags—and the purée—to the other side, then helped hoist one another over the gate. I baked two loaves of pumpkin bread in pans I borrowed from the school, shared one with my classmates, and kept the other for Christine and me to eat for breakfast. It was so worth almost having to spend a night sleeping in our school kitchen, and the pumpkin bread tasted even better with the schmear of triumph!

On Thanksgiving Day in the US, I made the move from my school to working my three-month internship in Carsoli, Abruzzo, a region in central Italy with picturesque towns sandwiched between the imposing mountains of the Apennines and the idyllic beaches of the Adriatic coast. European kitchens rely heavily on unpaid interns. In Italy, this internship is called a *stage* (pronounced *stahj*) and the intern is called a *stagista*. My assignment detail was lacking just that. It contained the name of the restaurant, a contact email, and the physical address. I had an iPhone, but it only worked when connected to WiFi. I sent a quick introductory email with my expected arrival time in Carsoli. Thankfully, I understood how to navigate the train system, as it was my only means of getting there. However, the regional trains are much slower than those connecting major cities, and I was late meeting Leonardo, the restaurant owner, who didn't hide his agitation when he greeted me at the station.

Leonardo reminded me of my dad. He was spirited, loved hats, and yelled—a lot. His son, Francisco, was the chef and his polar opposite. He was quiet, mild-mannered, and fairly aloof. He spent more time working on side projects than in the kitchen. The restaurant prided itself on offering the highest-quality products from Abruzzo and having the second-largest private wine cellar in Italy. Leonardo's daughter, Francesca, was the sommelier and the only one who spoke a little English. She was very kind and very pregnant, but wasn't around a lot, leaving me to rely on my awkward Italian.

The sous chef, Ricardo, ran the lunch and dinner service, but three women were the true backbone of the restaurant. Anna made all the bread, pasta, and gnocchi, while Franca and Grazia prepped the bulk of the food for lunch and dinner. They were hardworking and didn't put up with anything less from those around them. They were quite cold to me at first, but once I proved I was there to learn and work hard, I won their hearts. I also won their stomachs with the goodies I constantly baked for the staff! There were two head waiters—Hans, who was born in Germany and didn't drink any of the wine he knew so much about, and Antonella, whom I became fast friends with.

Leonardo's home was above the restaurant and the interns stayed in his spare room. Vicki, from Canada, had been there for the past few months and taught me the ropes—in English, thankfully—during the few days our stages overlapped. My main job was making the desserts. Every guest ended their meal with a plate of five different bite-sized sweets called *dolcetti*. I was tasked with keeping a steady supply of these and plating them during lunch and dinner service, in addition to making and plating the other desserts. Working the appetizer and pasta stations was also in rotation.

I arrived in the kitchen at 10 a.m. each morning, espresso in hand, wearing black-and-white checkered pants, a white chef coat, and a demeaning hairnet. All of us women were required to wear one, but Chef Francisco was not, even though his wild black curls were longer than any of our hair! I'd take inventory of the *dolcetti* and dessert, then I'd commence my prep. Before opening for lunch, we ate a quick family meal together, usually a simple but tasty pasta. Lunch service ended with dish duty. We had two dish pits—a double sink for the pots and pans, and a dishwashing machine for plates, glasses, and silverware. We rotated between the two, and I ended each lunch and dinner service washing dishes for at least an hour with the help of Franca and Grazia. The men never washed a dish—or shed a hair, apparently.

I'd leave the kitchen between 4 and 5 p.m. and do a quick Pilates workout or go for a run, despite the protest from my aching, worn-out body. After a particularly late shift the night before, I'd lie down in bed unable to move due to utter pain and sheer exhaustion. Returning to the kitchen at 6 p.m., requisite espresso in hand, I'd do it all over again, leaving the kitchen anywhere from midnight to 1:30 a.m. The restaurant was supposed to be closed on Wednesdays; however, every week in December there was a Catholic holiday leading up to Christmas that happened to fall on a Wednesday, so we would stay open for at least a long and busy lunch service, if not dinner as well.

So starts *The Stagista Chronicles*—bits and pieces from the journal I wrote in each night, usually at 2 a.m., when I was finally in bed. The first few entries were in Italian until I conceded to my physical and mental exhaustion from a thirteen-hour day of cooking while attempting to speak and comprehend Italian.

# SPERANZA

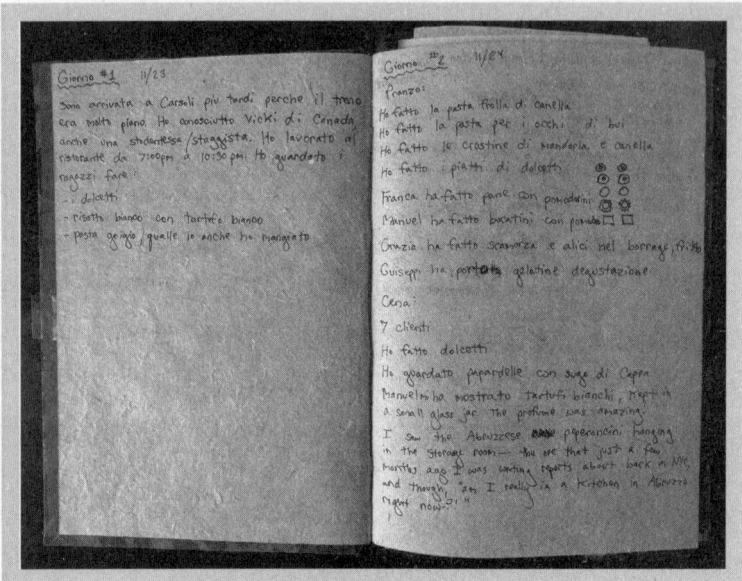

*Stagista Chronicles journal entry*

Giorno #5, 11/27
*There is no "sh" or "ley" sound in Italian, so everyone has a really hard time pronouncing my name. The many variations I've heard: Ashee, Asha, Assa, Ashland, Askey, and my favorite, Ashmee. Ricardo found out that I was born in Springfield and when I came into the kitchen tonight he'd made a name tag for me that said "Marge."*

Ricardo, the scrawny sous chef, was a little punk. Almost right away he started fondling me. He grabbed my butt while I was plating desserts, or grabbed my boobs while I was elbow-deep in soapy dish water, wearing big rubber gloves, and pretty much defenseless. While violating my personal space, he'd ask me to sleep with him. To my "no," he'd ask

*The day Ricardo nicknamed me Marge*

"why?" I'd explain my belief that sex is a sacred act for a husband and wife, and he'd laugh, saying that wasn't how he viewed it. At first I was furious at his manhandling and didn't know how I was going to put up with three months of it, but very quickly I made a choice. I could be mad at him the whole time, or I could brush it off, knowing that, if need be, I could snap him like a twig. I have three brothers and know how to hold my own. I also prayed a lot—for patience and love—the brotherly type! It was a good decision. Groping aside, he was sweet and funny, and we joked around constantly.

Hans, the German waiter, also took a liking to me. While I was loading the dishwasher at the end of a dinner service, he'd offer me a glass of leftover wine, to which I would always answer, "*Si!*"

He would exclaim, "*Buon vino, Ashmee!*" Then ask me out on a date to the Autogrille, a glorified rest area and the only place open at 2 a.m.

To which I would always answer, "*No.*"

After a few go-rounds, Hans started coming into the dish pit chanting, "*Ashmee Si, Ashmee No. Ashmee Si, Ashmee No!*" Then he'd grab my cheeks and ask, "*Toute okey, Ashmee?*"

*No, Hans, between the incessant chanting and cheek pinching, everything is not okay!*

Giorno #9, 12/1 *Giornoringraziamente!*

*I arrived at the restaurant on Thanksgiving, and as a way of celebrating my culture, Leonardo asked if I wanted to cook a traditional Thanksgiving meal for the kitchen crew the following Wednesday. I excitedly agreed and gave Francisco a list of ingredients. A few days ago, Leonardo informed me the only turkey they were able to find weighed thirty pounds. Mom cooked a turkey that size every year like a champ, but this was too big for them, so the whole dinner was in jeopardy of not happening. I stayed optimistic, and last night started preparing some items—currant "cranberry" sauce with orange and spice, dough for my apple crostata, pumpkin pie, and pumpkin bread. All the cooks scrunched their noses at the idea of a dessert made of pumpkin. "How can this be? Pumpkin in a cake? It makes no sense. Surely this can't taste good!" I just smiled and thought,* They'll see!

## THE STAGISTA CHRONICLES

*Ricardo stayed late with me helping to peel chestnuts, while Leonardo still didn't know if the turkey was going to arrive. But early this morning I awoke to him yelling, "Askey, la tacchino e arrivata!" The turkey arrived! I jumped out of bed, threw on my clothes—and hairnet—and ran down into the kitchen. I examined the turkey. It was about fifteen pounds and a real looker. I made a stuffing with roasted chestnuts and apples and got it into the blast chiller so I didn't give us all food poisoning. Never stuff a cold bird with hot stuffing! I got the turkey stuffed, trussed, and into the oven, then made an apple and mock-mincemeat crostata with an almond crumble, buttery herb biscuits, and mashed potatoes. It was madness, but I kept praying and everything turned out great!*

*Ricardo was supposed to help me, and when he finally strolled into the kitchen later this morning all he cared about was seeing where I had put the stuffing into the turkey . . . nel cullo! He insisted on opening the oven and showing everyone who came into the kitchen. After three hours I couldn't figure out why the internal temperature of the turkey was only registering 94 degrees, until suddenly I realized the oven thermometer was in Celsius! I quickly did the conversion, remembering the formula I'd learned in middle school: $F = 9/5 \times C + 32$ degrees and saved the turkey from near obliteration. Leonardo had invited a bunch of friends over and I was now feeding a group of twenty. He uncorked some wine as I served the dishes family-style, then Chef Francisco* *attempted to carve the turkey, looking at it like it was a foreign object. Before he butchered the poor bird, he asked if I'd carve it instead. They all sat in amazement as I removed the legs, carved the breast first, and then the dark meat. The meal was a hit! When it came time for dessert, I whipped up some cream and served a small slice of each of the three tortas. This was a tough crowd, but everyone cleaned their plates. This is one Thanksgiving I'll definitely never forget!*

Giorno #10, 12/2
*I saved a plate of desserts for Anna and Grazia and they loved everything. Anna said Chef Francisco had nothing on me. Francesca recounted to them everything I had made. It's so funny how astonished they are at eating turkey—you'd think I was serving them monkey! Meanwhile, they got two whole baby pigs today, broke them down, and boiled the heads to make coppa. Quite ironic!* Stasera (this evening) *as Ricardo was trying to grope me, he felt my arm muscles and was amazed. I told him I've done twenty-five push-ups every day since I was a teenager. He made everyone feel my muscles!*

Giorno #14, 12/5
*During dinner tonight, hottie truffle guy—a tall, blonde, handsome man—came into the kitchen in full camo gear and a headlamp, holding a bag of dirt-covered white truffles that sold for 3,000 Euros per kilo!*

## THE STAGISTA CHRONICLES

Giorno #16, 12/7
*Hope (n.)* speranza
*To hope (v.)* sperare
*Desire (n.)* desiderio
*To desire/wish for (v.)* desidere

*I had to look these words up because Ricardo won't quit with the "Ashley sleep with me" and I didn't know how to say, "You wish!"*

Revisiting this entry made me laugh out loud! Then, I got teary-eyed as I looked down at the word *speranza* tattooed on my wrist. I'd long forgotten about writing this in my journal, but that word had stuck in my mind. Years later, during some of my darkest days after contracting Lyme disease, I started each morning drinking coffee, obviously, and reading Bible verses about hope. I clung to that word, believing there'd be brighter days ahead, and I got it tattooed in Italian as if to say, *You won't just get better, you'll live a life of adventure again one day!*

Giorno #18, 12/9
*Busy lunch, busy dinner. I worked the service with Francisco. Ari, who helps out when we're busy, was washing dishes and started getting friendly with me, and Ricardo told me later that he was jealous. Hans wouldn't stop with the long stares and cheek grabbing. I then found out that Ari is Hans's nephew. Talk about a twisted love triangle I want no part of! When I left the kitchen tonight all three of them were standing at the door and I said, "Ciao ragazzi" ("bye guys"), and left.*

# SPERANZA

### Giorno #21, 12/12

*I read an amazing and comforting scripture—a psalm—before bed last night. Twice now a psalm has spoken exactly to my problems and fears. I made all the dolcetti, washed a bunch of dishes, and made desserts. I'm getting faster. At lunch Leonardo grilled pancetta in big strips like bacon and some sausage, and we all ate together, rounding out the meal with some bread and wine. He asked me to go into the meat fridge for more pancetta, and I noticed there was still fur on it! At dinner, Leonardo took me out to the grill to try the salame called "pigs' testicles" because two of them hang side by side from a wooden stick. To my relief, it's not because it's made from pigs' testicles as I'd originally thought!*

### Giorno #28, 12/19

*Christmas week is here! Francisco made a cake for a little girl's birthday and decorated it with doll figurines and assorted candy. It looked like a twisted scene from Katy Perry's "Candyland" music video. Francesca didn't like it and started yelling at Francisco, who in keeping with his mild temperament, didn't yell back. But soon, Leonardo joined in and made up for Francisco's silence. All day today, yell, yell, yell! I realized that growing up with so much yelling around me, I expect people, especially men, to yell when they're upset, and I'm actually surprised on those occasions when they don't. In so many ways, my upbringing tinted the glasses through which I look at the world.*

Oh, and Ricardo sprayed me with the steam oven hose while I was washing dishes tonight!

Giorno #34, 12/25 Buon Natale!
The restaurant closed for a few days at Christmas and Lex (my little brother) flew to Rome to spend it with me. Maggie came from her stage and met us on Christmas Eve for dinner and midnight mass at the Pantheon. On Christmas Day, Lex and I went to the Vatican for the Pope's address. It was thrilling listening to him say "Merry Christmas" in about twenty different languages and hearing the crowds from those countries shout and cheer.

Giorno #39, 12/30
I made the crust for the cheesecakes that Francisco asked me to make for New Year's Eve, using hazelnuts which I toasted and skinned. It's a nice feeling to be comfortable working with almost any ingredient. I added mascarpone, vanilla bean, and orange zest to the filling. They call cream cheese "Filadelphia," and I once saw Hans eating it by the spoonful! Tomorrow is New Year's Eve. I found out there is some tradition about giving/wearing red underwear. Leonardo asked me what size I am?!

Giorno #40, 12/31
This morning there was a package on my doorknob containing red lace underwear, a red garter, and a love letter from Leonardo. Yikes. I prepped dolcetti and made the passion fruit glaze for my cheesecakes. I learned that

## SPERANZA

*it's supposedly good luck to wear red underwear on NYE, as well as to eat things that are round like money. People also throw belongings they no longer want out of their windows, like small appliances, which could be lethal considering how many people live in multistory apartment buildings. Tonight I breaded lamb meatballs and plated three different* aperitivi *for our 150 guests. I helped Rosso with the* panzanella *and* pasta a la Grigia—*a creamy pasta made with pancetta—and every diner got a mandarin after their meal for good luck. After I had peeled about fifty of them, Ricardo finally told me I was supposed to serve them whole. My fingers were almost bloody! I also made a ton of dolcetti.*

*At midnight, there were fireworks, lots of rosé prosecco, and bagpipers who came through the kitchen playing traditional music, followed by karaoke which lasted until 3 a.m.! Everyone was wishing one another Happy New Year and I joined in saying, "Buon Ano" which I later found out I was mispronouncing and wishing everyone "good butthole." It's "Buon Anno"—a long "n" sound! Leonardo asked if I had gotten his gift and note, and then French-kissed me. What is it with these men! At least the cheesecake was a hit. Francisco and Francesca loved it and said it got loads of compliments from the diners. I washed dishes with Franca, Ricardo, and Rosso until 3 a.m. It was the first time a man had been in the dish pit, and we had so much fun!*

# THE STAGISTA CHRONICLES

Giorno #45, 1/5

*Another Wednesday I don't have off. Made the marmellata di arancia with Grazia. I have a wicked head/neck ache and there's a vertebra bulging from the back of my neck. Leonardo showed me his pre-Castro bottle of rum, aged in Oloroso sherry oak casks and let me taste thirty-six-year-old Demerara rum that was delicious! Notes of brown sugar, caramel, tobacco, asphalt, tar, and leather. So strong it made my mouth tingle and go numb! Sadly, not potent enough to dull my pain. Will it ever end?*

Giorno #62, 1/22

*Tonight was my last night at the restaurant. Antonella and I went to the bar afterward, but no one was there so we went "in giro" to the hilltop town I always admire on my jogs. It was beautiful. As we were driving through, we were listening to an American Country station and the song came on, "I'm leaving on a jet plane, don't know when I'll be back again." It was so ironic!*

Giorno #64, 1/24

*Well, I've survived my stage! It was sad saying goodbye to Franca. I'll miss her and all of the women. The men on the other hand . . . ciao ragazzi!*

I reunited with my classmates in Colorno for two days of commiserating about our stages, giving ample feedback to our teachers, taking our final exams, and celebrating our survival at a banquet our school threw for us grads.

## SPERANZA

The next day, I took the train to Venice to meet my older brother, sister-in-law, and two little nephews for a week of sightseeing. Leaving my family was the hardest part of living in different countries and I always felt torn between two worlds. When I'd left for Italy, my younger nephew wasn't talking yet. They called to tell me their flight from Paris was delayed, and I heard a little voice say, "Hi Auntie."

I replied, "Oh, hi Logan!"

The voice countered, "No, this is Blake!"

That was the first time I'd ever heard him talk! We made priceless memories that we still relive and laugh over when we're together.

Pain aside, those days in Italy were some of the best I'd ever felt—and would ever feel again. I worked long hours, but with a singular focus. It was so different from the fifty items on my to-do list now, all urgently screaming for attention. I left a piece of myself in that haven of profound inspiration and planned on going back every few years. Then life happened. Hopefully one day soon. *Speranza. Sigh.*

*Grilling lamb chops, Season to Taste kitchen*

Twelve

# FINGERTIP SALAD

IT'S INTERESTING HOW we inadvertently gravitate toward certain jobs. I was listening to at least some of my body's requests when I was drawn to cooking. I'd always struggled with fatigue and mornings were not my friend, but I didn't mind staying up late, and my broken body felt better when I was on my feet and moving around than it did when I was sitting down. Spending my days in the kitchen the past nine months checked all these boxes, but more than anything, it reawakened me to the power of food—the way it brings people together, transports us to another time and place, and delights and nourishes us too.

I worked for a year in Tampa, Florida, at a catering kitchen built by Outback Steakhouse, where we cooked banquets for up to six hundred guests. At my very first event, we set up food stations around the ballroom. Our chef assigned me to the slider bar. I struggled to focus on the pedantic task, as my dad's admonition, "You'll spend your life flipping burgers," mocked me with every turn of my spatula. I learned the ropes of large-scale catering and discovered that I had a knack for making food look like art—excelling at the precision of plating hundreds of bite-sized appetizers, building a lavish dessert platter, or crafting barnyard cake pops for a child's birthday party. Growing up in a family that lived to throw a party, I learned from the best!

Just before my twenty-seventh birthday, I moved back to Boston and went for an interview/trial shift at Season to Taste (STT), a farm-to-table catering company that mirrored my cooking philosophy. I worked next to Elissa, with her silky brown ponytail and warm chestnut eyes, as she animatedly told me she had recently moved from New York City, starting at STT as a prep cook. We chatted the whole time, exchanged phone numbers, and then she actually texted me that evening saying how great it was to meet me! I had so little self-worth, I was shocked to get her text.

STT hired me as a prep cook and we both quickly moved up the ranks. We catered high-end events and had a chef's table in our kitchen where we held private dinners showcasing delicacies from local purveyors, including farms, distilleries, and cheesemakers. In large part, this kitchen made me the chef I am today. I was surrounded by people who were passionate and genuine—traits I have always been most drawn to. My cooking skills were nurtured and honed, and I grew in confidence as a chef, a leader, and a person, mostly because I spent my days with people who *saw* me.

It wasn't so much that I let my defensive walls down, but more so that I was surrounded by people who didn't ask if they could breach them—they just did. And it was exactly what I needed. Elissa

# FINGERTIP SALAD

*Cooking with Elissa, Season to Taste kitchen*

instantly lifted the energy and spirits of every room she walked into. She was unabashedly settled in herself in a way that showed me I was also safe to be me. We quickly became best friends, spent countless days cooking side by side, and eventually we ran STT's kitchen together.

George, STT's general manager, had a larger-than-life personality and way of seeing right into the core of who I was. He enthusiastically brought out and applauded my most valuable traits. While working with him, my confidence soared. He soon nicknamed me "Scrappy," recognizing my grit and determination. Our sous chef, Fern, exuded warmth and sarcasm, and gave me freedom to blossom under her gentle guidance, while keeping our kitchen thumping with music and full of laughter. Chef Paul lauded my attention to detail while lighting a fire under my ass to hurry up on tasks that didn't require such precision.

STT's owner, Robert, like many visionaries, often made my life hell due to his over-ambition for what our small kitchen could handle. Even though I often wanted to strangle him, he was equally endearing. He promoted me to management while recognizing the ways I struggled with communication and leadership, and his gentle guidance helped me grow into my roles. Laura, our operations manager, had a big heart, was fiercely opinionated, and set a high bar, but on rare occasions she made it known that I was doing good work—like when she casually announced that because of my exactness, I'd lowered the company's food cost by a whole 10 percent.

The most profound things we can do for someone else are to encourage their strengths, recognize their struggles, meet them where they are, embolden them, be their cheerleader, and *see* them!

One morning, as I was buttoning my chef coat, I got a call letting me know that my dad was in the ICU after suffering a massive heart attack. My sister and I dropped everything to be at his side and help in any way we could. He was put on several medications and discharged with orders not to do any strenuous activity, and to lower his stress levels. He "obeyed" by promptly going outside and chopping wood. My sister and I were upset and afraid, and I lost focus while cutting up vegetables for a salad and chopped off my fingertip. My dad was enraged as I frantically bandaged my bloody hand, our collective anxiety pulsing like my wound. *This anti-stress campaign was off to a great start!*

Never in my life did I hear the words "I can't" come out of my dad's mouth. He didn't like the side effects from his medications and was determined to get off them. After researching his options, he decided to go vegan and fat-free. We're taking about someone

# FINGERTIP SALAD

*Barnyard cake pops*

with 100 percent Slavic roots who lived on kielbasa and potato salad with extra mayo. He consulted a functional medicine doctor, actively worked on his response to stress, and joined a men's prayer group at his church. God slowly healed my dad's heart, figuratively and literally. After a year, my dad was off his medication and had reversed his heart disease!

My dad's faith became a tangible part of his life. He had more patience, less anger, and a softness I'd never seen. I thank God every day that he spared my dad's life and for the way he used this trial as a turning point in our relationship—one that became rooted in deep love, and eventually, safety.

As my dad healed, I wish I could say my health was following suit. Instead, I was having worsening GI issues, fatigue, and hormonal and thyroid imbalances. It was clear that I was not getting anywhere with conventional medicine. A naturopathic doctor suggested a plethora of dietary changes, which I was skeptical about, but seeing the impact my dad's change in diet was having on his health was the push I needed. We forged a bond through our commitment to our well-being—encouraging, inspiring, sharing new research, and bouncing ideas off each other. I made it my mission to cook food for my dad that was heart-healthy but tasted so good he never felt he was missing out.

*I love watching your eyes light up with delight when you see your food bring a smile to someone's face! But it runs so much deeper than that. You know the darkness of pain, and you don't want it for anyone else. You can't yet see the wounds that are driving your own beliefs and actions. But you see the wounds of others and are compelled to lessen them—through appeasing, even when it means squashing your own opinion, and by pleasing, even when it means taking on a heavier load yourself. Aren't you tired of holding the fate of other people's happiness on your shoulders?*

*With Elissa in Julia Child's Cambridge kitchen*

Thirteen

# GIGS AND GIGGLES

USING THE DRIVER'S side fish-eye mirror, I move mere centimeters in reverse, just to stop, crank the wheel in the other direction, shift gears, and watch the nose of the truck inch forward. The engineers of Cambridge's cobblestone streets and alleyways, dating back to our country's Revolution, didn't foresee fifteen-foot box trucks careening down them. I just returned from Cape Cod, leading a diverse team of chefs as we set up a field kitchen and cooked an exceptional meal on cast-iron skillets set over charcoal fires. There were no trout cheeks on the menu, but recalling my childhood experiences, I felt most exhilarated cooking in these places.

One of the many amazing things about life is that we never know how all of our seemingly unconnected experiences will prove to be extremely useful later on. I was usually the only one who had the courage and training to operate these vehicles of all shapes and sizes, including box trucks, refrigerator trucks, ones with hydronic tailgates, and Sprinter vans that are so top-heavy they feel like wind in a sail. The first time I ever drove a truck for a catering job in Boston, and once it was safely parked back at our kitchen, I immediately called my dad. I thanked him for his driver's ed obstacle course and we chuckled at the irony of how that skill was being put to use now.

Catering is like the Girl Scouts of cooking—you learn very quickly to be prepared for anything. I so wish I had kept a journal during this time, but I wasn't the spring chicken I was during my stage in Italy. What's more, eighty-hour workweeks left little energy for writing. But there are a few events I'll never forget.

The wedding on Cape Cod for two hundred guests, where the Peruvian purple mashed potatoes never made it onto our truck. I got the call from the kitchen as I was about halfway to the Cape, so I quickly phoned one of my cooks, who was scheduled to meet us on-site, and I asked him to stop at the grocery store and buy all the potatoes they had. Per usual, we were setting up a field kitchen where most of the dinner would be cooked on grills. I boiled the potatoes in the small guesthouse kitchen, used a milk crate to strain them, and once mashed, mixed in some red beet puree that was a component of the salad course, making them somewhat purple-ish.

For another wedding, we hollowed out two hundred Cinderella pumpkins, brûléed the tops, filled them with pumpkin soup, then garnished each with a homemade cheese straw, which I stayed in the kitchen until midnight making. The venue was a tent on the rocky coast of Maine, and after the five-course dinner, we served a late-night snack of fried chicken and soba noodle salad. I saw women so wasted, they didn't even realize they had dropped fried chicken into their cleavage.

*Plating a salad, Season to Taste kitchen*

# SPERANZA

There was the time I drove our Sprinter van right across the perfectly manicured grass of the Harvard Quad and simultaneously ran events in three different locations at Harvard Medical School. At a dinner party in Cambridge, I realized partway through that everyone attending was a swinger. For a fashion show on Newbury Street, we set up a makeshift kitchen in a closet, which doubled as the dressing room for the models—a gig the young male cook working with me will never forget!

My dating life at the time was equally eventful. My cousin met her husband on Match.com, bolstering my confidence that I, too, would find the love of my life through online dating. If I was matched with someone who seemed compatible, I'd ask him out for a drink, which occasionally turned into a second date over dinner, but rarely went further than that.

One of my first dates when I moved to Allston, Massachusetts, was with a police officer who, at the end of our date, asked me if I wanted to come up and see him dressed in his cop uniform. After I gently declined, he harassed me via text message until I blocked his number.

There was the guy who halfway through my glass of Malbec asked, "Do you smoke pot? Because I'm a total pothead. Actually, I'm about to be fired from my job because of it." He then went on to argue that Moses was tripping when he saw the burning bush.

At a loud Cambridge bar, every time I talked to my date about work, I was met with the response; "He-he, you call your jobs *gigs*? Like a band? That's so funny. He-he."

On a second date with an MIT grad, he explained, "I consider myself Christian because I work in aeronautical engineering, allowing people to live in space, close to the heavens." He then told me that the movie *Ratatouille* changed his life, and he watched it every night.

There was a first date where the guy talked about his Myers-Briggs type and confided, "I'm most comfortable when I'm by myself, solving the answers to complex questions" as we struggled through awkward small talk.

Partway through another first date I found out the guy was a health and safety inspector, a loner, and a germaphobe. He advised me not to use the silverware that was set before me, and when I asked if he enjoyed his holidays, he answered, "Yes! I spent Christmas with my dog. I cooked him a really nice dinner."

I made it through a few dates with an uber-intellectual and joined him and his friends for trivia at a Cambridge bar. One of the categories happened to be recreational drugs, and I was the only one on our team to answer them all correctly. Those were the only questions I got right. I had a lot of explaining to do, and let's just say he didn't find the situation nearly as amusing as I did. I didn't score any brownie points with his friends either—especially not pot brownie points!

Valentine's Day found me crying all alone in my Cambridge apartment even though shedding a tear was not something I ever did, even when completely alone. I'd been on a handful of dates with a guy I had high hopes for, only to find out he was after just one thing—and it wasn't my cooking. In truth, I had both missed the signs and given him the wrong signals, but I'm blaming it on my biological clock. There have been a few times in my life—this being one of them—when I've felt an overwhelming, visceral urge to be a mother that is so intense, it's made me ache in ways I didn't know possible. It's like going through life thinking the stately, predictable, wooden timekeeper in your living room is a grandfather clock, when suddenly, every few years, a bird pops out, screeching, "Cuckoo, cuckoo!" Oh there are so many joys of being a woman! This pain, though—this longing—led me to deep soul-searching and questioning.

In my twenties, I was, in so many ways, still blazing the trail of what I believed about myself—my value and worth, my aspirations, and my purpose—and about God, especially whether or not I was going to accept him as my moral compass. My thoughts often spiraled. *It would be so much easier to find a partner if I didn't care what he believed. Does that really matter? Why does everything seem so difficult for me yet easy for other people? You created Eve so Adam wouldn't be alone. Do you have a partner for me, God? Don't you want me to be happy? Is the Bible even pertinent anymore or did it just apply to a former time and place? Surely you want me to stay relevant with the times, right God? If the norm is having casual sex, why shouldn't I?*

Sitting with these questions actually strengthened my faith. Relative truth is a very slippery slope, because where do you draw the line if there isn't one to draw?

Attending Bentley a decade earlier was the first time I'd been in a secular learning environment, and right away I realized I had to stand for something. Even though I was mad at God, I did believe in his existence and that the world was created by him. So again, I chose to take a stand even though I didn't *understand*. I could let doubt drive a wedge between me and God, or we could agree to disagree for the time being while working it out together. As I was struggling to put this dance of faith and doubt into words, I read a chapter in *Mostly What God Does*, in which Savannah Guthrie nailed it once again.

## GIGS AND GIGGLES

When we work out our questions in the presence of God, answers may not be possible, but relationship can be. Faith simply invites us to coexist with the doubt and belief within us—to live with our questions and live with God, simultaneously, as opposed to all alone with one or the other.[10]

By this time, I'd moved up the ranks to executive sous chef and purchasing manager at STT and worked with about thirty different purveyors sourcing seasonal produce, grass-fed meat, sustainable seafood, local dairy, and the like. I calculated my beef demands months before an event, taking into account the loss from each cut and any scraps we could repurpose. Then, my broker, Andy, pieced the order together from local farms. I managed the inventory of all perishables and nonperishables and made pack lists of every item needed in order to execute our events. I also led many of those events each week.

It was absolutely thrilling work. I learned so much, was pushed hard—mentally and physically—and excelled at it. We won Best of Boston Wedding Caterer during those years! Being strong proved critical as my five-foot-four-inch frame hauled fifty-pound bags of flour and sugar up and down the stairs that led to our basement pantry, and carried eight-foot coolers through whatever maze we were setting up an event in. Cooking is hard work and hard on your body. You are on your feet for hours on end, bending over a hot flame or cutting board, trying to remember every last component that goes into a dish.

Being passionate about something doesn't mean it's without challenges. During wedding season, I often finished an eighty-hour week with an eighteen-hour day, setting up mobile kitchens, hauling coolers through rocky fields, putting out fires—figuratively and literally—and leading a team of chefs working tirelessly to cook the perfect meal on the perfect day the bride had dreamt of ever since wearing a tutu in the womb. Exhausting? Yes. But worth seeing the smile on the groom's face as he watched his bride savoring each bite? Worth seeing an embrace from the happy parents as they exclaimed it was the best meal they'd ever eaten? Worth knowing the guests didn't have to go to the McDonald's drive-thru as soon as the wedding was over? A big, *OH YES!* The cherry on top was getting to do this work side by side with my best friend, Elissa, as we laughed our way through even the most challenging of days.

Pain was my life, and I had accepted it. That said, the pain in my spine I'd lived with for over a decade was worsening and had spread all the way to my neck. I'd also developed severe TMJ—a dysfunction of the jaw joint from stress-induced clenching. And then there was the strange pressure in my skull. I popped Advil to dull the headaches that had become a daily occurrence, never thinking of the damage it could cause to my already-problematic GI system. Despite a clean diet, my health was steadily on the decline, and my functional medicine doctors were at a loss. As I grasped for control, that old vice of anorexia was threatening to regain its grip. Once again, I was overwhelmed at my own brokenness, but rather than stopping to let the pit crew refuel me, I pushed harder, my gauge hovering over empty.

I was compelled to exceed all expectations, which naturally resulted in a mountain of overwhelming tension. As a detail person, I could see the nuances of what each menu and event needed for it to be flawlessly executed, but I was contending with a steep learning curve as well. I was terrified of falling short of the high—and sometimes unreasonable—standards I set for myself, which led me to seek someone much wiser and more capable.

I remember lying sleeplessly in bed the night before the first wedding I ran on my own. I was lock-jawed and panicked. But that fear sparked memories of other instances when anxiety threatened, and in looking up for help, God had come through. So that night, and many thereafter, I prayed for peace over my mind and strength for my aching body. I started having a conversation with God, telling him specifically what aspects of the job I was most afraid of, what shortfalls I saw in my own abilities, and what potentially damaging variables could arise. I even mentioned what I foresaw happening to me if I didn't succeed. Rather than ignoring my fear completely or running away from the challenge and giving up before trying, this honest dialog with God about my struggles allowed me to yield them to him. Surrender led me to change the way I related to my work—and to my worth.

I can't control everything. *There, I finally said it and wow did it feel good!* Since God is the one who created my unique talents, I honor him by working to the absolute best of my ability. By shifting my priority from the praise and accolades of other people to the glory of God, I began to see that my worth doesn't need to be tied to my work. That revelation allowed me to hand my fear and worry over to God, trust him with control, and break away from the pressure of perfectionism I had been living with for so long. As I made prayer a habit, and replaced my striving with God's strength, I started to hear it—that still, small voice. Divine presence. The Holy Spirit, who understands the complexities of my swirling thoughts better than I do, and fills me with wisdom, clarity, and peace when I listen to his whispers.

*Playing dress-up, a few weeks post-foot surgery*

Fourteen

# PACIFIC OCEANS

I'M SITTING AMONG a handful of strangers, fidgeting and uncomfortable, scrolling through a list when a word suddenly catches my eye: *microfinance*! I was attending a prayer service at my church, which was *way* out of character for me, but listening to that still, small voice, I heard it nudging me to go. Our pastor divided us into small groups, and with a list of church partners, we were encouraged to choose a few to pray over. The microfinance organization was called PEER Servants, a Boston-based nonprofit that supports indigenous Christian microfinance organizations (MFOs) all over the world. Microfinancing involves providing small-scale financial services to low-income individuals and small businesses lacking access to traditional banks. Such services include helping to facilitate loans, savings accounts, and insurance. PEER Servants has over a dozen MFO partners and a worldwide volunteer network, which I

# SPERANZA

quickly became part of.

Microfinance, my old college dream that I never really had a chance to pursue—was calling me! For a short time after culinary school, I had a chocolate confections business I named MicroSweets, the profits from which I used to fund microfinance campaigns. That was short-lived as the inferno that is Florida made it impossible to temper and transport chocolate. The opportunity to volunteer with an organization like this was what I'd been longing for! I thought I might use my little knowledge about microfinance and economics to change someone's world in a small way. Instead, it was *my* life that was about to be profoundly changed.

Remember my New York City days when I had bunion surgery? Ever since then, I had worsening pain in my right foot. I finally saw a surgeon in Boston who told me the joint was set out of place, causing massive damage. I needed reconstructive surgery to open the joint, which involved removing a chunk of bone from my foot and securing it with screws. I was completely non–weight bearing, in a cast, on crutches for three months and had to take a leave from work because not even Wonder Woman could cook on crutches.

Bone pain is its own level of hell. I had to keep my foot elevated much of the time by lying on my back, which exacerbated my spine discomfort. I developed a one-legged Pilates routine because I was unwilling to let an injury keep me from staying in shape, and I excitedly discovered that using crutches was quite a good workout too. Being as active as possible helped reduce my pain—or at least I convinced myself it did. Occupying my mind did the same.

I'd been volunteering with PEER Servants for about a year, and from the start, I had been placed on Team Philippines, partnering with the Center for Community Transformation (CCT). CCT is the

## PACIFIC OCEANS

gold standard of MFOs, and organizations from all over the world train with them. CCT has a loan portfolio with a very high repayment rate, and they manage savings circles for their clients. Between these programs, they operate with a cash surplus, which they use to fund a host of beneficial projects.

One such project provided kids living on the streets with a home and education at one of their boarding schools. CCT was looking to PEER Servants to assist with a child sponsorship program. I used my recovery to help with as many CCT and PEER Servants initiatives as I could. I was in awe of their selfless devotion to helping the materially poor, and the ingenious ways in which they were doing so. It was such rewarding work, I didn't want my culinary hiatus to end.

Once I was off crutches, I returned to my catering job in Boston for another year while continuing to volunteer on Team Philippines. My teammate, Griffin, was spending a gap year as an intern with CCT in Manila, working on the child sponsorship program. As his term neared its end, CCT asked us for a new intern, and that still, small voice growing inside of me got the loudest it had ever been. I heard God tell me to GO!

There was an ever-present void in my soul—a relentless hunger that wouldn't quit no matter how many online shopping carts I filled, hours I worked, or dates I went on. Saying yes was a move so big it would take supernatural strength, courage, and trust. It would also turn my tepid faith into a consuming fire. Years ago, I'd decided to get into the ring and become a chef instead of watching from the sidelines; now, once more, the way forward meant putting on my gloves, ducking under the ropes, and stepping into the match. I was ready to be put in a place where alone I'd be crippled and powerless, because I knew God would show himself in ways I had never experienced and could never begin to imagine!

I was humbled by this opportunity where my life, which had once been blanketed in darkness, despair, and hopelessness, could be used to illuminate a path to freedom for others. At some of my lowest moments, God stepped in and demonstrated his unbounded love through people who, quite possibly, had also timidly said yes to that still, small voice.

My yes was a prayer: *God, use my life to be a blessing. Show me more of you, more of myself, and more of this world you've made, and fill me to the brim with light, love, and compassion so I can extend that back to others. I want to see your handprints everywhere!*

The amazing thing is that in just saying, "Yes, I am going to obey the calling I heard God speak into my life," he strengthened my faith, covered me in his peace, and gave me sign after sign that he was right by my side, even before I left Boston.

Around this time, Hillsong United released what is probably their most iconic song, "Oceans."[11] The first time I heard it was at church one Sunday, when the reality of my travel commitment was setting in and fear was threatening to take over. I'd made the mistake of watching that movie set in Southeast Asia, where a family on vacation from the UK gets swept away by a tsunami, and I started having nightmares that I was drowning in the floodwaters of a typhoon.

Amplifying my anxiety, my doomsday prepper brother gave me a thoughtful going-away gift of survival gear, complete with a solar-powered lantern and a straw that turns a puddle into potable water. *Note to self, add tsunamis and typhoons to my list of why I am terrified to be doing this! What did I just say yes to? The Philippines? It's a third-world country. There are remote jungles with snakes and dengue fever, and the people probably eat bugs!*

## PACIFIC OCEANS

It is still completely astounding to me that I willingly walked into the scenario that, as a child, topped my list of fears of what might happen if I handed the reins over to God and trusted him with my life. (FYI, they don't eat bugs in the Philippines, but I did eat several different kinds of them in Cambodia, including deep-fried tarantula!)

It was always in the hardest moments that God's peace was most real to me, spurring me to continually hand my fears over to him. I had no idea just how much more I needed to bulk up my faith muscle for what was later to come. But, back to "Oceans." I heard that song and felt God blanket me with his peace. I felt him right beside me. I sensed him saying, *I see you, my child. I see your fear and I see your courage, and I am right here with you every step of the way. Remember, I am your anchor! I see you and I will see you through.*

And did he ever.

I was moving halfway around the world to a place that, if you'd asked me to point it out on a map two years earlier, I don't think I would have been able to. I put all my belongings in storage, sold my car to fund my trip, and with my earbuds in—"Oceans" playing on repeat—I flew into Manila right between two typhoons.

*With Michelle, Penny, and Sarah, somewhere in the Phillippines*

Fifteen

# ALL THE SINGLE LADIES

NOTHING COULD HAVE prepared me for the world I walked into. The sheer number of inhabitants, the traffic, the pollution, the crowded streets and sidewalks, and how many people called them home. The naked children and the elderly squatting on the side of the road—the only toilet they had. The puddles of soiled water that pooled in potholes and in the cracked pavement. The stench of exhaust and human waste. Yet toothless smiles lit up faces, and gleeful shouts were heard at a game of soccer played by barefoot kids on a street corner. I'd often get a polite "Hello, ma'am" as I walked past a group of young men, and even more to my surprise, I was constantly approached by little girls asking me to sing "Let It Go" from the Disney movie *Frozen*. Apparently, they thought I was Elsa incarnate, and after repeatedly disappointing them when I didn't know the words, I memorized the chorus and sang it to their squeals of delight!

## SPERANZA

I had never been so constantly aware of the striking dichotomies that exist as I was during those nine months living in the Philippines. Joy amidst pain, beauty despite suffering, perseverance through trial, contentment while having so little. This duality was also a fitting encapsulation of my own story—I'd done so much living despite whatever difficulty I'd endured. It was through the darkest chasms that light had found a way to shine. Now here I was, helping to create a brighter future for children in the Philippines. And who knew that the most important job qualification was having blonde hair!

CCT provided a condo on the thirty-fourth floor of a building overlooking Manila Bay, with its barges that looked like battleships and sunsets that painted the sky. My flatmate, Sarah, was an intern from Singapore and had a charming British accent. Right away, when I saw the fierce tiger tattoo on her back, I knew we'd become fast friends. Sarah didn't care what anyone thought of her and said whatever popped into her mind. *What's that like?!* I wondered. We both loved to explore and wanted to see everything. She showed me how to navigate this wildly foreign place, starting with public transportation.

I took it everywhere—often, many different types in a single day. The FX was a small SUV that would have sat five people in the States but instead squeezed in eight and cost P15 (about 35 cents). The train system, called the MRT, lacks the efficiency of most urban subways systems. Many Filipinos work in telephone customer support jobs. That 1-800 number you dial when your refrigerator breaks, likely rings in Manila. During a shift change, it took several hours of waiting in line just to reach the train's platform.

Jeepneys are repurposed US Jeeps from WWII. With their

*The "Mother Mary 2" jeepney, Manila, Philippines*

open backs and long bench seat on each side, they pack in passengers at a price almost everyone can afford. Each one is ornately decorated, many with religious themes, as the Philippines is a deeply Catholic country. These jeepneys leave big black puffs of smoke from the exhaust pipe in their wake. The destination of each one is written on the front and side of the vehicle, and to hail the one I wanted, I'd stand on the street holding up my hand. If I was with a group, however, I'd hold up the number of fingers corresponding with the number of passengers we were.

If the Jeepney had enough room for more passengers, it slowed down, but it didn't actually stop. I'd have to hop on in the back and crab walk down the middle isle until I could find a spot on a bench to squeeze into. I'd tell the driver my destination and pass down my fare saying "*bayad po*," meaning "here is my/our payment" in Tagalog, the national language of the Philippines. When I wanted to get off, I'd either tap the roof or yell "*para po*" (please stop here), and the Jeepney slowed down a bit while I hopped off the back. The open sides were great for taking everything in—the chaos in the streets and, unfortunately, the fumes that constantly hung in the humid air. There didn't seem to be any traffic laws, nor were there many crosswalks. Pedestrians dodged cars as they maneuvered across the street, probably saying some Hail Marys as they went.

My first impression of Manila was a bit amiss. It was like being dropped off in Times Square and thinking all of New York City is like that. But as I had more time to explore, I found other areas—the Sohos, and the financial, historical, and garment districts of the city. The immigration office, where I went on the regular to renew my visa, was in the old district of Manila called Intramuros, a walled-in area, with Spanish architecture from Spain's reign in the 1600s. It is where two of the original eight churches established in the Philippines still stand—the ornate Manila Cathedral and the Cathedral San Augustin.

Malls are the most popular modern structures. They serve as air-conditioned sanctuaries from the oppressive heat and frequent monsoons. Our local mall was a relatively small one, yet it still boasted five levels and a surprising number of familiar stores and restaurants. I quickly learned that karaoke isn't reserved for bars and nightclubs; every department store had a machine, so I frequently shopped while being serenaded by off-tune renditions of Adele's and Bruno Mars's most popular songs.

Public bathrooms are called "comfort rooms," although they're far from it. Often, the toilet was a hole in the floor, and, as I learned the hard way, most do not have toilet paper. Either you took paper from the sink area before heading into the stall—on the rare occasion there was any available—or sometimes there was a handheld spray hose attached to the toilet, similar to a bidet.

My first purchase was a mini roll of toilet paper that fit in my purse, my second was a SIM card for local calls and texts, and my third was a pocket WiFi device that supposedly allowed me to have WiFi anywhere, but it only worked intermittently. The internet in general was maxed out due to the sheer volume of people trying to use it. Over 20 million people live in Metro Manila alone! Even at our office and cafes, the WiFi was unpredictable. I once tried downloading an episode of *Top Chef Boston*—my lifeline to home—and my screen said, "Download time: 25 hours remaining."

While Tagalog is the national language of the Philippines, English is the official language due to the country's history under US colonial rule. It is spoken by everyone who attends school, but I quickly learned that Filipinos refer to speaking English as "getting a nosebleed." Nevertheless, my poor co-workers had to speak it with me, as Tagalog was much more difficult to learn than Italian. CCT's head office, where I worked, was a thirty-minute public transit adventure from my condo. In the morning, I took the FX, and in the evening, I either walked or took a Jeepney, depending on the traffic and weather. I'd never experienced rain like I did in the Philippines. One minute there'd be hazy blue skies and the next minute a deluge. Inadequate infrastructure, a hallmark of the third world, meant drainage systems were minimal, and the streets flooded almost instantly. I'd hear raindrops while sitting at my desk and know it was going to be a long trip home.

The sun set around 5 p.m., so on rainy nights I emerged from the office to dark, flooded streets. I'd walk as far as I could, always coming to an area of such deep water I didn't dare wade through it. But in true Filipino ingenuity, teenage boys stacked cement blocks above the water line and ran long wooden boards between them, forming a bridge. Then, they would charge a fee to everyone who wanted to use it. Sarah convinced me to take a pole dancing class with her in the evening, assuring me that it was a fully-clothed, high-intensity workout. It was pouring rain, and after trying various forms of transportation, we walked the whole way. What should have taken twenty minutes took two hours, and we missed the class. Defeated, wet, and sweaty, we cooled off with a froyo from Red Mango instead. But we did get our exercise!

Many of my colleagues were around my age and, after becoming fast friends, we were dubbed "the single ladies." I was inspired and convicted by their selfless devotion. Penny and Leah left lucrative jobs in Shanghai and Singapore to utilize their skills at CCT. Gieza hardly slept in one place for longer than a week, as she met with teams all over the three thousand islands that constitute the Philippines. Michelle shared a room with five other girls to afford living close to the head office in Manila. They were slow to complain about the unpredictable internet, crowded cubicles, and meager pay, and quick to share their struggles, triumphs, joy, and pain, as they sought to serve God with their lives.

They took me to sample gastronomical delights such as Sizzling Sisig—pig face and intestine, finely chopped up with aromatics and cooked in a ripping-hot cast-iron pan. Everywhere we went, I stuck out. One night, at our favorite mom-and-pop Korean restaurant, a complete stranger jumped into our booth, snapped a selfie with me, and ran out of the restaurant! It didn't take much to make us laugh, but this had us roaring for the rest of the night, and every time we ate there after!

Over days and months, through a lot of laughter, and as they bore their souls, we forged deep, lasting relationships. They spoke perfect English, but listening to them was like learning a new language. Their vulnerability showed me that sharing my heart could be safe, although I still kept so much under lock and key, including the physical pain I lived with. *Talking about it isn't going to change it in any way, so what's the point?*

Sometimes, though, I was forced into accepting help. One morning, traffic was especially boisterous and every FX that passed me was full, so I decided to walk. The streets were buzzing with college students heading to class, and lines of teleworkers spilled from the train platforms overhead and down into the stairwells and the chaos below. There were motorists of all sorts weaving around me, and as I approached an especially congested area, I made the mistake of looking up for too long. My foot plunged into a deep pothole, and I fell face-first into a puddle of black, soiled nastiness, closer to sewage than clean water.

My laptop bag splashed into the hole with me. Horrified and panicked, I quickly jumped up, wiped the stinky, gritty water off my face with my shirt, and half-ran the short distance to the office. In hysterics, I called Penny from the lobby, and she rushed downstairs, always stylish in colorful tones and cute flats, while I felt like a sewer rat. We surveyed the damage, and my laptop was thankfully unharmed. Penny took my bag, and I jumped on a Jeepney back to my condo to shower, change, and decompress, then worked from a cafe for the rest of the day. When I got to the office the next morning, one of the sweet Ates (a polite term for an elder, pronounced ah-teh) had meticulously scrubbed the gunk off of my bag. It was cleaner than it had been in months! Her compassion was selfless and beautiful.

The overall unsanitary conditions were nearly impossible to avoid. I developed asthma from the polluted air and often struggled to breathe. The water was also heavily contaminated, and despite using five-gallon jugs of filtered water for everything—even to brush my teeth—I had frequent bouts of food poisoning and dysentery. When I was too sick to leave my condo, an Ate from work brought me fruit and juice and made sure I was ok.

I was a walking Pepto-Bismol commercial. Each day, I never knew which combination of symptoms I was going to be dealt. This was a unique challenge, as one of my tasks was travelling to remote towns and villages with less-than-stellar facilities. But some of the greatest blessings of my time in the Philippines were these weekends celebrating victory.

A country's geography plays a large role in its economic standing, and I was seeing first-hand why a country in a typhoon belt remains a third-world country—the people can never catch a break. The typhoons I arrived in were far less damaging than typhoon Yolanda, which had leveled entire villages and stripped countless people of their homes and livelihoods the year before. CCT responded by meeting with local officials in some of the hardest-hit towns to discuss both immediate relief and long-term recovery, and so the Nehemiah Project was born.

CCT set up vocational schools in these towns, providing certified training in carpentry, plumbing, electrical work, and masonry. The towns then hired these graduates to rebuild homes, hospitals, grocery stores, churches, community centers, and schools, thus

## ALL THE SINGLE LADIES

*The sunset over Filipino rice patties*

restoring livelihoods and their surroundings. Without this training, these men would have likely joined the thousands of street dwellers Manila is notorious for. Organizations from all over the world funded the Nehemiah Project, which also included providing new homes and fishing boats, and organizing co-ops so the fishermen could invest in farming and transportation enterprises, allowing them to diversify their livelihoods and bounce back quicker from future typhoons. I was asked to attend the vocational school graduations and dedications, sometimes saying a few words and gathering information to report back to the donor organizations.

The areas that were hardest hit by Yolanda were already some of the poorest regions of the country. The airports I flew into were bare-bones, yet the airport personnel welcomed us with singing and synchronized dance. On my first of these weekend trips there was a miscommunication between the head office in Manila and the employees of the branch I was visiting. Apparently, they were expecting the Filipino employee, Ashee. When I landed in Tacloban and called my local contact, she started speaking to me in Tagalog, then Ate Regie finally came to meet me, but her English wasn't great, and my Tagalog was all of about five words.

We took a Jeepney to the Van Van terminal, where a Toyota minivan of sorts awaited. These vehicles are crammed with five rows of seats, spaced about two feet apart. Ate Regie got me into the Van Van with no more instructions than to get off at the last stop where Josh, a CCT staff member, would be waiting. I got a flood of texts from some of the CCT team telling me that they were praying for my safety, which I read as, "You are headed into a dangerous place!" Thus began an extremely bumpy and frightening five hours. Most of the roads were unpaved and often had more potholes than gravel. The van's bouncy suspension made my seat feel like it was on a pogo stick, and shockwaves of pain coursed through my spine with each jolt. Seventeen people were crammed into the van, and as we left the terminal more people ran after us, jumping onto the back to hitch a ride.

We headed to Eastern Samar, close to an area overrun by Muslim insurgents, and went through several security checkpoints with armed guards. It was dark and the men shined flashlights into the van, looking directly at me with accusatory eyes. I was frantically trying to piece together all the Tagalog words I knew in case I had to explain why I was on that van and that the purpose of my trip was to help. Every time I felt scared and helpless, I prayed, and as I joined my prayers with my teammates', I felt a shield of protection around our Van Van. I put the rest of my focus into not peeing my pants as there were no bathroom breaks, and the facilities at the airport and terminal had consisted of a flooded hole in the floor. At close to 11 p.m. we arrived at the last Van Van terminal and Josh picked me up in a pedicab. I was never so relieved to see a complete stranger!

There were over one hundred graduates at each ceremony, ranging in age from sixteen to sixty, and their excitement was contagious. For many, this was their first time receiving a degree. In the mayor's graduation speech, he said that, where before they had only a single-level health clinic, their new skilled workers would build a two-story hospital, and the old market would be replaced with a hyper-mart. "Build Back Better!" Throughout the graduations, I was recognized as a "representative from PEER Servants in the US" and thanked for attending, which I wasn't that comfortable with because all I had done was travel there. Everyone else in attendance had done the hard work. But I hoped my presence made the graduates feel special and loved. I was later informed that throughout the ceremonies, people repeatedly—in Tagalong—noted: "She looks just like Barbie! Her eyes are so round, and her hair is so blonde!"

Another graduation was in a community center on the beach. Afterward, the local fishermen caught and cooked a seafood feast to show their appreciation, while one of the CCT staff cooked a literal bucketful of rice. We cracked open the shellfish with bare hands and I sucked every last drop of juice from the impossibly sweet crab and lobster as it dripped down my face. Then we simply washed our hands in the ocean!

The water was crystal clear and shallow for about fifty feet, until

## SPERANZA

*Beach shack made from a relief tarp, Eastern Samar, Philippines*

reaching a partially exposed sand bar suspended in its deep cerulean pools. The water then magically flowed over the obstacle and faded into the infinite Pacific. This stunning vista continued as we drove to the next graduation. Jungle-like mountains and rock formations studded with caves rose out of the aquamarine sea. It reminded me of the Amalfi coast, except Italy's brightly colored houses were replaced by shacks made of relief tarps, coconut branches, bamboo, cardboard, and tin scraps.

    I saw shattered footprints where beach resorts once stood tall, remnants of boats that used to take vacationers to explore the hidden caves, and where markets once sold freshly caught seafood. But what I never saw was a crushed spirit amongst the Filipino people I met. Everywhere we went they were quick to offer up the little they had and always with a smile from ear to ear.

## ALL THE SINGLE LADIES

One night, we stayed at a house-turned-inn that a woman opened to guests and relief workers after Yolanda. At the back of the property, tranquil rice patties extended as far as the eye could see. A five-star resort held nothing to the simple serenity of this place, except for some of the facilities. This was my first encounter with a "water closet" or WC. When my colleagues said they were going to take a shower, that sounded wonderful, as I was covered in sweet seafood juice. But I was confused when I didn't see one anywhere. Finally, after taking some clues, I figured it out. In the center of the property, there was a row of rooms with tiled floors and a drain in the center. Some had a toilet at one end, others had just a hole, and there was also a low faucet on the wall with a bucket next to it to collect water. It was one-stop for all your hygiene needs. You used the toilet, took a shower by filling the bucket up with water then pouring it over yourself, and brushed your teeth with bottled water, which you'd spit onto the floor afterward. But hey, it got the job done!

As the sun set over the rice patties, large lizards making a loud squeaking noise appeared all over the walls. Josh came running out of his room, shrieking that there was a frog inside and he was terrified. Had it been a snake, we would have had a problem, but frogs—I spent my childhood catching them! I can't help but laugh as I write this while watching my pup, Spritz, live her best life in our Florida yard hunting lizards!

Before my next mission, I made sure a CCT staff member was going to meet me at the airport, never to be left alone again! Ate Connie and Sheila were waiting for me and recognized me by my "Barbie-like" appearance. My reputation was preceding me. This trip was going to be a mix of graduations and home dedications, and after praying over the family and their new dwelling, the CCT staff insisted I take a picture with each of the proud recipients. So started the "Barbie Goes to the Philippines 2014" photoshoot!

To visit these homes, we walked through villages or "barangays" on narrow dirt paths lined with curious locals. All the while, we had to dodge stray cats and dogs, step over free-range chickens and roosters, and tiptoe through pig pens, trying not to land our feet on any of the droppings, and avoiding the small streams of sewage water trickling from drainage pipes.

The families we visited excitedly explained how their houses were now sturdier than before the typhoon. Some were concrete with tin roofs, some brick, some plywood, and one was made entirely of bamboo, which grew in the mangroves and was suspended on stilts over murky, brownish-green water. As we padded gently over a creaky, zigzagging bamboo plank for about twenty feet to reach the door, I prayed fervently not to fall in. Once safely inside, I noticed that even the walls, floors, and furniture were intricately crafted from bamboo.

The generosity of these families was soul-stirring. From the little they had, they offered us snacks of rice cakes, candies, cookies, spaghetti, coconut custard, and once a huge bag of prawns. It was worth trekking through soiled streets and over murky water to meet these joyful Filipinos who were grateful for a secure shelter to call home, for a good night's rest before facing a long day of work, and for being part of a community working by the grace of God to become whole again.

On these trips, I experienced even more modes of transportation than I did in Manila, including a tricycle, known locally as a "traysikel," which is a motorcycle with an attached sidecar that was about the size of a large cooler. At any time, these tricycles would hold the driver, two passengers sitting on his motorcycle seat behind him, five passengers inside the sidecar, a passenger sitting on a rod extending from the sidecar, two passengers perched on the metal protruding from the back of the sidecar, and a couple of passengers sitting on the roof. It was like a clown car, only there was no mystery about how many people were going to come stumbling out of it!

We delivered donated school supplies and backpacks to children in the province of Iloilo by riding a tricycle through fields of sugarcane and corn and then taking a small boat with bamboo outriggers to our destination. After hitting sand about one hundred feet from the island, we slipped off our shoes, hiked our pants up to our knees, and made our way to the outstretched hands of families greeting us on shore. After handing out their gifts, I prayed over the children as a young boy climbed a coconut tree and shook down its fruit. One of the men used a machete to cut a square into the top of the coconuts, then we poured the juice into a pitcher and used the cut portion of the coconut to scoop out the tender flesh. The flavor was intense yet pure and made all the coconut water I'd had up to that point taste like the cheap coconut shampoo I doused my hair with as a teenager.

Once back at the local Capiz branch, my CCT hosts cooked our gifted bag of prawns in a Crock-Pot with Sprite and a seasoning packet. These meals afforded me the chance to hear their backgrounds, the high points and struggles of their work, and their prayer requests. Their joy was palpable. They loved to laugh and were constantly teasing one another, although much of the teasing had to do with me because the boys kept secretly snapping candid photos of me! Almost everywhere I went, the first question the Ates asked me was, "Are you single?" *Had my dad called ahead?!* I should have walked around with the name tag "Single Barbie."

*Bringing gifts to the children in Ilollo, Phillippines*

*Fishing boats in Capiz, Phillippines*

*Sampling my first durian in Davao, Philippines*

## Sixteen

# BEAUTIFULLY BROKEN

I WAS TASKED with building a crowdfunding website for the child sponsorship program and writing the children's stories. Most of them had been born on the streets; some knew their parents and others did not. The kids often started sniffing solvent as a way of forgetting how hungry they were. Many began this habit as young as six years old. By twelve, girls were sleeping with older boys for protection, and some boys were forced to commit murder for their gangs. Learning about their lives was heart-wrenching. They'd lived through unthinkable pain, abuse, poverty, malnourishment, and abandonment. But in spending time with these smiling, grateful children, you'd never know the horrors of their past. Having a safe environment to live and learn in, and being nurtured physically and spiritually, gave these precious children a new start.

Early into my stay, I met a sixteen-year-old named Gale, whose parents paid to send her to Manila when she was fourteen, with the promise that she'd be gainfully employed. Instead, she was sold into a sex-trafficking ring—a common occurrence—and had been rescued only a few days before I met her. Her beautiful eyes were devoid of life and her dark brown hair was streaked with gray. The torment, fear, and suffering she had endured is incomprehensible, and brought new meaning to my work.

I frequently visited CCT's two boarding schools and became fast friends with the precocious kids there. I played soccer with the boys and games like ring-around-the-rosy and duck, duck, goose with the girls, although they mostly wanted to play with my blonde Barbie-doll hair. The older girls taught me how to make the Filipino dessert called Turon, which is an egg roll with cinnamon, sugar, and banana inside. The schools offered many extracurricular activities, such as choir and dance, and they grew vegetables, raised milkfish, and had a bakery where they sold their product to local townspeople. I often left the schools with an armful of gifted vegetables and, each time, a little bit of my heart remained behind with the kids.

One morning while working on the sponsorship project, I needed an extra jolt of caffeine and ventured from my office to the Dunkin' Donuts next door. Coffee shops didn't have brewed coffee readily available, so they brewed it to order. As I was waiting for my cup o' joe, a little boy came inside and started asking me for money. I brushed him off because it was usually the parents sending the children out begging, and if I gave him money there was no way to know if his needs would be met. He left, then returned soon after, and I sadly repeated *no*.

I was staring at the case of donuts, thinking of the fun I'd had bringing my nephews to Dunkin' and watching as they excitedly picked out their favorite, when I had an idea. I jumped up, asked the barista if I could add a donut to my order, then I called the little boy over and told him to pick one from the case. A smile lit up his face as his eyes grew wide. He pointed to one while saying, "Thank you ma'am, thank you ma'am, thank you ma'am!" The barista also had a big smile on her face, as did a couple who were sitting at a table. I got my coffee, went outside, and found the little boy sitting on a perch, happily munching his donut. He thanked me even more, and I eked out a "Jesus loves you" as I fought back tears.

I saw so much poverty, so many dirty, sickly children roaming the streets, so many broken families and homes, and so many mothers with sad eyes because they didn't know where their family's next meal was coming from. Even with the vastly transformative work of CCT, it was hard not to lose hope, and even harder not to let my heart break. And so, I did.

Every morning over a cup of instant coffee, I read the Psalms, prayed, and journaled. Following David's cue, I poured my heart out to God. David, a mighty king known as the man after God's own heart, often wrestled with deep pain, grief, hurt, betrayal, loss, frustration, and the list goes on. Yet no matter where he was in that chasm of emotion, David had experienced too much of God to do anything other than magnify him as King of his life. I wonder if David had any idea the weight his words would hold for generations to come.

As I let myself be honest before God, I began to see that having emotions isn't wrong. It's beautiful, it's human, and it's divine. Showing my emotions isn't a sign of weakness—it's a reflection of the very nature of the One whose image I was made in. I'm not loved less when I let myself be vulnerable—I'm actually loved more fully and completely, because when I keep my struggles hidden, I miss out on all the ways God wants to show how much he loves me. Sometimes it's through whispers of that still, small voice. Sometimes it's through the embrace and listening ear of a friend. And sometimes it's even through pizza, which we'll get to soon! Exposing my emotions to the light helps lift me out of darkness.

Living in this new place—and in my role as Elsa—I was growing in so many ways, but it didn't mean I suddenly stopped being me. I was often focused on how I was going to meet my first-world demands in a third-world land, while surrounded by some of the most selfless people I'd ever met. I struggled with the feeling that I was a misfit—an imposter. It was also very isolating not being able to pick up my phone and get in touch with anyone back home. With the twelve-hour time difference, I had a small window each morning and evening when I could make a call to the States, but it was prohibitively expensive.

One weekend, I was especially homesick and lonely, and my friends were occupied, so I decided to explore a new area—a series of malls, restaurants, stores, and beautiful gardens. I gravitated to these places as a haven from the chaos of where I spent my weekdays. I was walking along with the overwhelming sense that *no one in the world knows where I am,* and all of a sudden, there in front of me was my favorite Neopolitan-style pizza place from Manhattan: Motorino. I stumbled in, half blinded by shock, and read on their menu that indeed, they had two locations in NYC and one in Manila.

In her book *Eat Pray Love*, Elizabeth Gilbert recounted eating pizza in Naples that was so delicious it caused tears of joy to stream down her face. As I ate my Margherita, I was also teary-eyed over the

*Tasting kopi luwak coffee in Davao, Philippines*

fact that God, who has the whole universe to tend to, saw my loneliness and knew exactly how to prove to it to me. The voices in my head chastised me for craving comfort and told me I should toughen up and be grateful for my abundant blessings. But God wrapped me in his arms of love—not because of anything I'd done to deserve it, but because demonstrating the enormity of his love is his favorite thing to do.

## SPERANZA

*It's going to be glorious when the Son breaks through, and you see how recklessly loved you have always been!*

This love penetrated the deepest parts of my soul, and I knew I couldn't be loved this deeply by accident. Experiencing God's love proved my worth in his eyes. I was not a mistake. Time after time, as I leaned on God in my solitude, and poured my heart out to him, my Creator showed me that he always sees me, knows me intimately, and loves to delight me—usually in ways that involve food!

As a chef, the details of the food culture were endlessly fascinating to me. The grocery stores near my condo didn't have much fresh produce or dairy. Everything came in a plastic packet: Cup-a-Soup and instant noodles, three-in-one coffee (coffee, sugar, and creamer), seasoning packets (MSG, salt, and flavoring), dried fish and crustaceans, fried pork rinds, and other salty snacks. Some of my co-workers ate this fare three meals a day for $1.50–$2.00. I bought fruit from a vendor, whom we lovingly called "Ate Fruits," and veggies, such as carrots and Chinese long beans, from nearby produce stands. But to find a grocery store stocked with more options, I had to travel quite a way and pay a hefty premium. A jug of almond milk or a box of cereal sold for five times what it cost in the States.

I quickly realized how much I took for granted jumping in my car and driving ten minutes to a Whole Foods. To grocery shop in Manila, I took the MRT train for about an hour and then walked another thirty minutes. The train was quieter on the weekends, but there was still standing room only. At all of five-foot-four (on a good day), I was often the tallest woman on the train. For nine months, I felt like the only blonde-haired, blue-eyed, pale-skinned person on the planet. I was stared at constantly, which gave me lots of reasons to smile back—if only to show I was real. Women came up to me, touched my face, and said, "What big eyes you have" and "What a big nose you have." Such comments left me feeling like the big bad wolf, but it also made me laugh a little.

It was often dark by the time I left the stores I'd ventured great lengths to find, and since I didn't feel comfortable walking alone to the train, I'd hail a cab, which cost about $2 for a fifteen-minute ride. It felt safer than walking, but I always feared being kidnapped for a ransom. If I was at a mall and connected to WiFi, I would book the taxi through an app that could be tracked; otherwise I'd text the cab number to a friend. I don't know if these fears were warranted, but I once got off at the wrong MRT stop and had to walk a long distance alone at night. A group of men started following me, so I got out my cell phone and pretended to be talking to a friend about meeting up with her. I had regular nightmares about being abducted, and other fears plagued my dreams. As I read my psalms in the morning, I started writing down verses in my journal, listing my fears, and paraphrasing the psalm in light of them. I'd then meditate on those truths.

October 3, 2014
*Psalm 91:1 "Whoever dwells in the shelter of the Most High will rest in the shadow of the Almighty" (NIV).*

*My peace comes from trusting in God's sovereignty. What can man do to me?*

## SPERANZA

*I rest; I take full comfort; like coming home to safety after being away on a journey.*

*Walking in dark streets I am cloaked, not exposed.*

Without even knowing what I was doing, I was reframing my experiences and creating new neural pathways of safety. This practice helped ease my mind, but I was far from experiencing any safety in my body. I couldn't see yet how intricately linked these two dynamics were.

I wasn't used to sitting at a desk all day and my spine hurt even more, but in response, I punished my body for being sedentary and pushed through pain. The more my surroundings felt unpredictable, frightening, and uncertain, the greater I sought security in controlling my body—no matter the cost. My friends liked to work out and sometimes we'd stay late at the office and find an empty conference room to do the Insanity Workout DVD, a version of Tae Bo. Our co-workers mimicked our high kicks and laughed.

I'd meet up with friends or running groups on Manila Bay and jog on the boardwalk of sorts—an area about twenty-five feet wide, technically closed off to vehicles, though sometimes people still drove their cars there when they felt like it. The boardwalk was paved in a mishmash of concrete, pavers, brick, tile, and a Lego-like material. Patches of grass and trees periodically lined the middle of it. It was filled with street dwellers who made their "home" there, as well as a fleet of workers taking breaks. Street performers were scattered amongst curbside nail salons, tattoo parlors, and massage and reflexology spas offering a sixty-minute massage for all of six dollars! A cat man laid out blankets and small dishes of food and water for about thirty of Manila's feral felines.

Families were out for a stroll, couples were sharing the romantic sunset, and horse-drawn carriages rolled along, which meant I was constantly dodging horse droppings. It all made for great people watching, when I wasn't looking down at my feet. The ten-minute run from my condo to the Bay was another obstacle course of crowds, puddles, broken sidewalks, stray cats and dogs, vendors, and motorcyclists. At first I didn't feel safe running this stretch at night, but as my confidence grew, and I came armed with my psalms, I thought, *I'm already running, so if something happens, can't I just run away?* And off I went.

As an alternative to the Bay, I ran down the stairs from the thirty-fourth floor of my building, then all the way up to the roof deck, often taking the stairs two at a time. I'd cap off my workout with push-ups, crunches, and squats on the roof. On my non-cardio days, I brought up my yoga mat for a Pilates or yoga routine. People stared and sometimes asked to join in.

One day, while doing yoga on the rooftop, my face was pressed into my mat after coming into child pose, and I smelled my dad. The mat had picked up dirt from the cement, and the beads of sweat from my forehead mixed with the always-present gasoline fumes suspended in the humid air. Instantly I was back in my parents' garage where my dad's work boots, jeans, and plaid button-down shirt hung over his woodpile so he didn't track dirt through the house. Dust, sweat, and exhaust was my dad's hard-earned cologne. Sacrifice was often on my mind these days, and I thought deeply about how tirelessly my dad worked for our family and what it cost him.

There are no sick days, let alone mental health and self-care days, when your entire business is your responsibility. I have a mug that says, "Coffee . . . because adulting is hard," to which my sister-in-law once responded by saying my dad's generation would have never dreamt of complaining about "adulting." True, his was an era with an unparalleled sense of duty, but there was also a societal prohibition against a healthy expression of emotion. For my dad, that suppressed emotion built up under the pressure of obligation and then erupted. Maybe vulnerability didn't feel safe for my dad either.

The more I sat in introspection, the more I started to understand the forces that had shaped my life and family dynamics. But I was merely scratching the surface. The idea that my beliefs or emotional pain—past or present—could be contributing to my physical symptoms was not even on my radar, let alone on my mind. Besides, I had bigger issues to tend to.

One unusually clear afternoon, Michelle and I were walking from the office to the small cafeteria where we often ate lunch. I had my sleeves rolled up and was enjoying the sunshine on my skin, while Michelle was using an umbrella to shield her beautiful cafe au lait hue from getting any darker. As we talked and laughed, a worm popped out of my mouth. I didn't know what was happening until I grabbed the white squiggly creature and stared at it squirming in my palm. Trembling and trying not to throw up, I showed Michelle, and we promptly headed back to the office to see Doc John. He gave me an anti-parasitic to take for the next week, and I tried to forget it happened. Easier said than done.

Our condo had no AC, and the temperature outside never dropped below 80 degrees, so we left the balcony door leading into the main room/kitchen open. Giant cockroaches walked or flew right in, completely unphased by us, and at night, through my closed door, I'd hear them buzzing around the kitchen. I started waking up with giant itchy welts on my rear end—a very

*A cockroach on my electric toothbrush*

inconvenient place to scratch in public. My friends informed me they were cockroach bites. Apparently, they have an affinity for the derrière and for electric toothbrushes, as I'd often come home to find one perched on mine.

## SPERANZA

The humidity level in Manila was close to 100 percent, 100 percent of the time. Moisture-absorbing beads are sold for use in damp rooms and when they are saturated—usually after about two weeks—you exchange them for new ones. I put some around my bedroom and bathroom, and after one day they were a pool of liquid. It was quite a fitting analogy as my "little bucket" was constantly maxed out to overflowing from all the toxins.

Black mold lined the bathroom walls and all porous surfaces, including my luggage, which doubled as my closet. If you remember from my childhood, mold is my kryptonite. MSG was in most of the food, and I'd immediately get a raging headache, pounding heart, and flushed skin. But it was many months before I made the association. I was highly inflamed all of the time, which drastically increased my pain and made sleeping unbearable.

I didn't know it, but the strange pressure in my head that had been getting worse since my Boston days was due to increased levels of cerebrospinal fluid, exacerbated by changes in barometric pressure. The frequent rainstorms contributed to my debilitating headaches. I'd lie awake at night in a pool of sweat, praying for a few moments of sleep, drifting off to nightmares about coach roaches, typhoons, and kidnappers. Mornings brought a fresh tension headache and intense pain in my neck, jaw, and back, and my days were filled with fears of what food-borne or environmental toxicants might make me sick. I felt powerless, and watched as that old adversary of control reclaimed all the ground I'd fought so hard to win. Yet again, I began severely restricting what I ate.

These were difficult days that often had me crying out to God, pleading for relief, questioning why this was happening, and questioning my life choices as well. But more than the whys, these trials showed me Jesus, and a glimpse of what he had done for me. He left a place of perfection and unity with his Father to take on full humanness and live in this broken world, with all of its enormous pain and heartache. He personified complete humility, service, and love, and was crucified for it, enduring not only the most horrific suffering imaginable, but taking on the sin, darkness, and weight of the entire world, separating him from his Father. And Jesus loved me this much while I was rolling joints with pages torn from the Bible and listening to music that made a mockery of him.

Dwelling on Jesus' love gave me strength to go on. His whole life was a sacrifice. So how was I to model Christ if I never gave up anything to do so?

*Wearing traditional Filipiniana at the TEE banquet*

Seventeen

# THANK YOU, ANG BABAIT NINYO

CCT HOSTED AN annual microfinance conference, bringing together thirty attendees from twelve countries spanning four continents. I was the conference liaison, scribe, and a group leader. We commenced with an exposure week similar to one CCT had taken me on when I arrived, seeing the many ways CCT was empowering the materially poor. It was thrilling to have come full circle as I answered participants' questions and expounded upon what they were seeing at each place. Mostly, though, I just listened to their stories of how microfinance and discipleship were bringing transformation. I was in awe of their love for God, which overflowed to others. And I was amazed at their compassionate hearts and their commitment to doing everything in their power to make a better future for the people they were serving.

One of the breakout sessions each day was focused on

# SPERANZA

discipleship based on the verse in Matthew 28:19, where Jesus instructed his followers, "Go and make disciples of all nations" (NIV). This isn't about promoting a religion, but rather it's about developing relationships as modeled by Jesus. His relationships were deep—he invested in people. They were wide ranging, too, as he made friends with those of all different backgrounds. And these relationships were rooted in love. I pictured friends and strangers gathered around my table, enjoying a meal and an honest conversation. Whatever the next chapter in my life held, I knew discipleship needed a place.

I was part of the CCT choir and for the conference kickoff we performed several songs, which required my wearing traditional Filipino formal attire called "Filipiniana." A friend let me borrow her two-piece ensemble, which was bright yellow and made of gauzy cloth. I looked like a giant pineapple. But itching aside, these were the memories and experiences that took me from being an outsider looking in, to embracing the place that became my new home.

The same was true of eating the Filipino delicacy balut. It's a boiled, fertilized duck egg with an embryo that can be in any stage of development. Tasting it had been on my to-do list since arriving—not because it sounded appetizing, but because as a chef, it's kind of my job to try everything. CCT gave the participants the chance to do so, and Andre, whose microfinance operations served the Gypsy population in Ukraine, quickly volunteered with me to cheers of grossed-out onlookers. Seasoned balut eaters guided our steps as we peeled the top and drank the embryonic fluid, called the "soup," exposing the purplish-grey bird within. Its limbs and feathers were compressed into the shape of the egg and a bright yellow yoke appeared beneath that. I was trembling the whole

## THANK YOU, ANG BABAIT NINYO

time as adrenaline coursed through me, but ultimately it tasted like a very rich hard-boiled egg with a little added crunch! Andre commented that it would have been better with a shot and some pickles, and I had to agree!

Fall arrived, and even without the familiar change of leaves or chill in the air, I found myself missing my Auntie Lor and craving a taste of home. Browsing the grocery store shelves—one of my favorite activities—I found a lone can of Libby's pumpkin. I was so excited until further inspection showed it was dented and expired. I acquiesced to living without pumpkin for a year, and besides, our condo didn't have an oven. Shortly after this, my ever-thoughtful cousin Lily told me she was sending a package and asked what I'd like. I immediately responded, "Pumpkin!" She mailed the package in the beginning of November, and three weeks later, when it hadn't arrived yet, I started to worry. All I could do was pray that it would arrive by Thanksgiving.

Thanksgiving morning I received a sweet email from my Auntie Linda, telling me she was baking away. The scent of pumpkin bread—from the same recipe that almost had me locked in my culinary school overnight—and my Auntie Lorilee's famous sweet potato casserole were filling her kitchen. I could smell the warm spices as I read her email, leaving me quite homesick and craving these comforting tastes of tradition. I decided I'd request the pumpkin bread at the next holiday I spent at home, then I moved on to read my next email informing me I'd received a package! Penny and I dodged Jeepneys and other wild motorists as we excitedly made our way to the post office.

Once back to the confines of my cubicle, I opened the box and found it brimming with pumpkin goodness. There was pumpkin spice coffee, pumpkin crackers, and something wrapped tightly in tinfoil and plastic. As soon as I began to open it, I was hit with the unmistakable aroma. It was Auntie Linda's pumpkin bread! Lily had baked me a loaf, studded with chocolate chips that helped keep it moist. As I broke into it with my bare hands, I had the biggest smile on my face. I savored that initial bite. It didn't matter that it was now three weeks old and had traveled halfway around the world—it was the best!

My first thought was that I couldn't let anyone know about my treasure. I'd take it to my condo and slowly eat it over the next week—or eat half of it that night for Thanksgiving dinner! But the more I thought about it, the more I knew I would enjoy it most if I shared it. That's what I love about being a chef—seeing the delight on people's faces and knowing how nourishing to their souls sharing a meal can be. All night I kept smiling when I thought of this series of events—from missing my family and our Thanksgiving feast, to my amazement and delight when I opened Lily's package and found the pumpkin bread inside.

The next morning, my breakfast consisted of a chunk of pumpkin bread and a steaming mug of pumpkin spice coffee. I then cut the loaf into pieces, just like when I was a kid helping my mom on Thanksgiving morning. I left a piece for Sarah and brought the rest into work. As I unwrapped the pre-cut loaf, I shared with my co-workers the story of the pumpkin bread; how it's from my aunt's recipe, which we enjoy at every holiday, and how my cousin baked and shipped this one all the way from the US to Manila. Together we finished every last bite, and they kept exclaiming, "*Masarap!*" Delicious!

# THANK YOU, ANG BABAIT NINYO

November 29, 2014 *(over sips of pumpkin spice coffee)*
*God has made it so easy to delight in him. He never fails me. He daily blesses me more than I can fathom. I'm so often focused on my "needs," and I still worry about "what I will eat and what I will wear," yet God continues to bestow his blessings. My prayers in coming here—the desires of my heart—were to experience God in new ways, that he would be even more real and more powerful to me. He has not only shown his omniscience, but he has also shown that he knows me intricately and loves to delight me in the details. He is my reward. And my vindication is the justice he is bringing to my cause—the life-changing work I get to be a part of with CCT.* (Paraphrased from Psalm 37:3–6)

After Thanksgiving came Christmas, although carols had taken over the sound waves in September while trees went up and lights were strung. I'd spent the past several years catering holiday parties for complete strangers and was excited for the time and opportunity to bring the magic of the season to the precious kids now in my life. CCT had several parties lined up. The first was for the children in the sponsored boarding schools, organized by a church in Manila. A few days before, Penny, Michelle, and I met with a group of the church women to fill over one hundred backpacks with the toys, books, school supplies, T-shirts, and Bibles that the church members had provided. The kids were squealing with delight when they opened their bags filled with gifts! Gale, the precious girl saved from sex-trafficking, joined in our games with a shy smile. As she laughed and played, for the first time I saw a twinkle in her eyes. Hope. *Speranza.*

# SPERANZA

*A Christmas card from an American student*

I joined Penny and a group of her friends throwing a party for kids in CCT's shelter for street dwellers. Some of the children arrived bare-backed, and most were dirt-stained and malnourished. They eagerly received a T-shirt that said, "I am a child of God." Each leader was assigned a group of about twelve kids, and I later learned that mine lived under a bridge and came to the shelter the night before to attend the party. A young woman in my group named Russel had a hard edge. But I watched her compassionately act as a mother to this group. She sat with bare feet, picking lice out of the hair of one of the boys—something I saw the street kids doing often and something I feared contracting.

They decided on *"Torrepinest"* as our team name, and I figured, like most Tagolog words, it was one I didn't know the meaning of. When it was our turn to chant, I pumped my fist as we yelled, "*Torrepinest!*" Everyone looked at us with questioning stares, and I suddenly got worried. Penny came to my rescue and asked the kids what *torrepinest* meant, and they answered it was the name of their group on the streets. *Were we chanting a gang name?!* For fun, these kids swam in the filthy water under the bridge they called home, and they climbed up the tower (*torre*) that rose from the water in order to jump back in. To them, it was the "finest tower." Many Filipinos pronounce the letter *f* as "p," thus our chant, "*Torrepinest!*"

Lunch from a local fast-food favorite, Jollybee, garnered the most excitement, yet many of the kids saved some of the meager chicken nuggets to bring back to their families on the streets. At the end of the party, the kids sang us a popular Filipino Christmas song, "Thank You, Ang Babait Ninyo." The title repeats in the chorus, translated as, "Thank you, thank you, you are such a blessing. I'm so thankful for you this Christmas." They sang with eyes closed and hands stretched out in gratitude, as we stood with tears in our eyes—our hearts bursting with joy at their joy, and brokenness for their circumstances.

A local Christian high school arranged a Christmas party for the children attending the CCT-sponsored schools in Manila. I again joined Penny to help, and as kids started filling the rented gym on busy EDSA street, we realized the high school students were MIA. Penny and I had a gym full of more than fifty six-year-olds to entertain! The only Christmas music we had was on the phone of one of the mothers—an inappropriate mash-up of Christmas carols and pop songs—and every game we tried ended in a sea of kids pushing us in all directions and playing tug-of-war with one another's limbs.

## SPERANZA

An hour and a half later, the high school students finally strolled in. They didn't have much of a program planned but brought more gifts than there were children. They asked if we could use them elsewhere, and Penny and I excitedly said we could bring the gifts to the next Christmas party in Payatas. One of the mothers had a Jeepney and volunteered to transport the presents to CCT's office. We loaded the gifts inside, and it looked like Santa had arrived in the Philippines driving a Jeepney!

Payatas is home to the Manila dump, and CCT operates a school and community center there. We only had a budget for the forty students enrolled in school, and Michelle, Penny, Gieza, and I had gone to Divisoria—the huge warehouse shopping district—and haggled our way through stalls to find the best deals on school bags, water bottles, coloring books, and school supplies. The leaders in Payatas asked if our party could include the kids who weren't in school but were part of CCT's savings circle, where their meager savings earned interest in CCT's banks. With no extra resources, we had regretfully said no. But now, with the overflow of presents, we were able to include the savings group after all! However, we feared we didn't have enough gifts for all of them.

The kids were dressed in their best clothes for the party, and another hip-hop Christmas carol mash-up played in the background. When "Boots with the Fur" came on, I noticed one of the girls was literally wearing boots with fur! Michelle led an animated program of action songs, games, and a Christmas story, and the highlight was always a Jollybee lunch. During the story about the star of Bethlehem, the kids were asked rhetorically, "Have you ever seen a really bright star?" They all answered, "No!" Of course not, with the thick smog you can't see stars in Manila!

## THANK YOU, ANG BABAIT NINYO

During the party, one of the teachers counted all of the extra presents that were to go to the savings group, while we counted the additional kids. There were 150 savers in Payatas who had joined our party, and 151 gifts! We were speechless in amazement at God's provision for these children!

To cap off the most wonderful time of the year, during the early fall I had asked my family if their elementary-aged kids would join with their classes to make Christmas cards and hold a fundraiser for CCT's boarding school in Malungon. With its remote location in the southern Philippines, the kids were left out of the Christmas parties. My family rallied and sent close to two hundred handmade cards as well as a generous sum. The teachers in Malungon purchased a backpack and imitation crocs for every one of the one hundred children at the school. The kids had never had backpacks, and, with them strapped to their backs, the teachers said for the first time, they felt like real students! Most walked several hours each day through rugged terrain wearing only flip-flops, so the new shoes were most welcome. The handmade cards, whose messages came from the lips of children in the US, expressed God's love for the children in the Philippines. One of the real gems was this note:

> Merry Christmas! I hope you enjoy your Christmas and I hope you know that you are special and that God has a plan for you. You shouldn't worry about anything because God will always come through and will always care for you. I am not you but I think that you are going to enjoy this card.

## SPERANZA

December 22, 2014

*I can't count the number of times this past month that I've been overcome by the outpouring of God's blessings on the children here. That he would use me as an instrument of his love is the greatest Christmas gift I could ever receive.*

I promptly flew from one of the poorest cities in the world to one of the wealthiest so I could spend Christmas and New Year's in Singapore with my Bentley friend Jag, who'd lived there for the past six years. I was so used to the puffs of black smoke whooshing from Manila's vehicles that one of my first questions upon arriving in Singapore was if all the cars were electric. The answer was no; they merely had adequate exhaust filters! Singapore is known as "paradise" with its immaculate streets, nonexistent crime, and architectural feats, but all of that comes with a hefty price, including fines for littering, chewing gum, and for the operation of radar sensors monitoring speeding and other activities.

Singapore is a fascinating mix of historical and modern architecture. A convergence of cultures also shape the place and the food scene. We ate dishes prepared from generations-old recipes at the city's best hawker centers and sipped Singapore Slings at the swanky Fullerton Hotel. While Jag was at work, I luxuriated in the opportunities to pop into a yoga class and then later have a nutritious smoothie or celery juice. And throughout my visit, I was breathing clean air and walking unsoiled streets. No longer fearing my environment and everything I ate, I felt my coiled nervous system begin to relax. Pain is a relative thing. My days in Manila were excruciating, but once removed from its many assaults, I bounced back to "baseline shitty" pretty quickly, which felt downright pleasant.

# THANK YOU, ANG BABAIT NINYO

*With my instructor at Tokyo Sushi Academy, Singapore*

# SPERANZA

I explored the Tiong Bahru neighborhood where pre-war Art Deco buildings housed modern stores, bakeries, and cafes influenced by the terroir of the place. I roamed the stalls of the many wet markets, enthralled by the unfamiliar sights everywhere I looked. I took a course in the fundamentals of sushi-making at the acclaimed Tokyo Sushi Academy, knowing that in a few months when I returned to the States, I was going to launch my business as a private chef and teach cooking classes. I relished being back in a kitchen!

Jag hosted a New Year's Eve dinner party with friends, and I excitedly sourced ingredients from the wet market for our feast. Jag grew up in Thailand and developed an affinity for Thanksgiving food in college. She requested my Auntie Lorilee's sweet potato casserole, which swaps cloyingly sweet marshmallows for a brown sugar and pecan streusel. Also on her wish list were my famous balls—made of ricotta and ground pork, which I topped with a pistou made from local herbs. I found dirty squid that still contained the briny, black ink sacks, and I stuffed the squid with fragrant red curry lentils and a garnish of crispy yellow chives. I rounded out the menu with a colorful salad of star fruit and local vegetables. Dessert was DIY parfaits of ginger-spiked Thai mango, Australian apricots, and Malaysian passion fruit, layered with whipped coconut cream and an oatmeal crumble. Jag was transported back to our college days in Boston, and the exotic ingredients and enthusiastic guests rekindled my joy in cooking.

I loved rolling up my sleeves and getting my hands deep into the dough of each new land. I visited Jag several times and Singapore quickly became one of my favorite places on earth, although the more I saw of Southeast Asia, the more I felt that sentiment everywhere I went.

*Tuk-tuk taxi with Elissa in Siem Reap, Cambodia*

Eighteen

# SOMEBODY FEED THE FEMALES

THE TIMING OF my worst bout of food poisoning couldn't have been worse. My BFF, Elissa, made the trek from Boston to Manila, and I was too sick to leave my condo to meet her at the airport. Elissa, with her endearing personality, had befriended a woman on the plane, who, when I didn't show up, let Elissa use her cell phone so I could tell her how to take a cab to my condo. My excitement outweighed how weak I was, and I rallied to spend the next week in Cambodia and Vietnam living the female version of our favorite Netflix series, *Somebody Feed Phil.*

In Siem Reap we were whisked around in a tuk-tuk by our driver, Mr. Pov, who smiled with piercing eyes and cheerily spoke about five words of English. We marveled at Angkor Wat's vast corridors and intricate stone carvings, and in the dense jungle en route to Bayon Temple, we spotted a large pig, monkeys, and a man riding an elephant. I kept waiting for Mowgli to come swinging through on a branch! The beauty of Ta Prohm was enhanced by the obtrusive jungle, as monstrous trees grew right out of the rock, their weaving roots choking the stone structure. As the sun peaked through a canopy of leaves, I noticed a deep serenity about this land, and a calmness in my whole being that I rarely experienced. I half expected fairies and wood nymphs to appear, yet I also pictured Indiana Jones cutting away vines with a machete in search of ancient relicts.

Mr. Pov, who proved to be a stellar tour guide, took us to a floating city—a village comprised entirely of boats. As we climbed from our small vessel onto a souvenir boat, I noticed a little canoe next to us. On one end sat a mother with a baby sleeping peacefully in a tiny hammock strung between the two sides of the canoe. On the opposite side sat a young boy with a boa constrictor wrapped playfully around him. After a muffled scream, I took a picture of this surreal scene and quickly walked away, but the little boy started chasing me with his snake until I paid him for the picture I'd snapped!

We tasted traditional Khmer (Cambodian) cuisine, including banana flower salad with chicken and local herbs—one of the most delicious bites of our trip—and we enjoyed fish amok curry, the national dish of Cambodia, which was delicate yet immensely flavorful, with tender fish and a local greens chiffonade for welcomed texture. The most memorable and tasty meal—possibly of my life—was literally from the side of the road. A woman squatted down and cooked flatbread that puffed up like a balloon over a small brush fire. A man tended long bamboo skewers filled with meat that would have

*Butcher shop at a Siem Reap Market*

*Seafood stall at at Siem Reap Market*

been discarded in most other places—charred chicken butts, small quail with the egg still attached, and a whole frog, splayed open and stuffed with spicy curry sausage. There was an array of local fruits—green mango, olive fruit, grapes, cherries, and a host of others I didn't know the names of—seasoned with sugar, salt, and chili.

We bravely sampled an assortment of fried bugs—mealworms, crickets, cockroaches, and tarantulas. I viewed eating them as my ultimate revenge on the pests that haunted my dreams in Manila, and besides, I'd already had a worm come out of my mouth, so what could be worse than that? We washed down the meal with Angkor beer, hopefully sterilizing our insides. Like the hawker centers in Singapore, street food is the true essence of a place. Made by artisans, who, out of necessity, are skilled at coaxing the most flavor from humble, local ingredients, cooked by whatever means are available.

The markets in Siem Reap were as fascinating as the temples. Rather than rows of neat stalls divided into categories, there was a chaotic blend of items strewn about. Women sat on the ground filleting fish—a mound of bok choy next to them. Low tables held piles of vegetables, fresh fish, dried fish, curries and fish pastes, seafood, fruit, and fresh rice noodles. Because the women sat cross-legged on top of each table, it was nearly impossible to take a picture of ingredients without also capturing a random foot in the shot! The meat area was vast and impressive, showcasing every cut from whole carcasses to expertly broken-down steaks.

We watched people leisurely enjoying the famous "fish spas" and, like everything else, we gave it a try. Elissa and I sat side by side on a bench and apprehensively lowered our feet into the tank. Instantly I was attacked and started shrieking! The nibbling fish

*Siem Reap fish spa with Elissa*

simultaneously tickled and pinched, and I couldn't stand to have my feet in the water for longer than a few seconds at a time. So much for a gentle or relaxing experience. The fish bit so ferociously that upon later examination, I saw that they had eaten off some of my nail polish! Not only did I pay for this torture, but I also had to dole out money for a new pedicure! Elissa and I laughed so hard we drew stares from everyone around us.

We left the tranquility of Siem Reap for the sensory overload of Hanoi—its bustle of bicycles, scooters, and cars with blaring horns, dodging people as they walked with long sticks over their shoulders, balancing produce on each end. It reminded me of the Richard Scarry books I read growing up, filled with an array of characters in miniature cars. Lining every road were adults with coffee in hand. They perched on tiny chairs that looked small even for a

*Bubbling pots of broth on a sidewalk in Hanoi*

*Hanoi storefronts*

# SOMEBODY FEED THE FEMALES

*Eating a bowl of pheasant pho in Hanoi*

child. In Hanoi, life happens on the sidewalk, and at every turn we were enthralled by the sights and smells.

One alleyway had several large pots of glistening broth with an aroma so intoxicating I wanted to jump in. On another corner, we saw a man in an open-air restaurant/meat shop, knife in hand, holding a rabbit strung up by its foot. Our jaws dropped as in one swift movement he pulled the fur right off the bunny and plunged it into a bubbling pot. Our quest to eat the best pho in the world was what brought us to Hanoi and each one was better than the last, as the collagen-rich broths nourished my waning frame.

I passionately shared the events of the past several months with Elissa, and we had deep conversations about faith—her beautiful Jewish heritage, and the profound meaning I'd come to see in Jesus' life. We talked about struggles in our younger years, and for the first time I admitted how much anorexia had consumed my life. Ever guarded, I couldn't muster the words to convey that I was struggling with the same demon once again. My worth was still tied to how I looked and other people's opinion of me, and even with my best friend, I thought I had to prove I was strong in order to be loved. We'd have tears in our eyes while sharing our souls, and then something would pull us back into the present and make us gasp in awe or burst into hysterical laughter.

The friendships I forged with "all the single ladies" in the Philippines were deep and rich as well. We planned a weekend to the white-sand beaches of Boracay, but a late-season typhoon forced us to cancel. The wind during the storm caused the thirty-fourth floor of my condo to slightly sway and the rain came down in blinding sheets. But I survived yet another fear, and I didn't even need to break out my typhoon pepper kit my brother had given me for my safety! We did have other getaways.

Penny and I spent three nights in Taipei, with its modern skyscrapers covered with colorful billboards and engulfed in the lush mountains that surround the city. The streets came alive at night with larger-than-life markets and a sea of people. We sampled the famous soup dumplings where impossibly thin dough magically holds a rich broth-and-meat filling, sealed perfectly in its pouch. We also took a gondola to a traditional tea ceremony overlooking Taipei's skyline. I experienced my first communal bath house where men and women

*Riding a tricycle taxi with Michelle in Davao*

of all ages waded in bathing suits through a series of natural pools, some bubbling hot and others refreshingly cool. I didn't see the No Photography sign, and when I went to snap a picture, I was almost tackled and put on warning!

Michelle and I visited the Philippines' southernmost province, Davao, where the plush jungle and orchids growing in massive trees replaced the high rises found in Manila. We took motorcycle taxis, jumping on the seat behind the driver and hanging on for dear life as he maneuvered the winding hills of a Dole fruit plantation. We got stuck in a monsoon, and between the flooded streets and stalled vehicles, it took us eighteen different modes of transportation to get back to CCT's office, where we were staying. One of the highlights was a day at Pearl Farm—a stunning resort on Samal Island, where we snorkeled with Nemo and saw giant sea clams that looked like something from *Alice in Wonderland*. We ate crocodile-egg ice cream, and I tried my first durian—the fruit that smells like garbage and is banned in many places because of its stench yet has a cult following. I am not a member.

The Pope came to visit the Philippines and enthusiastic crowds from all over the country made their way to Manila, overrunning the streets. "Escape the Pope 2015" commenced in the middle of the night when Sarah, Michelle, and I hopped on a bus, then a ferry, to arrive at a modest island resort. For a few pesos we took a boat in the crystal-clear water around the island where I scooped up sea urchin—uni—with my bare hands. Prized for their explosion of salinity, I was tempted but didn't dare eat them. By that point, my body was completely unraveling.

February came—the month of love—and one evening while cooking dinner at my condo, I put on a sermon by my former pastor in New York City, Timothy Keller, that I had saved on my phone. The topic was marriage and singleness—still a sore subject for me. But as I listened, for the very first time I thanked God for all those bad dates and that night a year prior when I stood crying and heartbroken in my Cambridge apartment. If my life had gone the way I planned, I wouldn't have come to the Philippines and perhaps never would have understood God's consuming love and the life-changing sacrifices of Jesus. My body felt more broken than ever, but for the first time, my spirit was whole—filled with a deep joy rooted in God's love and grace. This joy, independent of any circumstance, was made even easier to inhabit because I saw it in the Filipino people everywhere I went—my single ladies included. I hosted a Galentine's brunch, celebrating my friends, whom I'd

*All the single ladies Galentines brunch at our condo in Manilla*

come to love so much, and who had helped show me the depths of God's love.

I'd grown in profound ways, and knew my future relationships were going to be that much stronger. When we don't know our own worth and are looking for a void to be filled that only God's love can, it's only natural to place unrealistic expectations onto a partner. But I have to admit, in the back of my mind I thought, *Okay God, I learned the lessons and am so, so grateful. So I'll go home now and find a husband and start a family and it will have been worth the wait!* Because isn't that how our minds work—expecting a kind of give-and-take? It was completely true. The lessons I learned would be invaluable for what was to come in the next season of my life, but not at all in the ways I expected.

# SPERANZA

February 11, 2015
*This morning before work, I was outside the condo talking to Mom. Over the fence and through the trees, I spotted a radiant beam of light, amplified by smoke from a small fire. I wanted to take a photo but couldn't while I was on the phone. As soon as I hung up, it was gone. I got on the FX to head to work, opened my daily devotional, and it read, "My peace is like a shaft of golden light shining on you continuously . . ."*

God knew how much I'd need to cling to his peace. A few days later, a profusion of parasitic worms started coming out of my mouth and actually looked like they were living in the lining of my cheeks. I had had an incident where a single parasite emerged from my mouth before, but this was a complete infestation! It was horrific and terrifying. Meanwhile, Sarah contracted head lice and wore a colorful turban while treating her mile-long locks. We were quite the pathetic pair. When the worms weren't clearing up with anti-parasitics, Penny took me to the hospital. I was paranoid I'd also caught lice, so while we waited for the doctor, she combed through my hair. We laughed at the absurdity of the situation, while I experienced, yet again, love that bore no conditions and asked nothing in return.

When the doctor finally ushered me into her office, she sat across her desk from me and exclaimed, "You have worms coming out of your mouth?" And laughing hysterically, she sent me away. In addition to the parasites, I had a severe sinus infection, my asthma was worsening, and I was dropping weight at an alarming rate. I feared for my life and made the difficult but wise decision to fly back to the States a few weeks early for medical care.

SOMEBODY FEED THE FEMALES

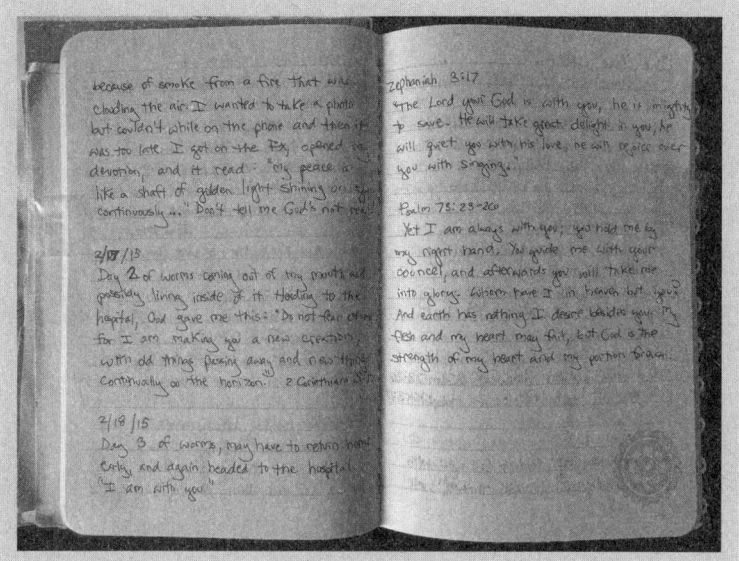

*"My peace is like a shaft of golden light"*
journal entry from Manila

Amid my fear, I was washed in that golden light of peace. I'd experienced too much of God not to trust him completely with my life. Nevertheless, the closer I got to safety, the more I acknowledged how dire my health situation was. There were blizzards across much of the US, and I almost missed my connecting flight to Massachusetts, where my mom—my biggest supporter, cheerleader, and prayer warrior—met me at baggage claim. I choked back sobs as I ran down the airport stairs to her outstretched arms and tears of relief. This was a scene that would play out again many years later and for a very different reason.

Saying my goodbyes a few days before had been extremely bittersweet. I was delighted to be seeing my family and grateful to have my parents' house to convalesce in, but I couldn't say I was excited to be returning "home." I no longer knew where home was. I had built a life in Manila and didn't want to leave my friends and colleagues. It was the most stressful and difficult environment I'd ever lived in, but simultaneously the most joyful and freeing. I left forever changed, with a bursting heart for the beautiful people, the beautiful place, and for the way my Savior had answered my prayers in abundance and had become so beautiful to me.

# SOMEBODY FEED THE FEMALES

*Last day at the office in Manila, saying goodbye to Michelle, Leah, and Penny*

*My dad and Spritz in my St. Pete back yard*

Nineteen

# SUMMER OF SPRITZ

"*I'M SORRY TO desert you, but if I stop paddling, the wind will turn my board and I'll fall in too,*" I yelled back to my date as the distance between us widened, literally and figuratively. He'd arrived at our rendezvous in a giant straw sombrero and couldn't stay afloat on his paddleboard for longer than thirty seconds before falling into the Bay, his hat making as big a splash as the rest of him. After recuperating from my many ailments—compliments of the Philippines—I'd moved to sunny St. Petersburg, Florida, with its Indy vibe that reminded me of Cambridge, the most recent place I'd called home. My sister and cousin Lily lived nearby and were both trying to get pregnant, so I had wanted to be near them and their babies—and hopefully start a family of my own too. There was plenty of clientele to support a luxury, niche business like private catering. And after Manila, I knew I preferred the hot and humid weather over the cold and snowy kind, without question. I excitedly traded my downhill skis for a paddleboard, although I needed a partner who could keep up.

Before my belongings even arrived from Boston, I was back on Match.com, convinced there was a Jesus-loving prospect in my future. After all, I had moved to the Bible Belt! But oh, if this doesn't sound familiar . . .

Toward the end of a first date, a guy excused himself to use the bathroom, then returned to the table and said he'd just looked at himself in the mirror and said, "I'm going to marry this girl." I soon found out he was sleeping his way through the traveling nurses who sublet in his apartment building. At least he wasn't a commitment-phobe?

Another guy did a mean George W. Bush impersonation then ran away to join the circus. The job he moved away for sounded equally as preposterous.

I took a nannying gig while finding a catering job, which I worked while also teaching cooking classes at the newly opened Sur la Table and launching my private catering business. The chef I'd interned for in New York City had recently published a book co-authored by a health coach, and although I didn't know what that was, I immediately wanted to be one. The more I learned about the growing field, the more I saw health coaching as a natural extension of my cooking philosophy and a meaningful complement to my private chef services.

In the Philippines, my friends and co-workers always wanted to know about the strange food I cooked for lunch as I excitedly shared the ways food can be used as medicine. Unassuming grocery shoppers slowly backed away as I gave dissertations on the many health benefits of cruciferous vegetables. Maybe I needed to ease up?

*With my dad after my knife skills class at Sur la Table*

But I was convinced that my attempt at clean eating had saved me from getting even sicker than I was. I enrolled in a year-long program to become a certified health coach.

What I never foresaw was the detriment that program would have on my well-being. I was still quite underweight but eating a healthy amount of clean food. The curriculum introduced me to the world of "anti-nutrients." Certain vegetables, grains, and legumes have survival traits that prevent them from being eaten by predators. While these naturally occurring compounds protect the plants, they can interfere with our ability to absorb and digest essential vitamins, nutrients, and minerals. Have you noticed the astringent quality of spinach? That's oxalate acid. Some people are more sensitive to it than others, but oxalates can increase joint pain, cause GI issues and kidney stones, amongst other things, and the list of threatening compounds doesn't stop there. There are phytates and lectins, and saponins—the soapy residue in the water when you cook quinoa.

We learned about every kind of diet—carnivore, vegan, frequent small meals, intermittent fasting, low carb, carb loading, no grains, only grains that end with z (yes, I made that one up), and the legitimate science behind all of them from health professionals who were leaders in their field. It was a dizzying amount of information, which I loved learning, but the contradictory aspect left me completely confused and afraid of everything I put in my mouth. Yet again, my environment felt unsafe, and yet again, I used control to mimic security. I no longer wanted to ingest anything that could potentially harm me. By the end of the program, I had few options left. I traded the "I don't eat anything until I'm about to faint, and then I eat a cube of cheese" brand of anorexia for orthorexia—an unhealthy obsession with eating only "healthy" food. Ironic, right?!

## SUMMER OF SPRITZ

My apartment in St. Pete was an old house converted into two rental units. I would often find piles of ancient termite droppings, which had fallen through cracks in the ceiling, and large cockroaches scurrying across the floor, but at least these didn't bite! The smell of fresh paint initially masked any other odors, but after a few months, I left for a weekend and realized that all my clothing wreaked of mildew. I started having severe fatigue, brain fog, and shortness of breath and thought maybe my thyroid was out of whack again. *Add finding a new functional medicine doctor to my to-do list.*

One night I came home from catering a wedding in Tampa and found close to a hundred flies in my bedroom. It was 1:30 a.m. and I couldn't call my landlord, so I sent him a text and slept on the couch. When he hadn't responded the next morning, I went to the hardware store for fly tape, and within a few hours it was covered. Finally, my landlord showed up and blamed me for attracting the flies with the sticky strips! An exterminator found rats living in the crawl space under the house; one or more had died and the carcasses were attracting the flies, which came into my room through the AC vent. Vermin aside, I liked St. Pete and decided to plant roots. I bought a new-construction home and moved in the same week as Rat-gate.

I always thought mold was one of those allergens you react to while exposed, and that once you're removed from the moldy environment, the reaction goes away. Well, that is fake news. Mold emits mycotoxins, which, after becoming aerosolized and inhaled, embed themselves in your tissues. They are highly inflammatory and damaging to your cells, nervous system, brain, hormonal and endocrine systems, and can cause cancer, and much more. I was diagnosed with severe mycotoxicosis. It was the first time I'd ever heard this term, yet I had high levels of several strains from a lifetime of exposure.

## SPERANZA

I'd also accumulated heavy metals. While living in Boston, I was diagnosed with a pituitary microadenoma—a small tumor on an area of my brain that controls hormones. My doctor had me monitoring it via annual brain MRIs with contrast dye, which I found out contains the heavy metal gadolinium. I hadn't had a period in almost three years, and a bone-density test showed significant bone loss in my spine. Some of the symptoms women in menopause experience are because certain heavy metals can be stored in bone, and as estrogen declines, bone loss follows, unleashing these heavy metals into circulation. My lack of a period had essentially put my body into menopause at thirty years old, and the heavy metal dump followed suit.

My new functional medicine doctor recommended IV chelation to bind the heavy metals, but my—thankfully, very strong—intuition told me I was too frail for that to be a good idea. He also had me bathing in ammonia, swearing it was the only way to eradicate one strain of mycotoxin that would otherwise give me cancer. I was on a seesaw between feeling terrified and being held in that golden light of peace. I endlessly researched my conditions and supportive modalities and consulted with other doctors. Determined to beat this, I threw all my energy into a rigorous detox protocol, including high doses of cilantro and chlorella for the heavy metals, intravenous ultraviolet-light therapy to kill the mycotoxins, diatomaceous earth as a binder, and daily Green Vibrance smoothies to further detox and support my system.

During this time, we had a year-and-a-half-long stretch of red tide—the noxious algae bloom that occurs periodically in the ocean and has neurotoxic effects. The fresh paint, tile, carpet, molding, drywall, and insulation of my beautiful new home were off-gassing volatile organic compounds (VOCs) and toxic chemicals, flooding my poor "little bucket," which hadn't even recovered from the deluge in the Philippines. Talk about a perfect storm of offenses.

One night I went to bed weighing around 105 pounds. I woke up the next morning ten pounds heavier and by the end of that month, I weighed around 130. And oh, was I sick. I had headaches that put me on the verge of blacking out. My brain felt as foggy as the Manila air. Searing bolts coursed through my bloated belly. And the pain in my spine was amplified tenfold. I also started having frequent panic attacks from the assault to my nervous system.

For several months, I barely left my bedroom floor, except to cook for a handful of weekly clients. But worse than the tremendous physical pain was the shame I carried. *This is all my fault.* My rigorous detox protocols flooded my already-overloaded body with more than it could handle. How was I to know that was going to happen? Yet I would lie on the floor, my mind replaying every move I'd made to try and help my health—every move that had backfired and caused this mess.

*If only I had done chelation. If only I had focused on my gut health first. If only I had taken stronger binders. If only I hadn't made myself gain weight. If only.* I was ruthless. These were dark months of intense physical pain and spiraling rumination. But little by little, as I focused on what I could do to take charge of my health, and I worked through another hefty list of treatments, including acupuncture to bring my hormones back in line, my symptoms started improving.

I'd slip in late to the church I started attending while the lights were dimmed and the band was playing, then leave right after the sermon, as if the light would expose my brokenness. I felt trapped in an imposter's body and thought that only when I fixed this mess would I be worthy of the world's love. One Sunday, I got in my car to drive to church, but I was frozen. *If only I could go back in time and do it all over again.*

I aimlessly drove through downtown instead, begging God to turn my situation around. While streaming the sermon entitled "How God Sees Us," I heard it loud and clear.

I was still placing my worth on how thin I was and in my ability to control my weight. With the extra pounds, I thought I was loved less and worth less—a lie I'd believed since I was a teenager. I had been deaf to that still, small voice for too long. C. S. Lewis nailed it in his observation:

> God whispers to us in our pleasures, speaks in our conscience, but shouts in our pain: it is his megaphone to rouse a deaf world.[12]

Rather than ruminating on my failure, I began meditating on this truth: *I am God's beloved child, created not by accident, but with intention and for a purpose.* And as I let this image permeate my being, I slowly shed the persona of unworthiness. I still wrestled with my weight and body image—and honestly, still do. Decades of deeply engrained body dysmorphia doesn't disappear overnight. But a few months later, I posted a photo on Instagram of me standing beside my niece in matching bikini tops and pigtails, with this caption:

> *Too many days I stood in front of the mirror judging my worth by how many bones I could count on my skeletal frame. Too many nights I stayed home alone, ashamed I could no longer fit into my size 00 jeans. I was a bystander on the sidelines, rather than someone who joined in on the game, until one day when God said,*

> "ENOUGH! Oh my sweet child, your joy and your identity must be found in me! You are my Beloved, on you my favor rests. I have molded you in the depths of the earth and knitted you together in your mother's womb. I have carved you in the palms of my hands and hidden you in the shadow of my embrace. I look at you with infinite tenderness and care for you with a care more intimate than that of a mother for her child. I have counted every hair on your head and guided you at every step. You belong to me." (Henri J.M. Nouwen, Life of the Beloved)

I couldn't reclaim the innocence of my youth, but I vowed, for my two nieces, to help them *never* for an instant feel ashamed of their bodies. That summer, for the first time in a long time, I wore shorts and crop tops. Some days I felt free, and other days I didn't dare look in the mirror, to keep the old demons at bay. I swam, and splashed, and laughed, and played—once again stepping from the sidelines into the ring. God heard my pleas for deliverance, but out of infinite love and wisdom, he didn't give me what I asked for. Instead, he opened my eyes and heart to his truth. He brought me to a place of thanking him for stripping away everything that was holding me captive—a prisoner to my own lies. For the growth I experienced in the hardest of places. And for the beauty he was weaving in my life's ragged and worn tapestry.

When I finally realized who I was—or rather, *whose* I was—I found my voice. With my worth rooted in God's intention and purpose for my life, I let go of the mindset that no one cared about my opinion or what I had to say, and embraced the truth that I had unique gifts, knowledge, and life experiences. I extended this thinking to my physical body as well. Just as no two fingerprints are the same, there can be no one-size-fits-all approach to diet and health. In a world of information overload, the most powerful voice of discernment is our body's innate wisdom. When the health coaching course I had been taking ended, I spent a lot of time researching, reading books, and listening to podcasts. I experimented with many different ways of eating, and finally came to a much more balanced place. Having done this work, I was now positioned to coach others through the complex and often confusing dietary maze that exists in our culture. I began incorporating health coaching into my business, with a focus on helping clients adopt special diets and protocols. For my body at that time, eating a whole-food, plant-heavy, gluten- and dairy-free diet helped clear space in my "bucket."

Dr. Jill Carnahan's definition of a toxin as "anything that decreases optimal vitality and function" brought new meaning to the term "toxic thoughts."[13] My rumination and blame were adding to the overflow of my "little bucket," while robbing my body of the precious energy it needed for healing. In this new place of surrender and acceptance, I started noticing bigger and bigger shifts in my physical symptoms. I would have made even greater strides if I'd considered how constantly analyzing my actions and judging my shortcomings was consuming energy and contributing to my persistent fatigue.

I still lived with my sidekicks—pain, fatigue, and my cranky GI and endocrine systems—and was going through some pretty invasive testing for dysfunction in my pelvic region due to having had my tailbone removed. On and off, my headaches raged, as did various symptoms from mold and what I now know was mast cell activation syndrome (MCAS). MCAS is a condition in which one's immune cells overproduce chemical mediators in response to certain triggers. The most recent deluge of offenses had heightened my body's reactivity to any perceived threat, and like an unpredictable toddler, my body threw a tantrum if the sun looked at me the wrong way. My nervous system was again on edge, scanning the horizon for danger. But none of this was keeping me from living. Every bout of intense symptoms and pain raised the threshold of what I tolerated as feeling "well enough."

Coming into a place of greater acceptance helped me soften a bit. I still pushed through constant pain, but traded 5ks, which were hard on my damaged spine, for power yoga that kept me strong and helped harness my breath. Chronic pain and nervous system dysregulation left my breathing choppy and shallow, but as I learned to focus on extending my inhales and exhales, my nervous system shifted to a more relaxed state, and my mind and body followed. I'd arrive to class stuck on a menu idea and suddenly, mid-pose, the dish would come together in perfect harmony. Yoga—much like cooking—was a way I got into a flow state.

My culinary business was flourishing. I made beautiful bites for swanky cocktail parties, crafted elaborate multicourse dinners, taught private cooking classes, and had exciting ideas for pop-up dinners and collaborations. My friend Jag's boss hired me to cater a party in Singapore, so we added a weekend in Thailand and made plans for many more Asia trips and dinners-for-hire. My dad admiringly attended one of my knife skills classes at Sur la Table, then regularly sent me photos of salads he made, showing off his stellar knife skills. After every gig, I'd send him photos of my creations, which he'd then blow up on his iPad, proudly zooming in to see every detail. He had finally acquiesced to the truth that I wasn't flipping burgers for a living as he had long feared.

My parents came to stay with me in St. Pete regularly and my home became an ongoing group project. My mom helped me repot plants and pull weeds from my yard, and still cheerfully washed my mountain of dishes. My dad turned my garage into a man cave, with custom-built shelving, tools for everything imaginable, free weights, and odds and ends. No matter what I envisioned for my home, or what had become problematic, my dad held the solution. The flamingo-pink bougainvillea I planted along my detached garage quickly outgrew every trellis I installed. One day I returned home from meal prepping for clients to find metal signposts anchored in freshly-poured concrete, with chicken wire strung between them, and the bougainvillea finally well-secured. My dad was covered in scrapes from the plant's massive thorns, but his sweaty face showed pure delight and triumph. And I must add, that monster of a bush survived several major hurricanes without a scratch.

I traded ducking in and out of church for an active membership and held a weekly yoga flow there with a short devotional and time for anyone needing prayer. I even gave a young adults group another try and made friends who showed me more dimensions of God's love. In this community, I came to see God as my friend—the really over-the-top kind, who surprises you with extravagant gifts, always knows just what to say, offers the best advice, and is there through thick and thin, anytime, no matter what.

I hosted parties, brunches, and holidays, where friends and strangers from all backgrounds sat around my table. While setting out the dishes, I'd think back to those times as a little girl when I helped my mom prepare for guests. I had stepped out of her shadow and was now living my dream, using my own home to offer

*A grazing table in Tampa*

hospitality. I had such a full life, focused on deepening connections and building community. You could say that I was living in discipleship! I had even deleted my Match.com profile. Though I still dated, I let it happen the old-fashioned way.

# SPERANZA

As mentioned earlier, after a twenty-year campaign, I finally got the puppy of my childhood dreams. I threw a "Summer of Spritz" party introducing her to the world. Of course, there was a sparkling Spritz bar. On my first day with her, I wrote...

January 4, 2017
*All I've been doing is carrying Spritz around, holding her close to my heart, letting her know she is safe and loved.*

I knew feeling loved and safe were paramount and I wanted that for my little fur baby. If only I'd realized the importance of that for myself.

Had my story ended there, I'd have had a perfectly nice life. Sure, I would have weathered some storms, but I would have powered through by my own brute force masquerading as safety. I was paving my own way, relying on my capabilities and strengths. I believed God created me to share my gifts with the world. But when it came to doing so, I can now see that I was using those talents to prove my worth to others—and to myself. I presented as this perfect package, while going through life like someone who is colorblind but doesn't know it. Somewhere, deep inside, I still didn't believe I was supposed to exist, and I carried that burden while God was longing to carry me, yearning to flood my eyes with vibrant blossoms born from being rooted in and reliant on him. Stubborn as I am, I wasn't going to let that happen easily.

*Fourth of July at the lake with my nephew, Ethan*

Twenty

# TICK, TICK, BOOM

OVER ONE JULY 4th weekend, my parents, siblings, sisters- and brother-in-law, nieces, and nephews—nineteen in total, plus six dogs—bunked together in our rebuilt (and mold-free) lake house in Massachusetts. The Independence Day weekend is my favorite of the year. We blast EDM on the boat and have a dance party while wearing stick-on mustaches and watching fireworks dazzle the sky. This year, though, the firecrackers seemed to follow me home.

Pain suddenly exploded throughout my body. No longer contained to my spine, it sent jolts through my joints and muscles too. And my brain felt like it was on fire. I'd go to bed with a pulsing headache, wake up with it still raging, and spend my day in a haze. Sending a text or making a quick phone call was overwhelmingly difficult, but the scariest symptom was that my short-term memory vanished. I was cooking at a different client's house five days a week and I suddenly struggled to remember their names or what ingredients I'd put into a recipe. I developed a system of moving an item to a lower shelf once I had used it, and I went through my days praying I wouldn't have to talk to anyone.

Initially, I also had a fever and flu-like symptoms and began a round of antibiotics for a suspected sinus infection. When my symptoms remained, and months passed, I began seeing specialists, baffling one after another. One of several neurologists sent me home with the diagnosis of "chronic persistent headache disorder"—a fancy reiteration of the symptom I'd sought help for. Adding to my pain, I developed severe joint instability. My knees, hips, jaw, and shoulders popped partially out of place, and at least once a month my pelvis shifted so drastically my belly button was several inches from the center. I'd be unable to walk for days, as a whole new level of torment wreaked havoc on my twisted body.

Over the Christmas holiday, one of these episodes was so severe I landed in the emergency room needing prednisone and painkillers. For the first time ever, I had to cancel cooking for a client's dinner party. I was devastated and couldn't continue on this trajectory. I knew I had pretty severe degeneration in my lower back and herniated discs throughout my spine, so the only explanation I could come up with—because doctors were no help—was that something had triggered widespread inflammation, increasing my spine dysfunction, headaches, and cognitive issues. Thus I focused on my spine and started researching alternatives to more surgery.

I listened to a podcast with a regenerative medicine doctor in California who had a background in anesthesiology and was performing innovative injections using stem cell derivatives. During a phone consultation, he walked me through how my two-week treatment plan would target all facets of my pain—cellular function, inflammation, my nervous system, and the nerves themselves. I was sure this doctor and these treatments were not only going to fix my problems, but that I was going to feel better than I had in decades. I had walked this painful road in silence and was ready to let people in. If my experiences could help someone else, my pain would have served a purpose. The night before leaving, I posted on my Instagram:

> *I HAVE EXCITING NEWS!!! I leave tomorrow to spend 2 weeks in California getting treatments from the most cutting-edge regenerative medicine doctor out there. I've lived in chronic pain for the past 15 years as a result of a fall when I was 18. I've had 3 spine surgeries to remove my tailbone, then the base of my sacrum, and to repair a herniated disc. And all of that has left me with major disc degeneration up my entire spine, 6 herniated discs, nerve impingements, constant headaches, and pelvic floor prolapse. BUT I am telling you all of this because I want you to get really excited for the ways that God is going to use this doctor to heal me.*
>
> *I have been scared for so long to take the steps needed to get better. Scared I'd be let down by yet another doctor. Scared of taking time away from work and having my clients abandon me. And frankly, scared of no longer having this pain as an excuse for not living out every amazing plan God has for me. But it's time to start living again and to not just exist. God has plans to prosper me and not to harm me—to give me a hope and a future, and that future is going to be*

*better than anything I could imagine in my wildest dreams. Out in California, I'm getting a series of nerve blocks, epidurals, injections, IVs, and other procedures that I will share with you as I receive them, so hang on tight. I am so ready for this!*

That night, my back went out on me, and I could barely walk through the airport, but I boarded the plane with my mom by my side and renewed hope for better days to come. On day one at the clinic, my veins wouldn't cooperate for an IV start—the first of many such struggles. I squirmed in my chair, wearing my best poker face, as pain lit up my spine. My nurse, Lisa, looked at me and said, "It's really hard being in your body, isn't it?" I almost burst into tears. *She sees me.* No one had ever said anything like that to me before. Lisa is now one of my closest friends, as are many of the people I met during that time—one of the multitude of ways God continuously poured out signs of his love for me.

Over the course of two weeks, I had about twenty-five injections around the nerves in my neck, jaw, and thoracic and lumbar spine, as well as a caudal epidural, where exosomes were injected into the base of my spinal canal with the goal of breaking up scar tissue from my tailbone surgeries. That was my ground zero. I was still as tender there as right after I'd fallen and was now holding fifteen years' worth of agony in a knotted bundle of fascia, nerves, and lament over all the times I had wanted to scream in pain but never did. The zing as the needle penetrated scar on top of scar, the pressure as the liquid forced its way into tight traumatized tissue, and the tears I choked back, all threatened to unravel me. But what was I, if I wasn't tough?

Much like the effects of fear, chronic pain engrained pathways into my nervous system, and my body kept choosing familiar hell over unfamiliar heaven. A unique aspect of my treatments was the use of ketamine to help me see past the pain, creating new neural pathways toward healing. On my ketamine journey, I saw several friends living their lives without a hang-up and while I carried a heavy burden. My subconscious knew I was holding on to pain to be worthy of love, and it was telling me it was safe to let it go—that I was enough without it. But I wouldn't come to understand that for quite some time.

Chronic pain can also keep you stuck in the sympathetic state of fight, flight, or freeze. My doctor used an injection around the vagus nerve, called a stellate ganglion block, to reset my nervous system back to its default mode of rest and digest—the parasympathetic state. This treatment can also be helpful for PTSD and other conditions derived from trauma. I also had daily IVs targeting inflammation, including the "youth molecule," NAD, which contributes to mitochondrial function. I had IV ozone—a potent detoxifier—but my toxic blood was so thick and black that in the time we should have completed five infusions, I'd barely gotten through one. That was a red flag I should have paid attention to.

I returned home sore and eager to see results. After nine months of suffering, I was ready to get my life back. I had a get-together with a few friends who'd been praying for me and holding hope for my healing, and I barely made it through the evening. All of my symptoms had intensified. My pain and headaches were so fierce it felt as if someone was crushing my skull while tearing the muscles off the bones of my jaw, neck, and shoulders, and stabbing me in the back. My memory and cognitive function were even worse, and I struggled to form sentences or do simple math. I used to do complex econometrics and calculus with ease! My heart raced every time I stood up, and I was often dizzy and short of breath.

My California doctor ordered the full panel of testing for Lyme disease and mycotoxins, even though I had spent several years working to eradicate them. Mold weakens the immune system, making it inept at fighting infections, thus mold and Lyme are often found together. After two more months of anguish, I returned to the clinic to find I was positive for Lyme disease and four other tick-borne infections—each with a unique fingerprint of destruction—and I still had high levels of several strains of mycotoxins. So began the most difficult years of my life.

Lyme disease and its co-infections are damaging to many systems of the body and had been ravaging mine for almost a year while undiagnosed. As Lyme is killed, it produces endotoxins which add to the inflammatory cascade. The dreaded Herxheimer reaction occurs when Lyme is killed faster than the body can detox it. It's like a boat taking on water quicker than it can be bailed out. This created a situation much like when I'd tried to detox the mold and heavy metals. I was no stranger to fighting for my health, and I was prepared to get sicker before I got better. I had resolved to do whatever it took. For the next three years, I traveled to the clinic in California every two months for one to two weeks of treatments. I poked myself with needles each day, administering peptide injections, and I took a host of tinctures and supplements. I started on potent antifungals that gave me such severe die-off reactions it felt like I had a constant hangover. I powered through IV ozone and IVs, and was often at the clinic for ten hours a day.

On each trip, I had about twenty-five injections—some directly into my spinal canal, some deep into the spinal facets and intraspinous ligaments, and several more caudal epidurals and stellate ganglion blocks. My doctor was determined to eradicate my pain and continually had new ideas, using regenerative tools with differing properties. I clung to hope through each agonizing injection and the days of worsened symptoms afterwards, praying it would be just the right combination or pattern that would finally give me relief. We both agreed that treating my body was like a game of Whack-a-Mole—one nerve would calm down just in time for another one to light up.

A few times, my whole body lit up, reacting to these foreign substances as intruders instead of peacekeepers. One evening, I left the clinic suffering from what felt like razor blades cutting through my skull. I barely made it back to my Airbnb before I started shaking uncontrollably. Fever, chills, and lightning bolts of pain coursed through my entire body. My breathing was strained and shallow, and I needed to call someone for help but was shaking so violently I couldn't use my phone. *Why is this happening to me? Haven't I been through enough?* In moments of lucidity, I begged God to bring me through, then in feverish dreams I was swept back to those sleepless nights in Manila, when I cried out to God for relief. I knew he was right there beside me, and loved me so deeply, I could trust the why to him.

That cranky toddler—mast cell activation syndrome (MCAS)—was back full-blown, making me hyperreactive and increasing inflammation and pain. There were other factors at play as well. I didn't know it, but my body was producing too much cerebral spinal fluid—a condition called idiopathic intracranial hypertension (IIH)—contributing to the constant, pounding, crushing headache

I lived with twenty-four hours a day. The injections were merely pumping more fluid into my overloaded spine. No wonder it felt like my head might burst at any moment!

I returned home from an especially rigorous few weeks of treatments with a worse headache and higher heart rate than usual, and the constant feeling that I was going to pass out. I drove myself the few blocks from my house to the hospital emergency room, where I was given a sedative and Benadryl, and where I also had an EKG and cervical CT scan to check for fluid on my brain or any other glaring culprits. The ER doctor proposed a lumbar puncture to check my opening cerebrospinal fluid (CSF) pressure, but in the typical patient the resulting fluid loss causes an even worse headache, which I didn't think I could handle. In actuality, it would have relieved the pressure and given me an important diagnosis I was missing. But here's one of the many times in retrospect I see God's knowing hand of safety at work. I also wasn't aware that I was at far greater risk of developing a CSF leak from a lumbar puncture, for a reason we're getting to. I was sent home with no answers, no relief, and the belief that even the hospital doctors didn't know how to help me. *Was I safe anywhere?*

I was accustomed to pain and a nagging headache, but this was an entirely different animal. I never got a break, even while I slept. The widespread agony, pounding head, blackening brain fog, highly alert and overstimulated nervous system, and panicked, racing heart, was all too much. My body had been hijacked but my brain was too inflamed to send out an SOS.

One of my favorite movies when I want a mindless laugh is *Get Smart*. There's a scene where the would-be agent gets promoted and steps into the soundproof glass box to scream, "This is the happiest day of my life!" Except he hasn't switched on the soundproofing.[14]

I felt as though the real me was trapped inside a soundproof glass box, watching helplessly as my body fumbled its interactions with the outside world. I no longer journaled, as my blurred mind could barely write down words. But every once in a while, I'd write a quick update to my supporters on Instagram, or jot down thoughts, Bible verses, or quotes. On one especially difficult day, I entered this in my journal:

October 24, 2019

*I hate the way this disease messes with my mind and affects my relationships. My parents are visiting and I'm having such a hard time not hating myself right now. I keep having to remind myself that it's not me; it's this thing that has a hold of me. I hate not being able to act and react the way I want to. The way I should. The way a normal person would. Always feeling like I am trapped in a body and mind that are doing whatever the hell they want while I watch from behind this thick glass, kicking and screaming, shouting all the things I really mean, only to have it fall on deaf ears—and one particular mind reader. I am only able to take comfort in the fact that God knows my heart, knows my mind, and his reckless love supersedes it all. The reckless love that drives him to leave the flock in search of the one missing sheep; the reckless love that welcomes the prodigal son home with open arms although he in no way deserves it; the reckless love that has erased my past and has given me a new start; the reckless love that finds me when I'm lost, and sustains and uplifts me time and again.*

## SPERANZA

I didn't know how to let anyone into my pain. Keeping everything bottled up was my familiar hell, and I thought I was safer that way. Bit by bit, I said goodbye to my former life, as any sort of interaction was far too difficult and stressful. A few faithful friends stuck around when the parties stopped, but I was usually too sick to do anything with them. I quit cooking classes and making multicourse dinners. I could no longer teach yoga or even attend church. I let go of my dreams of traveling, starting a family, and continuing meaningful volunteer work. I still meal prepped for clients each day, as a reason to get out of bed and to earn an income, but I'd lost my ability to get into a flow state while I cooked, or did anything else. Cooking had always been my outlet, my safe haven. No matter how much pain I was in, the kitchen had always transported me to a better state. Now every move felt as if I was fighting against myself, and tasks that were once second nature became arduous.

The first year of this illness was a very dark time. I'd cry out to God, begging him to heal me so I could go back to a life of purpose—as if I knew best what that looked like! One day at the clinic, my nurse friend Lisa asked me how I was holding up and if I ever thought about ending my life. This time, I couldn't keep the tears from flowing. Exiting the highway on my drive home, there was a curving off-ramp secured with Jersey barriers. More often than I wanted to admit, I thought about not turning my wheel and driving straight into the wall.

I couldn't see an end to my pain, but I was staking my life on the hope that God could. Hope. *Speranza.* The joyful expectation of what's to come. Thus, when I got that word tattooed on my wrist. I started every morning with coffee, obviously, and reading Bible verses about perseverance and hope. One of the promises of God I clung to—and still do—is from Philippians 1:6:

> And I am certain that God, who began the good work within you, will continue his work until it is finally finished on the day when Christ Jesus returns.

God had initiated this work in me. He'd saved my life from an overdose and addiction, nudged me to take a chance on him while in Italy, called me to go to the Philippines, and used that time to transform my faith. Now he was once again asking me to trust him, to not give up on him, because his work in me was not done yet.

*Speranza tattoo, waiting to board a flight home after a week of treatment in California*

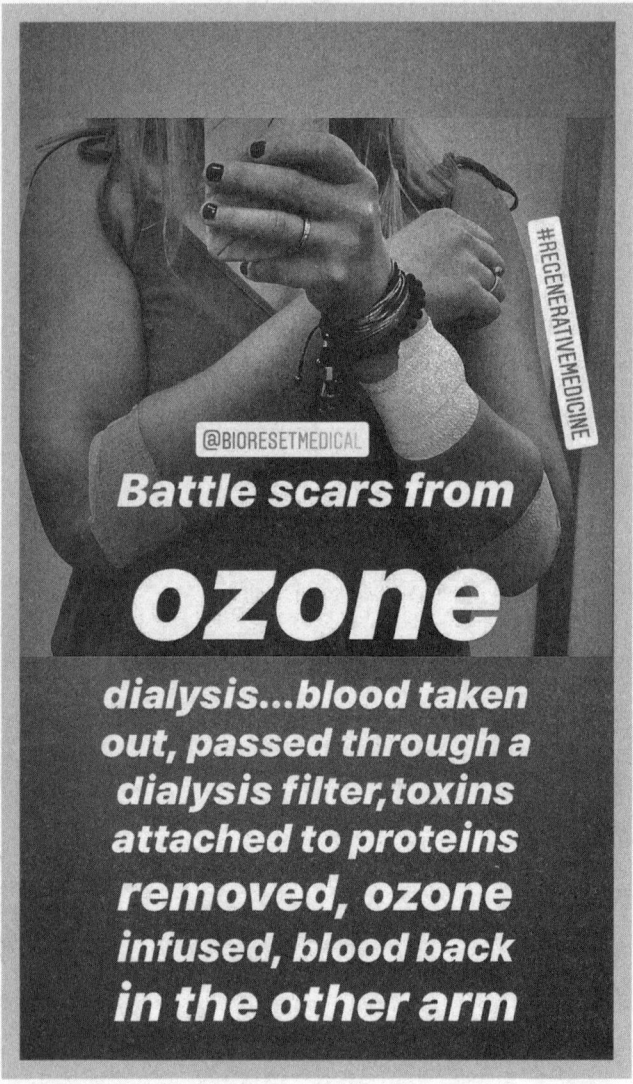

*Bandaged arms after ozone dialysis*

Twenty-One

# BOBBLEHEAD BARBIE

---

*Suffering produces perseverance;*
*perseverance, character; and character, hope.*
*And hope does not put us to shame,*
*because God has been poured out into our hearts.*
—Romans 5:3–5 NIV

I READ THIS verse over and over again while in the Philippines, trying to make sense of my own suffering and the enormity of it, which I saw all around me. This is what I distilled it down to: I don't automatically make the leap from hardship to hope. It happens as perseverance broadens my character traits and expands my trust in God's ability to see me through. Only then am I able to look past how hard the here and now is and shift my focus onto the growth my trials are producing, and the many ways God will use my challenges for good. There is no amount of pain God can't redeem—no amount of ashes he can't turn into beauty. So I put my hope in his promises because of the many times I have felt him carry me on his wings of love.

I'd seen this in the Filipino people. Their lives were difficult and full of setbacks, but their resilience and joy were palpable. Yes, everyone we helped said they were immensely grateful to have been given a home or a livelihood, but that was second to experiencing the life-changing saving grace of Jesus. It's because of him they lived with hope and could overcome anything. Their example continued to inspire me and also put my situation into perspective. On my very worst days, I had it better than much of the world ever did.

Every one of my needs were met in abundance, and I had access not only to doctors but to cutting-edge treatments. I made a list of everything I could do to improve my situation, however small. Optimizing my diet, improving my sleep, and getting more sunshine were on that list. Most profoundly, I began focusing on all I had instead of all I had lost, which doesn't mean I didn't have meltdowns on a semi-regular basis. But when so much is stripped away, there is room for the small, seemingly insignificant details and moments to be seen and to shine.

California quickly became my favorite place. In so many ways it's like Italy, with its rolling hills, cypress trees, vineyards, and farmers' markets. It's also like Asia, with its alcoves of immigrant communities who've replicated aspects of their former homeland. And then it has a magic all its own. I was constantly in awe of the way that, in my affliction, God brought me to a place that felt like home. As often as I could, within the limits of what my body allowed, I explored my surroundings, savored small pleasures, and celebrated every little win.

*Humorous quote at a coffee shop*

The other thing that kept me sane was finding reasons to laugh—especially at myself. I had a friend with complex health issues, and we'd text about the ridiculous situations we found ourselves in, sending each other funny memes that hit home. A few of my favorite quotes include:

Doctor: You have to start listening to your body.
Me: Oh, we're not on speaking terms.

My brain is giving me the silent treatment today.

## SPERANZA

Dear, whatever doesn't kill me, I'm strong enough now. Thanks.

I am awake. Please respect my privacy during this difficult time.

You've got it backward actually—I'm faking being *well!*

While humorous, they also reveal how I viewed my body, and that last quote was so true. I quickly learned that most people are highly uncomfortable with conversations about pain. Friends and acquaintances who genuinely cared about me would ask how I was doing, and as soon as I'd even begin to be honest, I'd see them squirm, look away, and regret asking. So instead, I made light of my situation, or simply stated that I was holding out hope, or I mentioned a small win. Eventually there were big victories to celebrate too.

My doctor was one of the first in the US to bring ozone dialysis and ozone plasmapheresis to his clinic. I was hooked up to IVs in both arms; blood was taken from one vein, infused with ozone, passed through a dialysis filter, then put back into the other vein. This added filtration gave my body a break from having to detox what the ozone was killing. It was the first treatment that didn't result in a flare-up, and I slowly started seeing improvement—especially in my cognition and memory.

The injections had finally brought stability to my lumbar spine, preserving my ability to walk. When it was all said and done, I had received over two hundred and fifty injections in my cervical, thoracic, and lumbar spine, jaw, and sacrum; five caudal epidurals; about twenty ozone dialysis treatments; and well over two hundred

IVs. I am unspeakably grateful to my parents, who made it possible for me to get this medical care, prayed for me every step of the way, and celebrated every victory. I am grateful, as well, to the team at this clinic, all of whom were my constant cheerleaders, holding my hand through many painful procedures and becoming like family to me.

I met so many other people at the clinic who greatly appreciated our doctor's wisdom and skill in treating their complex issues. A young boy had a condition called Ehlers-Danlos syndrome (EDS), which affects collagen production and weakens connective tissue—the body's glue. His ankles and knees wobbled when he walked, and he had come to the clinic in a wheelchair. After a series of injections into his ligaments, he was able to walk! His journey was hugely encouraging to me—and eye-opening.

As I thought back on my ligament injuries, weak discs, joint and spine instability, GI distress, and more, it suddenly clicked—EDS was the missing piece! Genetic testing confirmed I indeed had classic Ehlers-Danlos syndrome. I dove into research on EDS—or more like waded through research, given my very foggy brain. As I learned that it affects almost every part of the body—including the GI tract, blood vessel lining, spinal cord sheath, nerves, skin, tooth enamel, discs, tendons, and ligaments—I came to understand my broken body in a whole new way. Coming to this diagnosis through my own intuition, self-guided testing, and research, was empowering. I realized that I had spent my life putting far too much control in the hands of practitioners. While they were always well-intentioned, the bottom line is that no one knows my body, and my story, as well as I do. I still needed the knowledge and wisdom of the medical community—but I was armed with new agency in how I applied their recommendations. And it's a good thing, because . . .

# SPERANZA

At an appointment with a local EDS specialist, I scored a 9/9 on the Beighton test for hypermobility—the first test I wasn't trying to ace. A tilt table diagnosed postural orthostatic tachycardia syndrome, or POTS, which explained my racing heart when standing up. POTS can also develop after viruses or illnesses like Lyme disease, and there has been an uptick in cases since the pandemic. The specialist confirmed my MCAS diagnosis—another common comorbidity of EDS—and then told me something I will never forget: "I'll prescribe you medications to help manage your symptoms, and there are a few therapies you can try to slow your body's breakdown. But there's nothing you can do to reverse this condition, and if I were you I wouldn't even waste your time trying. Most likely, at some point, you will struggle to walk to the end of your driveway."

I left his office and sat behind the wheel of my car choking back tears, unable to move, yet unwilling to express the multitude of emotions coursing through me. I vowed to prove this doctor wrong. I would not only keep walking, but I would get better. The weight of my body's brokenness was heavier than it had ever been, but I was not going to let my spirit be crushed.

The field of epigenetics explores the impact of the environment on genes, for instance, the way outside factors turn genes on or off. EDS is a genetic condition where the body produces faulty collagen, and Lyme disease is highly damaging to collagen, especially the longer it goes untreated. I probably would have had mild to moderate symptoms from EDS had I not gotten Lyme disease, but that tick bite switched my EDS genes on and lit them up. I had broken the Whack-a-Mole switchboard. In fact, I often described my symptoms as my brain and body constantly short-circuiting. But if a damaging environment had flipped the switches on, couldn't a supportive environment flip the switches back off?

As some symptoms improved, a little fog cleared from my brain, and I started noticing a pattern. In the morning I felt somewhat okay, then just a slight movement of my neck, or even talking, would set off a cascade of intense air hunger, dizziness, brain fog, nausea, abdominal pain, fatigue, trouble speaking, a racing heart, pressure through my eyes, blurred vision, abnormal pupil dilation, sensitivity to light, difficulty looking up, and increased sensitivity to any stimuli. I had ringing in my ears and the feeling that my head was underwater. I would often lose my ability to taste from the pressure on my cranial nerves, and the muscles of my neck went into frequent spasm, causing my ears to bob up and down. My neck felt the best when my spine was in traction—*if only I could cook hanging upside down like a bat!* Throughout the day, I'd go into a forward fold, letting my head dangle down, and every vertebra in my spine would snap, crackle, and pop. My brain felt like it was being pulled downward before bouncing back against my skull, and my neck couldn't support the weight of my head. It was like I was one of those bobblehead dolls. Bobblehead Barbie.

Intuitively I knew this constellation of symptoms was connected and somehow keeping me systemically inflamed and stuck. Never underestimate the power of your intuition! A few years later, several prominent doctors confirmed what I was experiencing and published articles about an interplay of symptoms in those with complex chronic illness. This continuous loop connected EDS/hypermobility, POTS/dysautonomia, MCAS, chronic infections such as Lyme disease, autoimmunity, gastroparesis/slow GI emptying, and CCI (to be explained in a minute) or other structural anomalies—coined the Septad.

But these findings were a few years away, and I was barely

hanging on in the interim. Noticing my symptom pattern led me to again start digging. I was late to join the Facebook party, never really one for oversharing, which is ironic because you could argue this whole book is just that! But Facebook groups about EDS and chronic Lyme disease proved to have some useful information. I was reading a thread and came upon a comment about cranial cervical instability (yes, CCI) that explained my exact cascade of symptoms. If I could have jumped up off the couch and shouted without sending my heart rate through the roof and passing out, I would have!

CCI is a weakening of the ligaments that hold your skull atop your spine, a.k.a. the craniocervical junction—some of the most congested, complex, and vital real estate in the entire body. I learned that to diagnose CCI, I would need a dynamic cervical spine MRI, where my head was bent into flexion then extension, looking for signs of an abnormal shift of my skull off of my spine. I almost blacked out halfway through and it took me days to recover to baseline shitty. I sat in the parking lot with the radiology report, reading with validation that I had several levels of subluxations: abnormal shifts, signs of ligament damage, and nerve compression. The subluxations were affecting my brain stem, which controls the automatic processes of the body, and explained the racing heart, strained breathing, temperature dysregulation, brain fog, headaches, and the list goes on.

With these findings, my doctor in California gave me even more targeted injections, but the area was so unstable those injections didn't help for longer than a few days to weeks. Surgery was the next step, but there are only a handful of neurosurgeons in the US who treat CCI, and this was happening in tandem with the pandemic lockdowns. I emailed a renowned surgeon in South Carolina, but he couldn't help me remotely. I took my MRI to a local neurosurgeon who brushed me off and told me to come back to him if I had a real issue in the future. If my problem wasn't real, what was real in his book? Decapitation? Because that's where I was headed. I wrote in my journal:

> May 14, 2020
> *Knowing that something is majorly wrong with me, yet having so many doctors pass me over, write off my symptoms, and dismiss my pain, has made me even more steadfast in my pursuit of solutions. I'm not willing to accept that I will never be well. It's one time when my stubbornness will pay off! I know that if I keep searching for answers and pursue doctors who have wisdom and knowledge about my case, God will use them to heal me in his perfect way and perfect time.*

But in the meantime, I felt the entire weight of my illness resting on my ability to perfectly recall, at any given moment, every symptom and every treatment I'd had, just in case I came across someone who might be able to help me. Since my first week at the clinic, I'd kept track of every treatment, every injection, every supplement protocol, and every before-and-after symptom, and since then I'd added a daily play-by-play. The mental anguish was as difficult as the physical symptoms and pain. Talk about exhausting, to a body that was already running on fumes! Well, actually, I was running on adrenaline. I was constantly in fight-or-flight mode, with the overflow of cortisol ambushing my adrenals and feeding my system-wide dysfunction all the more.

My CCI symptoms continued to worsen, but I wasn't willing to fold. Instead, I treated life like a poker game—*I see you, pain, and I raise you.* I took on an even more rigorous schedule of clients, because I was

*My inspiration wall*

in agony even while doing nothing, so it was almost easier to stay busy. *Almost.* A few times I accidentally burned myself while cooking, then stood there scalding myself over and over again as the incinerated skin was an acute distraction from the blistering pain in my head and spine.

Every day I reached a point where I didn't think I could keep going, and I'd cry out to God to strengthen me. I had seen too much of him to know that he was anything other than completely good, completely loving, and completely kind. I didn't have any big epiphanies or hear God shouting, but day after day God found ways to make his presence known to me. Sometimes a song would speak directly to my situation. Sometimes, right when I was in a moment of deep despair, I'd get an encouraging text from a friend. Other times, it was a Bible verse I read that morning or one God put in my heart during the day. It was the constant, unwavering assurance that he saw me, was right there with me in my pain, and wasn't going anywhere.

Adrenaline is not a sustainable energy source and at the end of the day, I'd collapse in front of the TV. My favorite shows were medical dramas—probably because I felt like I was living one. In every episode, a scene unfolded where doctors scrambled to diagnose a mystery illness until finally an answer emerged. I'd lie on my couch imagining what it would feel like to be seen like that. *Is there anyone out there who will ever care enough to fight for me? Who will dig deeper below the surface, connect the dots, put the pieces together, and figure out what's going on? Will I ever be well again?*

*Cooking for a baby shower during the pandemic*

Twenty-Two

# STROKE OF GENIUS

---

*Do you ever feel like your body's*
*"check engine" light has been on and*
*you're still driving it like*
*"nah, it'll be fine?"*

CCI MIGHT NOT HAVE been quite so debilitating if my job didn't involve looking down all day, thus causing my cervical vertebrae to shift, compressing my brain stem and cranial nerves, and setting off a cascade of symptoms. Every article I read said a skull-base to C2 fusion was the only way to cure CCI, but the thought of cervical fusion was terrifying. My profession as a chef was significantly worsening my condition, yet the antidote—fusion—would leave me unable to move my neck, thus possibly unable to cook. What a cruel irony.

During an especially busy few weeks of cooking for clients, I went to the dentist to have a crown put in, which involved tipping my head back for a prolonged period of time, and forcefully pushing the crown into my upper molar. My dentist asked why I could barely open my mouth, and I mentioned my jaw pain and frequent dislocations. He saw elongated styloid processes on my imaging—small bones in my jaw area—and was concerned I had a condition called Eagle syndrome.

I left the dentist feeling even dizzier than usual, and with yet another diagnosis to explore. Then I drove to Target, where I almost passed out in the parking lot. I powered through my errands, and the rest of my week, but started having frequent episodes of lightheadedness that brought me to the brink of blacking out. I would stop cooking, put my head down between my knees, pray, wait for it to pass, and resume cooking when I could. This was happening close to a dozen times throughout the day.

It felt like my body had forgotten how to breathe without prompting. I was having frequent spells of confusion and struggling to form a coherent sentence. I knew something was seriously wrong, but I didn't have anyone left to turn to—every doctor I'd gone to for help over the prior four years had sent me away without a resolution. I used all my strength to research the symptoms of brain stem compression, and confirmed I was onto something there. I found the website of a PA who also has EDS, had undergone a fusion for CCI, and consults via a telehealth practice. She confirmed that I was dealing with complications from acute CCI, and told me I needed to be seen stat by one of the handful of neurosurgeons who specialize in this condition. As I was drifting to sleep that night, having to tell my body to take each breath, I didn't know if I was going to wake up the next morning, nor did I know if I wanted to. Whatever lay ahead was going to be a fight and I had no strength left. Yet, I rested, held in the assurance that my life was in the hands of the One who promises his strength shines brightest when I'm at my weakest. He would carry me through.

The next morning was even worse. My heart rate was uncontrollably high, and I was still struggling to take each breath. I called my parents in Massachusetts and my dad flew down to Florida the next day. As we sat on the couch that evening, his arm wrapped tightly around me, and with Spritz curled in his lap, his calm presence assured me that I wasn't alone. I had longtime clients whose son had severe food allergies, and they were celebrating his younger brother's first birthday. I was slated to make a baseball-themed birthday cake and a week's worth of meals for twelve people. I couldn't bail on them! My dad drove me to grocery stores and respected my silence as my jumbled brain was barely able to eke out a word, yet he somehow managed to make me laugh. He washed vegetables and helped chop them, showing off those stellar knife skills, honed by yours truly. As I looked down to pipe the red stitching onto the domed baseball cake—the finishing touch on all the food I'd made—my mind was fixated on the spinal fusion likely in my near future, and I thought to myself, *This is probably the last time you will ever do this.* I knew my life was about to change forever.

I made it through a cervical CT scan, chasing the Eagle syndrome rabbit hole—despite being on the verge of passing out—and added the images to the large collection of MRIs and other test results I was gathering for my journey ahead. My dad, Spritz, and I boarded a plane to Massachusetts, the start of Memorial Day

*Baseball birthday cake*

Weekend 2021. I gripped my dad's hand through the overstimulating airport and plane ride, all the while wearing my noise-canceling headphones, which played songs that kept my eyes trained upward and gently anchored my soul, as they had throughout all of my most difficult years.

# STROKE OF GENIUS

*Spritz cheering me up after I burnt myself
the week of my stroke*

"It felt like I had a stroke." That's how I explained my symptoms a few months later when I could talk again. Sometime during the following year, when I began working with my neurosurgeon, Dr. Henderson, he reviewed that cervical CT scan I'd squeezed in before my flight to Massachusetts, and informed me that indeed, I'd had an ischemic stroke. When my head was tipped back for the dental procedure, my shifting skull cut off blood supply to my brain. I was thirty-six years old trapped in a geriatric body and mind.

The day I left St. Pete, with every last ounce of energy and diminished brain capacity, I posted an update to Instagram, telling my friends and clients what had been happening with my health. I informed them that I would be staying with my parents in Massachusetts while I saw the handful of neurosurgeons who were my only chance of getting help. Suddenly, words came pouring out of me, turning into an entire testimony of God's faithfulness in my life. I relayed that it was his strength that had sustained and carried me all this time, and that I knew no matter what lay ahead, he'd be right beside me. After that, as much as I was able, I kept on posting throughout my trials and my triumphs—both as a way of keeping a lifeline to the world and as a way to offer encouragement to others.

Looking back at that post, I realized I'd said something very revealing:

*I knew I couldn't keep up this pace—something had to give. I knew I needed the next level of care even if it meant surgery. Mentally, I wasn't ready to do what my body needed, so it did it for me.*

Although it felt like my body was constantly betraying me, it was actually doing everything in its power to protect me! I couldn't see it yet, but I would in time.

I ended my post saying that although I didn't understand what was happening, I trusted God because *he is God, and I am not*. In his goodness, he is God. In the depths, he is God. When I wrote about the kind of faith I was searching for when journeying to the Philippines, I said *a supernatural faith* and God used those hard, painful days there to bring about just that. My abiding trust in God's goodness and sovereignty during my stroke was none other than the result of such supernatural faith.

Then I resumed posting about food, which is the subject of 90 percent of my Instagram feed. This was my next post:

> *I left Florida as our growing season had come to an end, and Massachusetts' growing season has just begun. The beautiful native strawberries are one of the many silver linings in suddenly having to uproot my life. "Sometimes when you're in a dark place you think you've been buried, but you've actually been planted."* (Christine Caine)

There was a reason this truth was speaking to me. In December of 2019, my dad was diagnosed with bladder cancer. He spent that first difficult year of Covid getting treatment from a functional medicine clinic in California as well as undergoing three bladder surgeries and several rounds of chemotherapy from a local urologist. It took a great toll on his health, but he was determined to get well, and at the time he came to my rescue, he'd regained his strength and vitality. In fact, a few months later, my dad's urologist told him that his cancer was in remission!

As for my mom, the stress of the pandemic and my dad's cancer caused dormant viruses to resurface. She was wasting away and spent much of the day in bed. I had barely seen them during the prior eighteen months, and when I had, their decline was frightening. I was acutely aware of the preciousness of life and determined to see and seize the beautiful moments that surfaced each day. There were many.

As I was barely hanging on to my own life, I made it my mission to nurse my mom back to health. I was able to help her navigate doctor appointments, medication, and supplements, and

# SPERANZA

*Massachusetts strawberries in May*

made simple, nourishing meals for us. I couldn't stand up for more than a few minutes before becoming faint, my hands trembled too much to hold my chef's knife, and my brain was too inflamed to use it. I prepped veggies with a paring knife while lying on the couch, bringing new meaning to the term *couch potato*. Slowly, we both started to heal.

As if CCI and having a stroke weren't enough, over the past six months I'd developed new symptoms in the lower part of my body. I was losing strength in my legs and walking became increasingly painful. My lower back and sacrum felt like they were being torn apart. I struggled to empty my bladder, and my pelvic floor was ripped with painful spasms. At night, sensations that felt like electrical shocks ran from my abdomen down my legs. Through my primary care physician, I consulted with a doctor in Spain, who ordered MRIs of my entire spine and diagnosed me with another comorbidity of EDS—a tethered spinal cord. The base of my spinal cord, which was both thick and brittle, was trapped in the lower portion of my spine, pulling my entire spine downward. He wanted me to go to Spain for his innovative surgery, but I couldn't even walk around the cul-de-sac our house was situated on, let alone travel to Spain. It did, however, give me one more piece to the complex puzzle.

I was introduced to a sweet friend who has EDS, as do her two children, and between the three of them, they'd had every associated condition and neurosurgery. I finally realized that my relentless, crushing headache was due to high cerebral spinal fluid pressure. I had four serious conditions that potentially all needed surgical intervention: Eagle syndrome, craniocervical instability, intracranial hypertension, and a tethered cord. It was going take a stroke of genius to heal me. What? Too soon?!

## SPERANZA

Those first weeks after my stroke were extraordinarily difficult. I was hypersensitive to any stimuli, I struggled to speak, and I couldn't voice what was going on in my body. I was often terrified. To make matters worse, I wasn't making any progress getting in with the surgeons I desperately needed to see. But this was my next post:

*The past few weeks have been a struggle. It's been overwhelming to think of how long I might have to wait for answers and for relief, and hard not to look at this as wasted time, as my days do not seem the least bit productive. It's getting harder and harder to hold my head up. The headaches are so intense, and even short conversations cause dizziness and worse pain. Fear has taken hold many times. Not fear of possible diagnoses and surgeries, but fear of being told by doctors they can't find anything wrong or they're unable to help. But I have to take the blind step out of fear and into trust and faith. I can do this because I know that God is FOR me and he IS love.*

After posting that, my phone died, and it was really nice being without it. Getting ready for bed, I realized that I had deep joy despite my circumstances, and peace, even with the uncertainty. Before drifting to sleep, I checked my email, and there was one from the neurosurgeon's office telling me they had received my (lengthy) intake forms and imaging, and I was scheduled for a video conference at the end of August—three months away!

*Hugs and kisses from my dad after a trip to see doctors in Manhattan*

Twenty-Three

# HAIL MARY

WHAT FOLLOWED WAS an absolute roller coaster. Buckle up. Over the next six months following my move to Massachusetts, I had appointments with:

1. An otolaryngologist in New York City, who ruled out Eagle syndrome. My sweet nephew Ethan drove me to the appointment. I hadn't been to the city I once called home in six years, and even though we only went to the hospital and grabbed a quick lunch, the familiar city smells and noises were exhilarating.

2. A urogynecologist in Boston. Although my conditions were usually seen in women twice my age and after multiple pregnancies, she didn't write me off because of my age the way my urogynecologist in Florida had. Instead, she diagnosed me with a neurogenic bladder and pelvic organ prolapse. She proposed reconstructive surgery but was hesitant due to my age and the

chance that I might still have children. Also, I had a few more pressing surgeries ahead.

3. A compassionate and knowledgeable EDS specialist in Rhode Island, who, over the course of six hours, went from head to toe explaining the manifestations of my faulty connective tissue. Unlike the specialist who told me rehabilitation was futile, this doctor gave me tools to preserve function and prevent further damage. He confirmed I needed neurosurgical intervention and suggested an appointment with the neurosurgeon I was already scheduled to meet with! He started me on periodic oxygen, midodrine to stabilize my heart rate, and a handful of medications for MCAS, but all of them made me much worse. He asked what my *Speranza* tattoo meant, and I told him it's Italian for "hope." He replied that it's his favorite word, and the next day, I posted:

*There's a reason it's referred to as "a glimmer of hope" and "the depths of despair." This morning after my doctor's appointment, as I was getting out of bed, everything around me seemed brighter, as if I'd been seeing in black and white and suddenly I could see in color. Even though I'm facing the possibility of four major surgeries, the mental anguish of not finding anyone able to fully diagnose and treat what has left me debilitated, has been as difficult as the physical pain. But I can see clearly now why God closed so many doors on doctors who weren't the right ones to treat me. Dealing with EDS patients requires deep knowledge of their complexities.*

# HAIL MARY

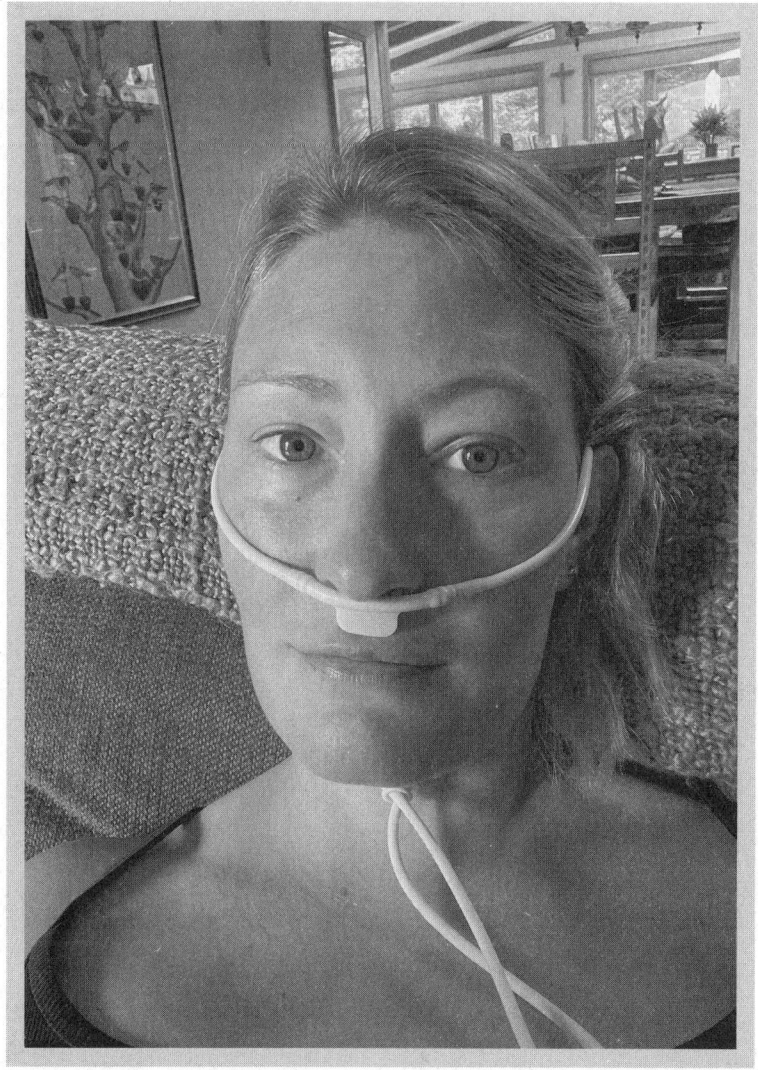

*Oxygen therapy at my parents' house*

I saw several more doctors in New York City and, considering that lying on my parents' couch was difficult, getting through the travel and appointments was a trial. But it was worth it, not as much for the doctors but for the time spent with my parents. Their fiftieth wedding anniversary was coming up that fall, and I treated them to a night at the Conrad with a stunning view of the city and Central Park, and to dinner at Hearth, where I'd interned wearing hot pink sneakers eleven years earlier.

My dad drove me to my appointments, and everywhere we went he had a story about a crushing or paving job in the various cities we passed. He told me all about the characters he met, the way he retrofitted each job, and the obstacles he overcame. His ingenuity and long hours often meant he finished ahead of schedule. I learned even more about his unparalleled work ethic, how much he sacrificed for our family, and his genuine interest in the people he worked with. It was decades later and he could still recall details about their lives as he animatedly spoke about them. I cherished this time.

But back to the doctors. Good news first: I was seen—truly seen—by a cardiologist who specializes in connective tissue disorders. After an echocardiogram to rule out any mitral valve or aortic complications due to EDS, he spoke words I didn't even know I needed to hear: "You are not in danger." That reassurance cut deep.

Now to the bad news: One of the top neurosurgeons in the city told me CCI was too rare, and therefore I didn't have it. He commented that I had a herniated disc in my thoracic spine—where only 1 percent of all herniations occur—and if I lost the ability to walk, to come back and see him. He couldn't see the irony in his statements, and in time his words would replay hauntingly in my mind.

## HAIL MARY

I was referred to a neurologist, whom another neurosurgeon used to screen his patients. She was supposed to diagnose CCI but used YouTube to look up how to measure the angles on my cervical MRI. I was about halfway through my medical history and symptom list when I saw it happen—her eyes glazed over and went slightly crossed. I'd overwhelmed yet another doctor. Then, instead of trying to put the pieces together and find which pieces were missing, she proposed Botox for headaches and medications for pain. The real kicker was when she said, "You're beautiful, smart, and successful. You're going to be fine." A few minutes later I almost blacked out in her office; she then left the room, had her nurse take me into another room, and never returned. Needless to say, neither did I. After that appointment, this was part of my post:

> *The biggest lesson I've learned through seeing more doctors than I can count over this 19-year journey is that we have to be our own advocate. Our symptoms are our body's way of telling us something is wrong. Any doctor who tries to cover up those symptoms without finding the cause is doing the opposite of "do no harm."*

Again, I was picking up on the fact that symptoms are how our body speaks to us! I was inching toward understanding.

Finally, I made it to the appointment I had waited all summer for—with the neurosurgeon who specialized in EDS and could potentially perform all the surgeries I needed. I'm throwing a lot of terminology out here, but maybe you've also been in pain for far too long, and this will potentially help you, a friend, or a loved one find a path forward too. He was the first doctor to tell me that I was very ill, and our telehealth appointment gave me validation. Remember when I had to rule out Eagle syndrome—those small, wing-like bones trying to take flight in my jaw? This surgeon attributed a different condition to the elongated styloid processes and diagnosed me with a condition called styloid-induced neuropathy of the glossopharyngeal nerve (STING). He confirmed a tethered cord (my trapped spinal cord sending distress signals to be let free), intracranial hypertension (fluid overfilling the water balloon that was my head), and craniocervical instability (the loose ligaments in my neck making me Bobblehead Barbie). He ordered a host of imaging, bloodwork, and scans; proposed two invasive diagnostic procedures under anesthesia; and ordered a glossopharyngeal nerve block with an ENT doctor to confirm STING.

My dad drove me to the ENT doctor in Queens and then double-parked a few blocks from the office. The doctor explained that he'd be injecting the back of my throat and that he was going in blind. There was no ultrasound guidance as used by my doctor in California. He warned that the needle might also get my vagus nerve, and I knew from my stellate ganglion blocks the unpleasant symptoms that follow—hoarseness, droopy eye, reduced reflexes, and more. I warned him about my history of autonomic dysfunction, including uncontrolled heart rate and near fainting, as he sprayed a numbing medication up my nose and injected the nerve.

Almost immediately I knew something was wrong. I grabbed his hand, partially yanking the needle out of my mouth, and started yelling and motioning for him to stop because I couldn't breathe and was going to pass out. My heart rate shot past 200 bpm. I tried further to tell him that I couldn't breathe, but I could no longer speak. Only groans were coming out of my mouth. He put his camera up my nose, then down my throat and saw that he'd missed his target and partially paralyzed one of my vocal cords as well as my tongue. I couldn't swallow and was choking on my own saliva. If I involuntarily swallowed, it would instead go up my nose, making me choke and gag even more. I figured out that if I spit into a cup and my mouth remained dry, I wouldn't choke, which helped me breathe a little easier. I also realized that my right arm was weak, and that in addition to losing my full range of motion, I had extreme pain in both arms and my neck. My right eye was nearly swollen shut from my vagus nerve being paralyzed. That was the only side effect I had expected.

The doctor was dumbstruck and texted the referring neurosurgeon, who instructed that I go to his hospital on Long Island where they would know how to care for me. I texted my dad, who once again came to my rescue and drove me an hour to the hospital. I still couldn't speak and was looking at the directions on my phone, then writing down an exit or turn on a piece of paper. I simultaneously drafted a short synopsis and my medical history for the hospital staff. I texted my mom and she sent my urgent need to her army of prayer warriors. All this while hyperventilating and having to spit into a cup so as not to choke on my own saliva.

At the hospital, it was extremely difficult to explain my situation while not being able to talk, and the staff was utterly confused. They did an arterial blood gas draw to check pulmonary function, but I was so dehydrated that it took a few painful tries getting the artery. I had an EKG and chest X-ray to rule out aspiration. After a few hours, the nerve block that was supposed to have lasted until the next morning started wearing off because I'd pulled the needle out of my mouth before the full dose of numbing medication had gone into the wrong places.

Slowly, I could swallow a little bit and say a few words as my breathing eased. We had a four-hour drive home and the hospital staff rallied to get me discharged at 7:45 p.m. when I was able to say enough to give my dad directions. Then my job was to keep him awake, which involved pit stops for coffee, Louis L'Amour on audiobook, polka music (his favorite), and Lauren Daigle (our compromise). One of my favorite songs came on, "Rescue," and as I was listening, I realized the deep calm I had experienced while in that hospital room. I pictured my army of prayer warriors holding me up in the grasp of their intercession and faith as God's blanket of peace covered me. My dad felt it too. He was so lighthearted, joking with the nurses and making me smile. And he was patient—a trait I didn't always see in him. My mom and I kept texting Romans 8:28 to each other: "And we know that God causes everything to work together for the good of those who love God and are called according to his purpose for them."

The "good" was what I learned from that episode. I didn't trust the wisdom of the neurosurgeon who recommended that nerve block and decided not to proceed with him. It made me acutely aware of the challenges I might face going into surgeries and the need to be that much more vigilant because of my conditions. I also discovered a growing trust in my body. Despite its brokenness, I was learning to admire its intuition and tenacity. I recently shared my story with a friend, and he commented that my body has always been watching out for me, has high-functioning survival skills, and wants me to trust it. It took me almost forty years to see that, but I certainly do now. We'll circle back to exactly how I got there soon.

In Providence, Rhode Island, I saw Dr. Klinge, one of the top tethered cord surgeons in the world. She was thorough and

# HAIL MARY

compassionate and explained that based on my MRI, I had been born with a tethered cord. Typically, symptoms surface early on, but sometimes it takes a traumatic event for it to reveal itself. In my case, it began making itself known when I fell and broke my tailbone. The reason my two tailbone surgeries never took away that pain was because the culprit was my tethered spinal cord. Finally, another huge part of my story made sense. She told me that I needed surgery. In the worst-case scenario, it would just halt the damage to my spinal cord and nervous system, which, as it continued to progress, could potentially leave me paralyzed. The best-case scenario was that it could reverse at least some of the damage. And the Hail Mary scenario was that it could also improve the symptoms of CCI and a host of other neurological conditions. I was scheduled for surgery six weeks later.

Right after seeing Dr. Klinge, my mom and I flew to DC for my initial appointment with another neurosurgeon who specialized in EDS and could address CCI, IIH, and any other issues that arose needing neurosurgery, which, at this point, wouldn't have surprised me. And good thing. She confirmed at least borderline CCI, based on my MRI, but the imaging was blurry and inconclusive. She found several herniated discs in my neck, and other issues needing more scans. I was so close yet so far, and was frustrated not to have a definitive diagnosis and plan. But I had my tethered cord surgery to get through before I could proceed with anything else. I was moving the needle and finally seeing some light at the end of the very long tunnel.

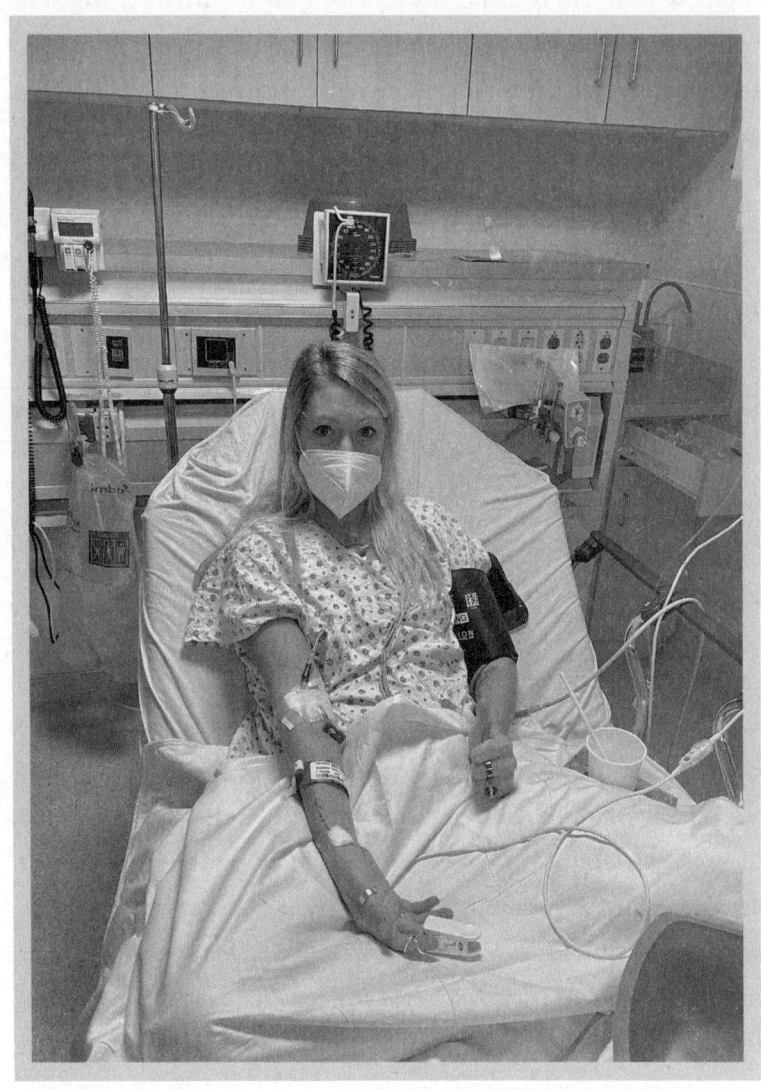

*Signaling I'm ok at the ER in Long Island*

Twenty-Four

# PROVIDENCE

ONE OF MY favorite names for God is "El Roi," which in Hebrew means "the God who sees me." In every procedure or scan, while lying on a cold table in a hospital gown, I took great comfort and strength knowing God saw me in my struggle, especially when it felt like no one else did. After months of bedrest between doctors' appointments, the acute inflammation around my brain stem calmed down enough for me to fly home to Florida, pick up some of my winter clothes, and check on my house, which was pristine, thanks to my sweet sister and niece who went there every week to water my plant babies. I had a one-week window in early November to do various tasks and get back to my parents, for pre-op appointments and surgery. The whole trip happened so quickly and last minute that no one knew I was there besides my immediate family. Yet, the most amazing thing I could have imagined transpired.

I arrived in Tampa, greeted by my sister and niece with flowers, hugs, and kisses, and then the eerie stillness of my home. Everything was just as I'd left it, longing to be lived in once again, yet it would be several months before I could return for good. I never told anyone, but since leaving, I'd wished someone who needed a place to stay could use my home. I woke up the first morning in my cozy bed, happy to be there, yet with great angst over leaving again. I opened my inbox and read The Daily Article email, in which cultural theologian Jim Denison urged us all to pray for boldness in the face of crises.[15] In that moment, I prayed for God to use me however he wanted, and asked for a measure of grace to not get in the way of his plans.

Next was an email from my friend Leslie, who is the volunteer director of PEER Servants and who had been praying for my health and following my journey for quite some time. The day before, another PS volunteer, who lived in Haiti with her husband and two young children, had emailed Leslie and said that due to the escalating political instability and gang violence there, they were no longer safe and were looking for a place to stay in the US, preferably in Florida. Leslie asked if, by chance, I'd lend my home to this family. I yelled "Yes!" so loudly my neighbors probably heard! I couldn't believe what I was reading. This was the answer to my silent prayer, and a very real answer to this family's prayer of faith. It was El Roi, showing his love, omniscience, and presence in a remarkable way.

What followed was a flurry of emails and WhatsApp messages making introductions and sharing our joy and awe at God's love, kindness, and provision. As I went to work unpacking, repacking, and getting my house in order for this precious family to live in, I had a whole new purpose for being home during this quick trip that I happened to squeeze in between doctors' appointments and surgery. I felt my house come to life in the same way it does when I'm entertaining friends or hosting family, and in the same way I always imagined it would if I had a family of my own. Rather than leaving it empty, I was welcoming new friends to come and make it their own. I pictured them stringing Christmas lights and baking Christmas cookies—both of which came true!

God had me back home at the exact moment, so I could make up beds and clear out closets, complete lists with WiFi passwords and security codes, stock the fridge, and add welcoming touches. I couldn't have done any of this from afar. I also spent those days in fervent prayer as the situation in Haiti was rapidly deteriorating. Flights to the US were being cancelled and a fuel shortage was, amongst other things, threatening internet connectivity, hence all means of communication. I flew back up to Massachusetts in the afternoon and the family safely landed in Tampa that very same evening. We became fast friends from a distance, and their faith was both encouraging and admonishing as they urged me to keep my eyes fixed on God—my Mountain Mover and Great Provider—and not on my situation.

The last time I had had surgery was to repair my foot eight years prior, and my body, in the gentlest of terms, had been through quite a bit since then. Now, nearing the end of 2021, my many conditions made surgery much riskier. But more than fear, I was filled with hope. There were a host of symptoms surgery might improve, and right before the day approached, I posted,

> *I am trusting my BIG God to use this surgery to heal me in BIG ways. That afterward, I'll feel better than I have in a long time. That I won't even need the other surgeries I'm slated to have because my God can do that!*

## SPERANZA

It had taken a village of doctors in Florida, California, New York, Massachusetts, Maryland, and Rhode Island to get me on track to have this tethered cord surgery. My surgeon, Dr. Klinge, cut through the muscle in my lumbar spine, removed a piece of bone covering my spinal canal, then cut into the protective sheath where cerebral spinal fluid came shooting out like a fountain—a sign that my intracranial pressure had indeed been extremely high. She had never seen the likes of it, and after surgery, for the first time in over three years, I didn't have a pounding headache.

The very bottom portion of my spinal cord, called the filum, was removed, and pathology showed that it was thick and brittle from abnormal collagen. It had been keeping my entire spinal cord trapped and unable to move within the spinal canal, and it was also failing at its job of regulating my CSF pressure. Dr. Klinge was hopeful I wouldn't have ongoing issues with intracranial hypertension. The surgery went perfectly, aside from a severe MCAS reaction to the antibiotics administered in recovery. Even in my extremely groggy post-op state, I knew what was happening from the time I'd had a similar reaction at the California clinic, and I instructed the nurse to give me Benadryl, which alleviated my symptoms. My body was on high alert keeping me safe, and I knew by then to trust my intuition!

I was ordered to lie completely flat for the first twenty-four hours post-op as my spinal fluid recalibrated, and I envisioned springing up from the bed, pain-free, with a new spine and a new lease on life. The reality was an excruciating few days in the hospital, struggling to stand and walk, as the hole in my back sent tidal waves of spasms through my spine. Before being discharged for six weeks of no bending, lifting, or twisting, I found out that one of my long-time school friends lived in Providence. I wasn't allowed any visitors

# PROVIDENCE

because of Covid restrictions but Mike is a pastor and played the clergy card to get into my room. Mike and I have known each other since we were preschoolers but had only seen each other once since high school graduation. He asked what had happened in my life since we were eighteen. *Oh, not much!*

Mike knew me during my angry, rebellious teen phase, when I was mad at God and looking for love in all the wrong places. I couldn't wait to share that God hadn't given up on me and had used the challenging situations in my life to show that he is all-powerful, trustworthy, faithful, and that he is love. The joy Mike and I had talking about our Savior's work in us and through us was palpable, and Mike told me he'd been praying for me for many years. We covered nearly two decades in two hours. I hadn't smiled that much in a long time. In fact, I still smile whenever I think about that afternoon in my hospital room—in Providence. A place that time and time again lived up to its name.

The story doesn't end there. Weeks later, I posted our reunion to my blog and Facebook, and I tagged Mike's wife since he doesn't have an account. In doing so, I saw her urgent prayer request for Mike's mom. Miss O'Brien had suffered a brain hemorrhage and was in the ICU. Immediately, I started praying for God to spare her life and for peace over her family. I got in touch with Mike, who kept me updated over a rocky couple of weeks, as she went on to suffer a series of seizures and was on a ventilator. At times they didn't know if she'd make it through the night, let alone ever resume normal functions including vision, speech, and processing.

I witnessed Mike's faith in a God who can part the sea, and it was an honor to pray with him to that end. Miraculously, Miss O'Brien was healed! She was taken off the ventilator, able to speak

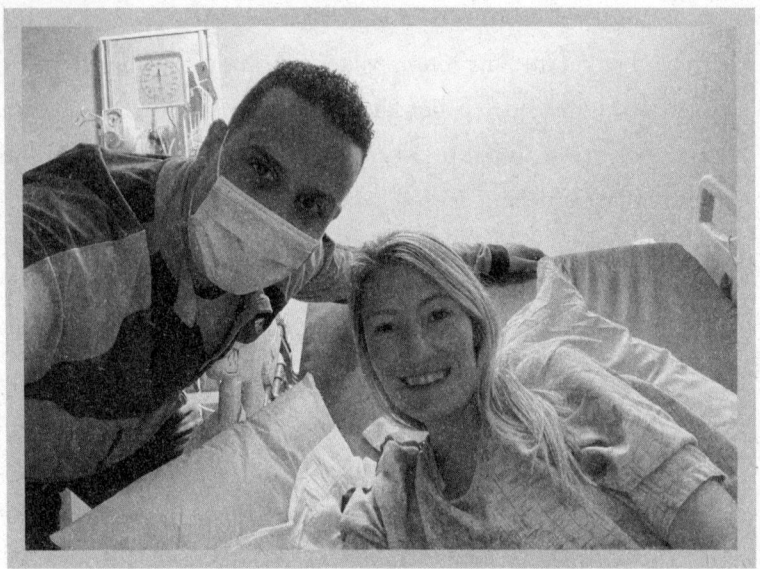

*Reunion with Mike in my Providence hospital room*

and process, see clearly, eat a meal, and smile at the camera. It was all truly awe-inspiring. The way God brought Mike back into my life to be a friend, prayer warrior, and huge source of encouragement during my surgery, the way God led me to post that story, and the way doing so led to my being there for Mike as we fervently prayed for Miss O'Brien's healing amazes me still. After adding her recovery to my post, I ended by saying:

> *There are miracles happening all around, and even when they come in ways I didn't expect, or the healing isn't physically my own, God uses these experiences to bolster my faith, show me his love, and lift up my downcast eyes towards his glorious light.*

## PROVIDENCE

Finally, 2021 came to an end. It was a year of numerous assaults on my body when my life could have been snuffed out many times. It was a year that threatened to crush my spirit at every turn—a year where a weak faith would have sunk me into the quicksand of hopelessness. But my life was built on the solid foundation of Christ, and every trial where I took a step toward him added layers to that bedrock. I was going to need every ounce of faith for what was still to come.

*Twinning with my mom in DC, headed to my first neurosurgeon appointment*

Twenty-Five

# THE GOOD DOCTOR

*I wanted to talk about it. Damn it.*
*I wanted to scream. I wanted to yell.*
*I wanted to shout about it.*
*But all I could do was*
*whisper, 'I'm fine.'"*

MY TETHERED CORD surgery reversed some of the damage to my spinal cord and alleviated several symptoms, quieting some noise, but my body was still screaming. I wrote this about it in my journal:

> January 27, 2022
> There have been so many days lately when every minute is a struggle. On a physical level, it's a challenge to get out of bed knowing it will mean 12 hours of agony, to keep

*breathing when every breath is a fight, and to take one step after another when my legs feel too weak to hold me up. On a mental level, it's difficult not to give in to despair, to keep pushing forward when I'm overwhelmed by it all, to contemplate what I have to be grateful for rather than dwell on all I've lost, and to keep engaging with people even in small ways instead of shutting out the world. On a spiritual level, it's hard not asking God "why" and instead, letting his love for me be answer enough, to trust that he will carry me when I have no strength of my own left, to keep praying even when it's for the same things, and to keep fighting those voices that tell me his promises aren't true, he doesn't care, and he has disappeared. But instead, to keep relentlessly seeking his presence. I'm learning that life is a fight. We do not advance in faith without a fight. We do not grow without a fight. We were made to fight.*

This journal entry could have been on repeat every day of the past four years, and many days before that. It's no wonder every muscle in my body constantly felt tense and tight. My whole body was balled into a fist, battling for my life.

Remember when I tried craniosacral therapy (CST) as a teenager after breaking my tailbone and I asked my mom if I could pretend to feel the flow of energy? I'm chuckling as I write this. Oh, how much has changed! Craniosacral is a somatic therapy that helps rewire the limbic system of the brain, which can cling to comfortable patterns, even if they are damaging, as if preferring a familiar hell. It aids in processing emotions or traumatic events, which, as you're learning, can have a profound effect on your physical body. And it's also helpful for calming the nervous system by restoring the flow of cerebral spinal fluid.

A few weeks after surgery, I began working with a caring and intuitive craniosacral therapist to help with rebound pressure headaches and other symptoms. During our CST sessions, I wasn't surprised to feel shifting energy, but I was shocked when I'd feel a coinciding emotion. Rather than suppressing those emotions as I'd done my whole life, I welcomed them with curiosity and even started tracing their origin. If you haven't figured it out by now, I always need to know the why!

I was living with my parents in the home I grew up in, and essentially did childhood regression therapy on myself. It was intense, uncomfortable, difficult, and completely foreign, but the more I uncovered, the more I carried on. I made huge discoveries about how my childhood perceptions shaped my life—the unworthiness that came when my mom told me I was an accident, and how I looked at pain as a means of earning worth and love. I saw how invisible I'd so often felt, and how finding my true identity as God's beloved child helped me find my voice.

Fear was the emotion I felt more than any other. My life had been driven by fear. *Of course, I'm holding fear after all I've been through—and am still facing. How could I not be terrified of my body?* So I just left that emotion alone no matter how many times it surfaced. But this newfound awareness regarding the connection between my body and my emotions was a huge first step!

Post-pandemic, there was an uptick in openly talking about mental health in a way that was once taboo, and *trauma* became a buzzword. I think it's now misused to describe any adverse event, but with it came insight into the way our bodies hold on to hardship and manifest it as physical symptoms. I began noticing that when my nervous system was relaxed, I was able to be present and express myself the way I wanted to. Conversely, and more often than not, I saw how my stressed-out nervous system coiled up, causing me to react instead of act. In those times, I felt trapped behind that thick pane of glass. I noticed how hypervigilant my nervous system was, surveilling my environment for danger and waiting for impending doom. I also realized how often I dissociated—feeling as if I was outside of my body—as an attempt to escape the terrors of being inside of it.

For as long as I could remember, I had felt trapped in a body I was at odds with, and I grasped to feel in control. Understanding the effects of my nervous system softened how I related to my body. It also offered a sense of control—or it would have, if every time I moved my head, my skull wasn't shifting off my spine, compressing my vagus nerve and sending me spiraling into fight-or-flight mode—the very opposite of control. The Hail Mary scenario—that my tethered cord surgery would help my CCI—was a miss. I was still Bobblehead Barbie.

Two months after my tethered cord surgery, I returned to the neurosurgeon in DC with my mom by my side, new imaging in hand, and one surgery checked off the list. Going into my appointment, I prayed for El Roi to give my doctor new eyes to see everything going on with me, and for the strength to plead my case. Despite my poise and ability to perfectly recount my medical history, the surgeon could tell I was in pain. She saw it in my eyes and kept trying to make me comfortable. We reviewed my CT scans, which needed another specialist's opinion regarding veinous congestion in my head, and then she was ready to dismiss me before addressing my CCI.

## THE GOOD DOCTOR

I'd spent so many years focusing on the positive, not on my pain, that it was actually harder to admit the depths of my suffering than to mask it with a smile. But in that moment, on the wings of my prayer and sheer desperation, I did something entirely unlike me: I spoke up. I told her that I lived in agony and could no longer cook professionally. I said that even a simple trip to the grocery store made my head spin and my brain foggy, I often couldn't remember why I was there, and I felt nauseated and seasick. I begged her to help me to be able to cook again! She asked if I wanted surgery, and I answered, "I want relief."

Every surgeon had performed the standard neurological exam, and I'd mostly passed, but those scores are relative. I worked hard at staying strong, but during her exam she validated how weak my arms were, as I explained that I'd gone from being able to do a dozen pull-ups to struggling through just one. She pressed on my neck, and I winced. She started reviewing my symptom list and her old measurements of my cervical MRI, and I pushed her further to look at my MRI again. Once loaded on her screen she said, "Wow!" commenting on how deformed the shape of my thoracic spine was. I told her how much worse that had gotten over the past year. I felt like Quasimodo! She reviewed my MRI in detail, and the more she looked and measured and commented, the more I could see her wheels turning.

Suddenly, I was a patient in the medical drama, *The Good Doctor* when the brilliant surgeon has a breakthrough and sees all the moving parts and how they fit together. I had two large, herniated discs in my lower neck that were stretching my spinal cord, causing a deformity in the curvature of my spine. I also had significant CCI, which was compressing my brain stem. She proposed two separate cervical fusions—the skull-base to C2, followed by C5 to C7—and said she couldn't believe what I'd been enduring. I told her God gave me the strength I needed to get through each day, and I thanked her for truly seeing me.

I left nearly in tears—both out of gratitude for having been seen and validated—and because the reality that I needed two major surgeries was sinking in. I was scared of what this meant for my future and afraid of making the wrong decision. One of the caveats with fusion is that the resulting lack of movement puts pressure on the surrounding discs, then those discs become compromised, resulting in a domino effect. I pictured an incision starting at my skull, traveling down my neck, through my thoracic spine, meeting the five incisions I already had over my lumbar spine, tailbone, and pelvic floor, thus leaving a giant fishhook of a scar. But as soon as I acknowledged my fear, I knew instantly God would lead me in his peace, as long as I kept a dialog with him. Besides, I now tell people my giant fishhook of a scar was from a shark bite—and boy does it have a story to tell!

While flying out of DC after my appointment, I saw a stunning sunset. The waning sun sat above the clouds, blocking the view of the city below. I knew the city was down there even though I couldn't see it, and what a powerful metaphor of faith that was! I took a video from the plane window and posted it to my Instagram with the caption,

Heading home—with hope on the horizon!

A few weeks later, I got an email with the neurosurgeon's notes. I read the words "significant CCI" and viewed the list of associated measurements that were "grossly" abnormal. For most people, the confirmation of a CCI diagnosis would have been one of the worst days of their life. For me? It represented victory. I broke down and wept. They were tears I hadn't let myself shed for so, so long. They were tears of pain for each agonizing day of putting one foot in front of the other and standing at my stove burning myself. They were tears of relief because I had been seen—especially after being dismissed and disregarded so many times before. They were tears of joy and gratitude that I hadn't given up on life and that God hadn't given up on me. They were tears of hope for brighter days to come. *Speranza*.

I had a follow-up telehealth appointment with the neurosurgeon a few weeks later, and she referred me to yet another specialist about putting a stent in my jugular vein. She also told me she was leaving the practice, but that I'd be in the best hands with her colleague, Dr. Henderson. Yes, the same Dr. Henderson I mentioned earlier, who diagnosed my ischemic stroke during my first appointment—a few months after this call. He is a leader in the field of EDS neurosurgery, having developed the superior hardware used in CCI fusion. I got off the phone and went to talk to my parents about the decisions I had to make. My dad listened intently, then asked to pray, and said he liked to picture us looking up at God through a small hole in the ceiling, while God looks down on us seeing the full picture—the entirety of our story. He thanked God for seeing every part of us, and knowing every part of us, so we might entrust into his loving care, every part of us. It was the most beautiful prayer my dad ever prayed over me—and the last.

Ten months after my stroke, I was finally returning home to Florida, and the day before I left, my dad went into acute kidney failure. His urologist attributed it to an enlarged prostate, and my dad underwent a double nephrostomy, a procedure that enables the kidneys to drain outside of the body through a tube. A few weeks later, just days before my thirty-seventh birthday, we learned that my dad's bladder cancer had been mismanaged by his urologist, was never in remission, and had instead metastasized to his pelvis, sacrum, back, and ribs. He was given weeks to months to live.

My dad called me the morning of my birthday and barely had a voice, but he sang "Happy Birthday" to me anyway. I spent the first half of the day in tears, knowing next year at that time, grief would fill the void his voice left. My dad was in and out of the hospital and in so much agony that conversations were few. But I got to tell him that I'd go through the stroke, and the most difficult year that followed, all over again for the time we spent together. Then, we muffled our sobs in a hug I wished would never end.

We celebrated my dad's eightieth year of life exactly three weeks before his death. My mom had the idea to decorate his cake to look like his rock yard. I ordered the supplies on Amazon while sitting in his hospital room, not knowing if he would be discharged in time for the party we'd been planning long before we knew he was sick. I covered the chocolate cake with turbinado sugar to look like sand, and added candy rocks, toy trucks, and pylon-cone candles. The day before his party, my dad asked his oncologist if he could be discharged on hospice. In a gravelly voice, he said, "There's nothing like twenty kids giving you a hug—I'll be going from heaven to heaven."

My mom, siblings, siblings-in-law, nieces, and nephews—all twenty of us—rallied around my dad and helped with his care in a beautiful way during those last months, and he did indeed make it home to celebrate his birthday. As we carried out his cake, singing "Happy Birthday" followed by "May the Good Lord Bless You,"

*My dad's 80th birthday cake*

my dad started to cry, and so did every single one of us—his entire family gathered around him. My dad said, "What a God, that he would take care of me like this, even in my last days. He knows every hair on my head, and the number of each grain of sand," as he pointed in amazement at his rock yard–themed cake. He then went on to talk about an analogy of death that had always stuck with him. "I think it's going to be like getting onto a boat and waving goodbye to everyone I love as they stand on the shore, then going into thick fog and emerging to another shore where I see the shining smiles of all those I've loved who had gone before me, waving hello and welcoming me with outstretched arms."

That assurance and peace is what my dad lived with right up until the end of his life. One day, sitting as I often did with one hand squeezing his and the other stroking his hair, my dad looked up toward the sky and said, "The colors, the colors are so beautiful!" I think he was seeing glimpses of heaven that awaited.

My brother and I held our dad's hands as he took his last breaths during Memorial Day weekend 2022—exactly one year from when he had flown to Florida and rescued me. Words can't express my grief—or gratitude—in seeing the many whys and ways God was working that year for my good: helping my mom with her health, the precious family from Haiti having a safe home to live in, reuniting with Mike and witnessing his mom's miraculous healing, and the priceless time spent with my dad. Seeing the why didn't lessen my heartache, but it was a vivid picture of God's love, omniscience, and faithfulness. During seasons of utter blind faith, I can look back with certainty and move ahead in trust, knowing God is indeed piecing together my pain.

My dad was always so strong. At seventy-nine, he outworked the twenty-year-olds, and there was nothing he couldn't do. My home is covered with his fingerprints—in some places quite literally—from projects we did together, and I always knew if I needed something I could call him. As my health declined, my dad often called me on a Thursday morning for an update before he met his men's group who faithfully prayed for me each week. That year after my stroke, his confidence brought me reassurance everywhere we went. Over the last decade, I had witnessed my dad come to a place of surrender. I had watched as God softened his rough edges and wrapped my dad's imperfections in his nail-pierced arms, the way God had done for me.

Returning home to Florida after my dad's funeral, thirteen months after being uprooted, was difficult for many reasons. I was picking up the pieces of a broken life. As I grieved, I realized that somewhere along the way, my dad had become my safety, and now my safety was gone. Yet there was also beauty in that. I spent much of my childhood afraid because of my dad's temper and outbursts, but by the end of his life he'd become my safe haven. I didn't know what to do with this revelation other than acknowledge it, and then try to forget it.

When I left my house after my stroke, I said I was ready to do whatever it took to stabilize my neck, even if that meant fusion. But I think that was the stroke talking. As soon as I was functioning again, albeit in a very dysfunctional way, I went back to my old tricks. I'd bury myself—emotions and all—in my work and put on a smile to mask my pain while barely getting through each day. I was willing to tolerate mediocrity because I wasn't willing to face the fear of what truly thriving would entail.

Over six hundred people attended my dad's memorial service. He was loved by many, was a pillar in his community, and left a legacy that had me thinking about the significance of my own life. *Have I accomplished anything? Left a mark anywhere? Done anything that matters?* Soon after returning home, I had the opportunity to become co-owner of a health clinic and jumped at the chance to apply the vast arsenal of knowledge I'd acquired and walk beside those struggling with their afflictions. Months back, I'd decided to shift my career in this direction, had been praying for an open door, and saw this opportunity as one God was dropping in my lap. I viewed the many red flags as hurdles to overcome, rather than as warning signs—much the same way I approached my health.

There's a reason they say not to make any life decisions after a traumatic event. There are big emotions swirling around, even if you don't recognize them. Becoming a partner in the clinic was driven, in large part, by fear. I was afraid of living an insignificant life and fearful that walking away would mean missing out on an opportunity and calling. Fear had been present my entire life in a multitude of ways, so it seemed normal that this was yet another situation where I had to take a step past fear into action.

I've talked so much about God's peace, but there was still a disconnect. Despite all I'd seen, part of me still viewed God in the same way my childhood self had. Then, and in this moment, I still thought living for him meant living in bondage to the frightful things he might ask of me. I didn't yet understand God's own words that he is a God of peace. The other part of this decision rested on the hope that if I shifted away from cooking and took a different career path, I might be able to avoid fusion. It's ironic the way I was driven by fear into making one decision and was running away from fear in another decision. Fear was truly piloting my life.

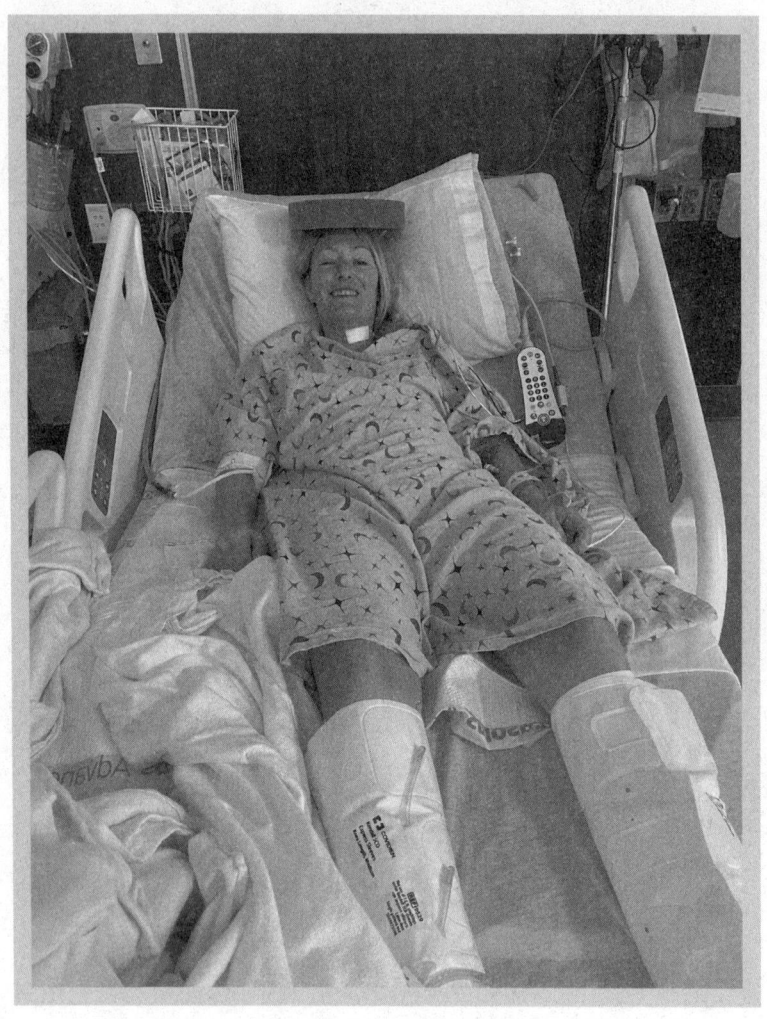

*Recovery room after my first cervical fusion surgery*

Twenty-Six

# SQUID GAMES

---

THERE WAS A good chance that, with the nerves in my spine finally functioning properly after my tethered cord surgery, the injections to stabilize my neck would be more effective. I also learned about other factors that were potentially exacerbating my CCI symptoms. I had not left any stones unturned when it came to alternatives to fusion, and so I started another dizzying round of doctors' appointments, treatment protocols, injections, procedures, and endless research. I'll give you the CliffsNotes.

Dr. Henderson, my neurosurgeon in DC, understood how complex and nuanced my conditions were and found several items of concern on my imaging. My cervical CT scan—where he first saw the signs that I'd suffered a stroke—also showed the compression of veins or arteries as a potential cause of my intracranial hypertension (those times when my head felt as if it was about to pop). That condition had improved for a while after my tethered cord surgery, but then returned. At a hospital in Baltimore, I had a cerebral arteriogram and angiogram, where they ran catheters through the veins and arteries, starting in my groin and continuing to my brain, and injected fiery contrast dye while taking X-rays. As I lay perfectly still, strapped to the sterile metal table, I pictured a battle between a squid shooting its black ink while being periodically zapped by an electric eel. If the study showed a blockage, I'd have a stent put in, which would be a somewhat simple solution to a complex problem causing a host of symptoms. I was convinced this scuffle was going to be the win I'd been waiting for. Instead, the study showed no blockage. There was a small aneurysm needing monitoring every few years, but otherwise the results were inconclusive.

I woke up the next morning defeated and beat up from the smoldering electric shocks and started asking God why. *Why'd I have to go through a grueling day at the hospital for nothing? Why couldn't even one step of treating my conditions be easy or clear?* I sat in my hotel room having one big pity party, until I started reading my daily devotional from Psalm 20:7. "Some trust in chariots and some in horses, but we trust in the name of the Lord our God."

It was another moment when that still, small voice became a shout, and I heard God say, "It will be *me* who heals you!" Right after, a client-turned-friend texted me encouragement to always remember I'm in the hands of the Great Physician. I wrote in my journal that morning,

> July 11, 2022
> *There is only one healer, and I call him Father. Once again God is surrounding me with signs of his presence and ministering to me right where I am—in my angst, in my frustration, in my fear, in my pain. He's gently saying, "I'm right here. Take my hand, see my scars, and trust how much I love you."*

## SQUID GAMES

I'd witnessed miracles, and had no doubt God could heal me with one snap of his finger, but kept wondering, *What does it mean that God himself will heal me?* From the get-go, Dr. Henderson tried every angle that might save me from needing the major CCI fusion. One of the discs in my lower neck was herniated and stretching my spinal cord, and there was a chance it was contributing to my CCI symptoms. Fusion at that level was much less invasive and a solid place to start. My mom and Spritz were beside me the whole recovery in DC and I was back to work three weeks later. Before surgery, Dr. Henderson prayed that I'd be filled with God's Spirit, for God to guide his hands, and for God to heal me. Suddenly I understood: My surgeon knew that his skill, his knowledge, and his ability to heal were only because God was working through him. Ultimately it is God who heals me!

At my three-month post-op, we were pleased with my recovery. The intense pain over the disc and down my arms was gone, and I no longer looked like the Hunchback of Notre Dame. But my symptoms of idiopathic intracranial hypertension were severe, scary, and escalating quickly. As this had been an ongoing issue, we decided on a diagnostic/therapeutic lumbar puncture to check my opening pressure and drain cerebrospinal fluid to give me temporary relief. Based on that, Dr. Henderson would put in a lumbar shunt to continuously drain the excess CSF. Since many symptoms of IIH overlap with CCI, relief from this procedure could prolong my need for the next big fusion and provide a huge increase in my quality of life. I fought fear all week leading up to it—not fear of the procedure, but of the thought, *What if this is another dead end or doesn't give me the clarity I need?*

That week my cerebrospinal fluid pressure got so high, I had

*Spritz by my side, headed into fusion surgery in DC*

CSF gushing out of my nose. Then, I almost didn't make it to DC for the procedure I so urgently needed. My flight was cancelled; so was the one I was rescheduled on; and in desperate determination, I slept at the airport, took a sunrise flight on a different airline into a different city, and rode in an Uber directly to the hospital. All with Spritz in tow and thirty minutes to spare! My mom, my partner through every step of this wild ride, met me at the hospital and took Spritz—who had been a champ during our twelve-hour day on planes, trains, and automobiles—back to our Airbnb, and then made it back to the hospital in time for my procedure. Crisis averted, back in business!

Before I went under, Dr. Henderson again prayed for God to heal me. Years back, when I'd driven myself to the emergency room for this very condition but didn't know what it was at the time, I was offered a lumbar puncture, which would have been profoundly helpful if it didn't come with the great risk of a CSF leak, which EDS patients are extra susceptible to. Dr. Henderson understood these complexities, and after draining 20 ml of CSF from my lumbar spine, he took blood from an artery in my wrist to seal the sheath around my spinal canal, providing what is called a blood patch. Aside from a blown vein, four missed IVs, and some very bruised arms and hands, I woke up feeling the improvement of many symptoms, along with relief—and hope. My opening pressure reading was high, but not high enough to warrant a shunt, probably because so much CSF had already leaked out of my nose in the days prior. Again, the findings were inconclusive.

I flew home and within a few days had a raging headache, legs that felt like every muscle had been ripped open, and an angry hornets' nest of pain in the area where my tailbone once was. It quickly escalated and I was in more agony than after any of my eight surgeries. Dr. H was concerned and checked in often. He prescribed medications, but they hardly touched the pain and didn't interact well with one another or with me. Through sheer grit, clenched teeth, and constant prayer, I made it through a meeting at the clinic, then flew to Massachusetts with wheelchair assistance.

## SPERANZA

When I saw my mom waiting at those same airport stairs I had run down to meet her when I was safely back from the Philippines, I burst into tears. I had never experienced pain like this, and it only got worse. I now understand why women scream during labor. Nothing gave me relief—not even THC, which, if you'd told my teenage self would someday be legal in Massachusetts, I'd never have believed you! My autonomic nervous system was so dysfunctional from CCI, the THC made me unable to control my heart rate or breathing, and on top of writhing in pain, I spent a panicked night on the verge of blacking out. The blood patch had aggravated my highly sensitive sacrococcygeal nerves, causing this unprecedented neuropathic pain, which lasted for six weeks until the blood patch dissipated, lessening the pressure on my nerves.

I returned to DC in the midst of this to discuss next steps with Dr. Henderson. He pulled some strings and, in the same trip, got me in with another doctor who specializes in neurological pelvic dysfunction. They performed a urodynamics test—yet another embarrassing procedure, where I had to sit on a computerized toilet at eye level with the doctor, wearing a see-through lab coat, while various catheters were inserted, and my bladder was artificially filled and drained. This humiliation pointed to CCI being a driver for my neurogenic bladder and colon dysfunction and gave me another piece of assurance that fusion was needed. I had exhausted all other possibilities and treatments, and my health was continuing to deteriorate in an even more frightening way. At night, the vertebrae in my neck were shifting, cutting off my airway as I'd jolt awake in a desperate fight to breathe.

It had been eight years since I'd moved to St. Pete from Manila, brimming with dreams and aspirations, and now I was struggling

# SQUID GAMES

*Morning coffee and writing about peace, from my Airbnb, the day before CCI fusion surgery*

to do the bare minimum each day. But with the decision to move ahead with surgery, relief was coming and that kept me going. As for my emerging awareness of God's peace—well, that was everything. What transpired in the months after making the decision to have the CCI fusion was a true turning point in the way I came to understand and experience peace instead of fear. I wrote this post the day before my surgery:

> September 26, 2023
> 
> Peace. *It's an often overlooked word in the busy, chaotic, hamster wheel of life I so often find myself on. But when I'm able to reject fear because I've found peace—and through*

*that peace the abundant life God has waiting for me—it becomes a life-changing word. Right now, left up to my own spiraling thoughts and meager strength, I would be paralyzed with fear. After exhausting all other options for the past five years, including more cervical injections than I can count, tomorrow I'm having surgery to fuse my skull-base to C2, and will never be able to move my neck again. Eight screws will be drilled into the base of my skull to secure a piece of hardware that will replace those cervical discs, and cadaver bone will be grafted over the C1 and C2 vertebrae, secured with four more screws. This surgery has always been a last resort, but ever since having a stroke, I've known I had to do whatever it took to stabilize my craniocervical junction. However, fear was still holding me back from taking this leap of faith, and as I've come to see, holding me back from the abundance I believe God has waiting for me!*

*Two years ago, I went to DC for the first time to start working with an incredibly knowledgeable neurosurgical group who specialize in CCI. In July, my surgeon and I made the decision to move ahead with this fusion after my imaging showed I was progressively worse, but I still wasn't sure it was the right move. So I started praying for peace. Every day I asked God to either fill me with peace or fill me with the opposite of it. I started meditating on Isaiah 26:3, and it took on a whole new power and meaning.*

*"You will keep in perfect peace all who trust in you, all whose thoughts are fixed on you!"*

## SQUID GAMES

*This verse promises not temporary calm, but says God will keep me surrounded by an unwavering peace when I lock eyes with him, rather than looking at the mountain in front of me, and that is exactly what he has done for me through the countdown these past two months. Every day, often many times throughout the day, God has affirmed this decision. Having that peace blanketing my mind has freed me to see handprints of God's love, promises, and victory in so many, many ways.*

*I've watched myself slip away these past 5 years, as month after month symptoms have chipped away at my resolve, drained my strength, and made it harder and harder to engage with people and in activities. I've buried my passion and zest for life beneath the weight of my condition and do the bare minimum to get by—but that's enough, right? In my own strength I'd keep backpeddling, clinging to what I am still able to do. But is that really living?*

*As I've read God's Word, I have seen promise after promise that God wants to give me full, abundant, victorious life, but it often means stepping right into the center of a battle. It's in the deep that God replaces my weakness with his strength; demonstrates his perfect love that drives out fear; covers me in abundant grace despite the mess I make; fills me with his abiding Spirit to intercede when I'm too weak to pray; produces a fountain of joy even in the face of hardships; and blankets me with perfect, unwavering peace.*

## SPERANZA

*This past week was one of the busiest I've had in a while, and it has pushed me to my limits while also being incredibly rewarding. I cooked an Italian feast for fifty people at a horse farm in Ocala, running through horse stables carrying giant platters of food. Then I threw the grand opening party for my integrative health clinic, which I also made the food for. They were exhilarating events and every day I thanked God for the strength to carry on. As I was doing some of the final food prep, I started imagining what it will be like after surgery. I was trying to chop while only moving my eyes downward, not my neck, and almost chopped off my finger. I started to panic, thinking surgery meant I'd never cook again. Almost immediately I felt God steady my hand, and I cried out to him that I knew he wouldn't bring me this far just to abandon me. A sudden sense of calm washed over me, and I went back to cooking. A little voice said to me, "hinge at your waist," and when I did so, I could chop just fine without moving my neck! The rest of that day I kept quoting Psalm 34:4:*

*"I prayed to the L*ORD*, and he answered me. He freed me from all my fears. Those who look to him for help will be radiant with joy; no shadow of shame will darken their faces."*

*Monday morning as I was making my coffee (my caffeine jolt is tangible proof that God loves me) and was getting ready to head to the airport for DC, I stood in my kitchen utterly amazed that I wasn't crippled by the fear of what could go wrong during this surgery, or by what it will mean for my future. I truly had God's peace, which "passes understanding." This level of inexplicable calm was beyond anything I could have attained through my own effort. Surely, it had come down from above. My mom, just minutes after, texted me that she woke up singing songs of victory! And I have to give a shout-out to her, as she has been an example to me of seeking God above all else and listening to the quiet voice of the Holy Spirit. She's been by my side through every single surgery—this will be number nine—and far too many procedures to count.*

*Will I have hard, painful days ahead? Yes. Will this surgery present new challenges that I'll have to deal with for the rest of my life? Yes. But do I have to rely on my own expectations for the healing that will take place, and for everything I will gain? Not in the slightest! Do I have to rely on my own strength to fight this battle? Not even a little. On the contrary, God is eagerly waiting to show up even more than I've ever seen before! Eager to show off his muscles, and eager to delight his child with the abundance he has in store! Regardless of the physical outcome, I am claiming healing and victory, because God has mended my misbeliefs about his love, and I've found my way home to his peace.*

## SPERANZA

*Please join me and so many others in prayer; for the hands of my surgeons tomorrow, for no complications, for perfect results, and for healing in more ways than I can even begin to imagine!! I know this is going to be a season filled with a lot of pain, but I also know there is nothing I can't overcome with God's strength.*

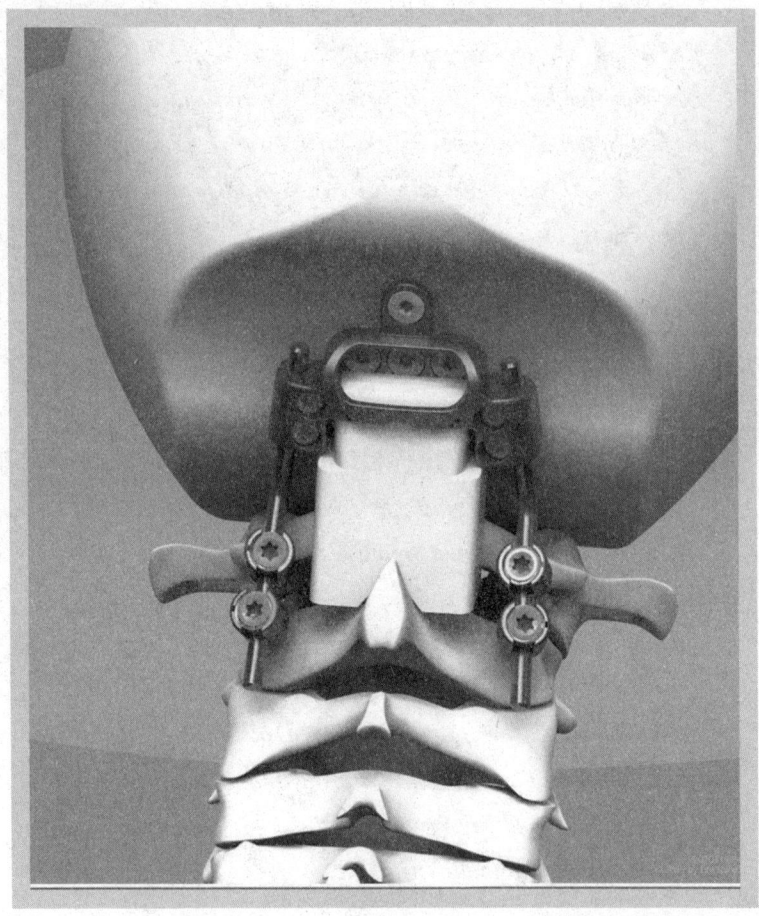

The hardware that was installed in my skull and neck

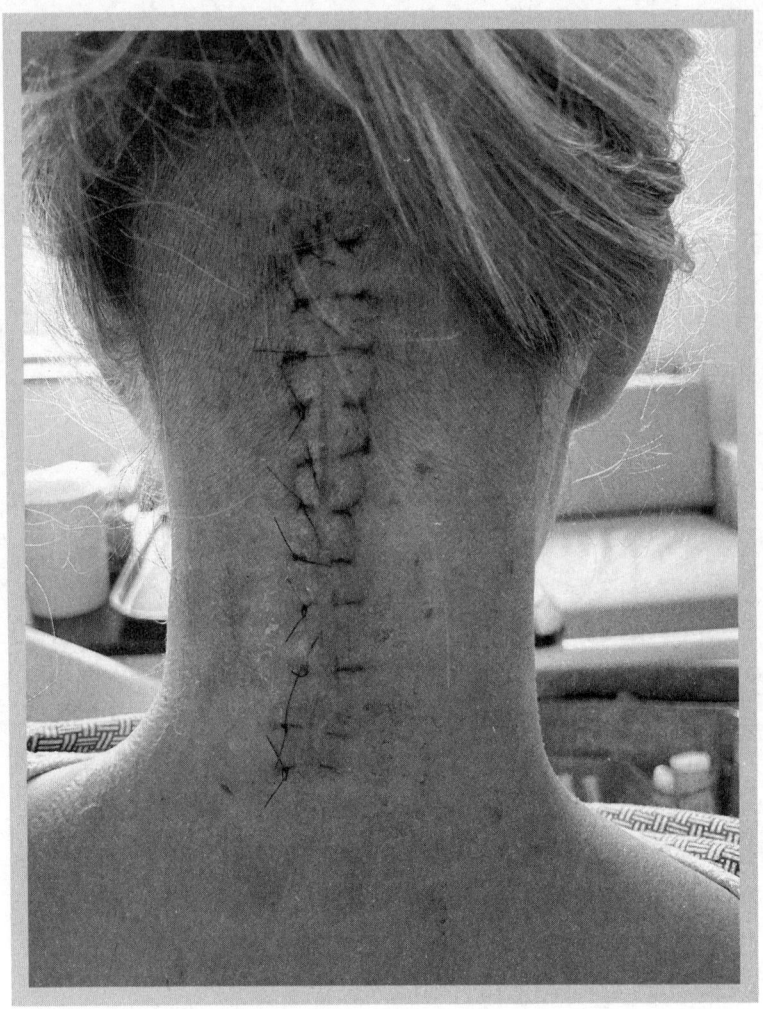

*Stitched up incision after my CCI fusion surgery*

# My Family's Holiday Table

I'm DELIGHTED to share with you one of my most cherished pastimes and to welcome you to my family's holiday table. This collection of recipes celebrates some of our favorite sweets and savories, as well as the warm and nurturing spirits of my mom, grandmothers, and aunts who lovingly made and perfected them. As these matriarchs aged or passed away, it was my honor and joy to carry on these traditions for both my relatives and my clients!

When several of my family members could no longer tolerate gluten (myself included), I modified the recipes and have included those substitutions here, with one exception. I have to be honest: I have yet to have any success with a gluten-free pie crust. Most end up in the trash, tears running down my cheeks in exasperation, because the crust doesn't roll out easily and my pie looks more like a kindergarten art project than the thing of beauty my grandmother's pie always was.

But here's where the "mostly healthy" part comes in. None of these recipes are something I'd make a habit of eating. But do I enjoy them on occasion? Yes! Because sometimes, the most nourishing choice isn't the one with the most ideal macros. Rather, it's the one that sweeps you back to your days as a child at your family's table, surrounded by those you adore, enjoying a delicious slice of your grandma's apple pie, and feeling her love in every bite.

# Grandma's Apple Pie

ONE YEAR, my sister couldn't make it home for Thanksgiving and asked our grandmother to give her the recipes for her famous apple pie and French meat stuffing. I hold dear my copy of these handwritten gems and am delighted to pass them on to you. At the top, my grandma wrote, "Hope you can read my hurried writing. Don't be discouraged with your first attempts—practice makes perfect!! You might find a better way—experiment!!"

And I agree. There is no better advice for approaching any recipe you set out to make!

*Makes 1, 8-inch or 9-inch two-crust pie (top and bottom)*

**Flaky Pie Pastry**
- 2 1/4 cups sifted, all-purpose flour (she preferred King Arthur)
- 1 teaspoon salt
- 3/4 cup shortening (Crisco)
- 5 to 8 tablespoons ice water (or very cold water)

**Apple Filling**
- 4 Granny Smith apples, peeled and cut into slices
- 4 Cortland apples, peeled and cut into slices
- 3/4 cup granulated sugar
- 1 teaspoon cinnamon or apple pie spice
- 2 tablespoons all-purpose flour
- 1 tablespoon butter, cut into small pieces

Mix together the sliced apples. Separately, mix together the sugar, spice, and flour. Set both aside.

**Making the pastry:** In a large bowl, mix together the flour and salt. With a pastry blender, cut in shortening until well incorporated. Sprinkle water over the mixture one tablespoon at a time, gently mixing with a fork until all particles stick together (I use closer to 8 tablespoons of water). Use a spatula to draw the mixture all together, then use your hands to form a single large ball. Divide it in half and place each ball of dough in plastic baggies or plastic wrap; then chill in the refrigerator until ready to use.

*The unbaked pie dough can be refrigerated for up to two days before assembling and baking the pie. Remember: The science of a flaky pie dough is to keep everything chilled until it goes into the oven!

**Rolling out the dough:** Place a linen towel or pastry cloth on the countertop and sprinkle flour on the cloth. Place one ball of pastry dough on the towel, flatten it a bit with your hand, then sprinkle flour on top and begin to roll the dough with a rolling pin. Tuck in the edges and continue rolling from the center outward to maintain a circle. Keep lifting the dough occasionally to make sure it's rolling out in even thickness (as thin or as thick as you want) and to ensure that it isn't sticking to the counter. When it's larger than your pie plate, gently fold the dough in half, lifting it off the counter and laying it into the pan. If it tears, use a little water on your fingers to patch it or use whatever else is needed to mend it. Leave about 1 inch of dough draping over the edges of the pie pan.

**Assembling the pie:** Place the apples in the pan evenly, mounding them a little bit. Sprinkle the sugar mixture over the apples and dot with butter. Moisten the edges of the bottom crust and place the other rolled pastry dough on top of the apples. Press the edges of the crust together and trim any excess. Press the pieces of dough together firmly and roll both pieces together underneath the top piece of dough, sealing the pie. Flute the crust decoratively. (I like to pinch the dough with two fingers and then make an indentation in the center with one finger from my other hand.) Cut vents in the upper crust to let out steam while baking. Brush the top crust with a little milk, and sprinkle with a light coating of sugar.

**Baking the pie:** Preheat oven to 450 degrees.

Place strips of aluminum foil on the edges of the crust to keep it from scorching, then remove them for the last 10 minutes of baking.

Bake at 450 degrees for 20 minutes. Then lower the oven to 350 degrees and bake for an additional 45 minutes. If the crust isn't browned enough, increase the oven to 375 degrees. Oh, always place the pie in the center of the oven.

*Christmas morning almond cake set against my mom's decorative table.*

# Bacci's Key Lime Pie

BOTH SETS of my grandparents wintered in Florida during their golden years. I was quite young when we visited them, but I can picture my Bacci (Polish for Grandma) picking oranges and giant grapefruits to accompany our breakfast. I also remember my delight that there were lizards everywhere, while my Bacci was terrified of them! In the evening she'd sit in the lanai with her back to the house, while my grandpa sat across from her. A mischievous grin would spread across his face as the little geckos—almost sensing her fear—gathered on the wall behind my Bacci, while she remained blissfully unaware. My grandparents often brought fresh juice from the Florida Keys up North with them (but left the lizards behind); thus, key lime pie was a Christmas staple. If you don't have access to fresh juice, Nellie & Joe's Key West Lime Juice is a widely available substitute that I use, and it makes a delicious pie.

**Graham Cracker Crust**
- 2 1/2 cups graham cracker crumbs (for a gluten-free substitute, use 2 boxes of Nairn's Oat Biscuits, pureed in a food processor until they are fine crumbs)
- 2 tablespoons granulated sugar
- 9 tablespoons butter, melted

Preheat oven to 325 degrees. In a bowl, mix to combine all ingredients. Press the crust mixture in an even layer on the bottom and sides of either a deep-dish pie pan or a 9-inch springform pan. Bake the crust for 15 minutes. Cool on a wire rack for 15 minutes or until cooled before adding the filling.

**Key Lime Filling**
- 8 egg yolks
- 2 cans sweetened condensed milk
- 1 cup key lime juice (you can add more or less depending on how tart you like your pie)

In the bowl of an electric mixer, beat egg yolks for 4 to 5 minutes until pale yellow and voluminous. Add the sweetened condensed milk and beat the mixture for another 4 to 5 minutes. Add key lime juice, gently stirring it into the mixture until combined. Pour the filling into the cooled crust and bake for 25 minutes. The center will be slightly jiggly. Let the pie cool on a wire rack for at least one hour, then refrigerate overnight. The pie keeps in the refrigerator for well over a week—it's just never lasted that long in our house to know exactly!

Serve with lightly sweetened whipped cream if desired.

# Mom's Godiva Party Cake

This dessert we call "Godiva" is one of my mom's signatures. She came across the recipe in a booklet from the Godiva Chocolate store and has served it at every Christmas Eve and family Christmas for over fifty years! When I was a kid, without fail, she'd commence making it close to midnight after finally completing the other items on her mile-long to-do list. I should have been asleep, but instead I'd tiptoe into the kitchen to help her tear the angel food cake into pieces, while periodically swiping the fluffy cake through the chocolate mousse and popping it straight into my mouth. For the past ten years or so, my mom and I have made it together. It's still often made in the late hours of the night, but now we divide the tasks rather than letting my mom do all the work while I merely licked her bowls clean. We've experimented with different brands, ratios, and methods of melting the chocolate, switched to gluten-free angel food cake, and tried to appease the nut-loving and nut-hating crowds. Still, after all these years, the Godiva turns out slightly different each time. And being a mousse means the ingredients must magically meld together in the refrigerator as it sets up overnight. Every Christmas Eve we hold our breath when it comes time to serve it, but either way, everyone scrapes their plates clean.

- 1 angel food cake (such as Duncan Hines, or Kinnikinnick for the gluten-free version)
- 2, 2.5-ounce dark chocolate bars (Lindt yields the best results)
- 4, 3.5-ounce milk chocolate bars (Lindt yields the best results)
- 10 eggs (it's important to use farm-fresh eggs as they will remain uncooked)
- 1 pint heavy cream (Horizon Organic or Organic Valley are best)
- 2 teaspoons vanilla extract
- 1/2 cup raw walnuts, broken in half

Prepare the angel food cake according to the instructions on the box and let it cool completely. We always make the angel food the day before making the Godiva.

**Making the mousse:** In the bowl of an electric mixer, beat the eggs for 5 minutes until voluminous and frothy. Meanwhile, break the chocolate into 1-inch pieces. Our preferred method for melting is to put the chocolate in a metal or glass bowl set over gently simmering water, stirring the chocolate frequently. Alternatively, you may melt the chocolate in a heatproof bowl in the microwave, stirring every 30 seconds. With the mixer running, add the melted chocolate in a thin stream into the eggs, mixing until fully combined. In a separate bowl with a hand mixer, beat the cream until it holds a stiff peak. Be careful not to over-whip the cream—it will turn to butter! Add the vanilla extract to the cream, then with a rubber spatula, fold the cream into the egg-and-chocolate mixture until uniformly combined.

**Assembling the cake:** Cut the angel food cake horizontally into thirds, then tear it into 1 1/2–inch pieces. Using either a 24 x 12-inch casserole dish, or two 9 x 13-inch pans, place the pieces of angel food cake on the bottom of the dish in a single, even layer. Gently pour half of the mousse over the angel food cake. We acquiesce to the walnut haters by sprinkling only half of the mousse with half of the walnuts and leaving the other half plain. Top the layer of mousse with another single layer of angel food cake pieces. Then add the remaining mousse in an even layer on top of the angel food cake. Make sure to cover all of the cake so that it does not dry out. Top the walnut half with the remaining walnut pieces. Refrigerate overnight to give the mousse time to set up, so when it is served, it holds its shape and can be cut into squares.

*Snow-covered cross and manger, hand-made by my dad.*

# *Auntie Carol's Pineapple Cheesecake*

My Auntie Carol has lived on Martha's Vineyard for as long as I've been alive and didn't always make it off the island for holidays. When she did, she and my cousin made up for lost time with a plethora of sweets. Some she'd bring from the famed Black Dog Bakery, and others she would make herself, including bite-sized black bottom cupcakes, and our family's favorite—her pineapple cheesecake. It became an Easter staple as the brightness of the pineapple lightens the rich cheesecake, yielding the perfect springtime dessert.

**Graham Cracker Crust**
- 2 cups graham cracker crumbs (for a gluten-free substitute use 2 boxes Nairn's Oat Biscuits, pureed in a food processor until fine crumbs)
- 1/2 cup granulated sugar
- 1/2 cup butter, melted

Preheat oven to 350 degrees. In a bowl, mix to combine all ingredients. Press the crust mixture in an even layer on the bottom of a 9 x 13-inch ovenproof glass dish. Bake the crust for 10 minutes. Cool on a wire rack for 15 minutes or until cooled before adding the filling.

**Cheesecake Filling**
- 3, 8-ounce bars cream cheese, softened to room temperature for 1 to 2 hours
- 2/3 cup granulated sugar
- 1 teaspoon vanilla extract
- 3 eggs
- 1, 15-ounce can crushed pineapple, drained

Increase oven to 375 degrees. In the bowl of an electric mixer, beat the cream cheese for 1 to 2 minutes until fluffy. Add the sugar and vanilla, then beat again until fully combined. Add the eggs, one at a time, beating in between each addition. Add the crushed pineapple and beat until fully incorporated. Pour the cheesecake filling into the pan on top of the crust, smoothing the top, then bake the cheesecake for 20 minutes. Remove and let cool for 5 minutes. Lower oven temperature to 350 degrees.

**Sour Cream Topping**
- 1 pint sour cream
- 6 tablespoons granulated sugar
- 1 teaspoon vanilla extract

In an even layer, spread the sour cream mixture onto the slightly cooled cheesecake. Return the cheesecake to the oven for an additional 5 minutes. Cool on a wire rack, then refrigerate until fully chilled, preferably overnight.

# Auntie Annmarie's Baked Brie in Crescent Rolls

No family holiday was complete without the presence of my Auntie Annmarie, Uncle Danny, and cousins from New Hampshire. I was always amazed at my aunt's ability to make the several-hours-long drive to our house, march into the kitchen with a cooler in hand, and within minutes, assemble a dish and pull a golden and bubbling hot beauty from the oven with ease. This level of comfort spilled over into my interactions with her as well. When you're a teenager and your aunts and uncles ask what's new, it can seem like a loaded question. But my aunt has never had an ulterior motive—just a genuine interest in my life. Especially regarding all I have been cooking lately!

- 2, 8-ounce packages crescent dough (substitute Dufour gluten-free puff pastry)
- 1, 8 to12-ounce wheel of brie, rind removed
- 1 large egg, beaten
- 1, 10-ounce jar of your favorite fruit jam

Preheat oven to 350 degrees. Using a rolling pin, roll out one package of the crescent dough into a rectangle slightly larger than the wheel of brie. Place the rolled crescent dough in the center of a baking sheet, then place the brie in the middle of the crescent dough. Spread your jam of choice on top of the brie. Roll out the second package of crescent rolls. Gather up the sides of the dough around the wheel of brie and add the additional dough to cover the top and any place where the cheese is showing. Press the dough evenly around the cheese, using your hands to gently seal the crescent dough around the brie. Use any extra dough to decorate the top or roll the dough into small rolls and bake them alongside the brie, which you can use later to dip into the cheese. Using a pastry brush, coat the pastry all over with the beaten egg. Bake for 20 to 25 minutes, until the pastry is golden brown. Let the brie sit for 10 to 15 minutes, then move the baked brie to a serving platter. Serve warm with crackers and fruit. Enjoy!

*The brie can be assembled ahead of time and refrigerated for several days before baking and serving.

# Auntie MJ's Crab Dip

My Auntie MJ always had an affinity for cooking, but it was when she married my Uncle Vito, whose parents emigrated from Naples, that she got a full-on culinary education—from her mother-in-law, Letizia, that is, who taught her all of the Caolo family recipes. My aunt, in turn, lovingly made many of them for our family. I have vivid childhood memories sitting around our table, enjoying my aunt's famous linguine and clam sauce, served alongside gorgonzola garlic bread. My Auntie MJ instilled in me both my appreciation for quality food and my discernment of superior ingredients, particularly those that "float my boat," as she often says. My aunt and uncle were even known to have a dedicated food suitcase that traveled with them down to Florida each winter and then back up to Massachusetts in the spring, containing all the staples they couldn't buy near them. Most of my conversations with my aunt still revolve around food, as she always wants to know what's on the menu for my clients each week and is eager to hear about how every one of my parties goes. And if I ever have a cooking question, my Auntie MJ is the first phone call I make!

- 2, 8-ounce packages cream cheese, left to soften to room temperature for 1 to 2 hours
- 6 tablespoons mayonnaise (I prefer Sir Kensington Classic Mayo or avocado oil mayo)
- 1/4 cup fresh lemon juice
- 16 ounces crab meat, drained (either claw meat, lump, or a combination of the two)
- Paprika for the top

Optional Add-Ins:
- 1, 16-ounce jar roasted red peppers, drained and cut into strips
- 1 teaspoon Cajun seasoning
- 1/2 teaspoon coarse black pepper

Preheat oven to 375 degrees. In the bowl of an electric mixer, beat the cream cheese, mayonnaise, and lemon juice for 2 minutes until fully combined and fluffy. Add the crab and beat until incorporated, about 1 more minute. Spread the mixture into a glass or ceramic pie dish (9 to 12 inches). Smooth the top flat and cover with a dusting of paprika. Bake the dip immediately for 35 minutes, until the edges are slightly golden and bubbling.

Serve the crab dip with crackers or crostini.

*The unbaked crab dip can be made ahead and stored in the refrigerator for 1 to 2 days, then baked just before serving.

# *Auntie Linda's Pumpkin Bread*

My Auntie Linda is a gifted baker. She covers our holiday table with all kinds of sweets, made by hand with the same love and care with which her presence fills our home. She's also one of the most thoughtful people in my life. No matter how old I get, she never misses sending me a birthday card, and whenever I haven't been home for a holiday, she always makes sure I know how loved and missed I am. The many references to this pumpkin bread throughout my book leave it needing no further introduction. So brace yourself for the addicting aroma that will fill your kitchen and ruin you for ever being able to enjoy any other pumpkin bread as much as this one!

*Makes 2 loaves*

- 2 cups pumpkin puree
- 1 cup neutral oil (I prefer sunflower or safflower oil)
- 4 eggs, whisked
- 3 cups granulated sugar
- 2 1/4 cups all-purpose flour (substitute King Arthur gluten-free all-purpose flour)
- 2 teaspoons salt
- 1 teaspoon nutmeg
- 1 teaspoon cinnamon
- 1 teaspoon cloves
- 1 teaspoon baking powder
- 1 teaspoon baking soda

Optional Add-Ins:
- 1 cup walnuts or pecans, coarsely chopped
- 1 cup semisweet chocolate chips

Preheat oven to 350 degrees. Grease two 9-inch loaf pans with cooking spray or line them with parchment paper, extending it over the sides of the pans. In a large bowl, whisk together the flour, salt, spices, baking powder, and baking soda. Separately, whisk together the eggs, sugar, and pumpkin puree. Add the dry ingredients to the pumpkin mixture and mix until just combined. Fold in the nuts or chocolate chips, if using. Pour the batter into the prepared pans and bake for 50 to 60 minutes, until a cake tester inserted into the center of the loaf comes out clean. (A bit of crumbs may cling to your tester—and that's fine—but make sure the batter in the center of the loaf has fully cooked.)

Let the loaves cool fully on a wire rack, then store them in a plastic baggie at room temperature for up to a week.

# Auntie Lorilee's Quattro Formaggio Bruschetta

My Auntie Lor was part of a "Gourmet Group" in her small town of Vermont, where she had many close friends. Every holiday she'd bring a new dish, and as we all finished our plates she'd exclaim, "It's a new recipe I tried from Gourmet!" My aunt's fearless enthusiasm for all things culinary encouraged me to experiment in the kitchen, try new recipes, and not be afraid to make mistakes—and always to get back up again! It's rare for a day in the kitchen to go by when she's not on my mind. My Auntie Lor is forever in my heart, and forever my culinary muse.

- 1, 8-ounce package cream cheese, softened to room temperature for 1 to 2 hours
- 8 ounces gorgonzola cheese, crumbled
- 10 ounces low-moisture mozzarella cheese, shredded
- 4 ounces Parmesan, finely grated
- 3 cloves garlic, minced
- 1/4 cup fresh basil, julienned, with one sprig reserved for garnish
- 1 large baguette, cut into ½-inch slices (substitute a gluten-free baguette or other GF bread)

Preheat the broiler on your oven to high. In a large bowl, mix together the softened cream cheese with the garlic and gorgonzola. Add the remaining cheeses and basil and mix until fully combined. Scoop about 2 tablespoons of the cheese mixture onto each slice of bread, and with a butter knife, smooth the cheese to evenly reach all edges of the bread (any exposed bread will burn!) Place the crostini on a baking sheet and broil on the top rack of the oven for 3 to 4 minutes, until cheese is deeply golden and bubbly. Transfer immediately to a platter and garnish with the reserved sprig of basil. Serve warm.

*The cheese mixture can be made several days in advance, but be sure to bring it back to room temperature before spreading it on the bread. Otherwise, it will count as your arm workout for the day!

*My parents' 12-foot-tall Christmas tree.*

Twenty-Seven

# FROM SURGERY TO SAVASANA

IT'S DECEMBER 30, 2023, exactly three months post-fusion, and I'm back at the horse farm in Ocala, cooking my largest solo gig yet—a three-course dinner for one hundred people. I put the finishing touches on the thirty-foot-long grazing table brimming with shrimp cocktail, cheeses, charcuterie, seasonal fruit, crudites, buttermilk biscuits, and preserves, then hop in the Gator to the apartment kitchen where I have five whole tenderloin and five sides of salmon awaiting in the oven. I still have a way to go in recovering from this massive surgery, but as I go through motions I've done countless times, I'm shocked—and oh so grateful—at how much improvement I already feel.

My entire recovery was much like that. Dr. Henderson gave me the award for the fastest patient ever to get up and walk, and within days of being discharged I was cooking simple meals for my

*Grazing table at the farm in Ocala, 3 months post-fusion*

mom and myself, albeit with a tremendous amount of pain that I downplayed. Surgery revealed significant brain stem damage from years of instability at my craniocervical junction, further confirming my need for fusion. I clung to validation, needing to prove this life-altering operation, for better and for worse, was the right decision. I also deflected my pain and continued to push my body despite its pleas, convincing myself this was resilience. I was unwilling to show any vulnerability or let myself become weak. This recovery was just one more opportunity to prove my grit and flex my tenacity. I was stuck in the decades-old belief that who I was, was not enough. That instead, I had to earn my worthiness through my strength. *But who am I so desperate to convince?*

At my two-week post-op, I went through yoga poses in detail making sure they weren't harmful. Yes, I did yoga in my neurosurgeon's office! Days later I attempted a virtual yoga class, although my "flow" was more like a "flop" as it felt like *all* my muscles had been cut through, not just those in my neck. The lower half of my head was shaved, and the eight-inch scar traveling down my skull and neck left me looking like the spawn of Frankenstein, but I joked I wouldn't need a Halloween costume.

Dr. Henderson locked my neck in place at a slight downward angle, making it that much easier to continue cooking. Within six weeks, I was back to meal prepping for clients and wasn't at all inhibited by the loss of movement in my neck! It can take up to six months for bone to fuse, and at my three-month post-op visit, Dr. Henderson reviewed my CT scan and said the bone was completely fused already. That CT was done only ten weeks out, and he was utterly amazed!

*With Kelly after my dad's memorial service*

Around that time, I posted this:

December 10, 2023

*At the end of September, when I flew from Tampa to DC before major surgery fusing my skull-base to C2, I arrived at the airport with my usual baggage—a pounding headache, searing pain in my neck and upper body, room spinning, and blurred vision. I could barely think straight enough to check my luggage, and I was on the verge of throwing up. All my energy was deliberate, putting one foot in front of the other. But when I got onto the escalator to go up to my gate, as I had done countless times over many years of feeling like this, I said to myself, "Mark this moment! It is the last time you will feel this way!"*

*Kelly, my BFF from high school, recently got married and I flew to Connecticut for her wedding. I have tears in my eyes as I write that riding the escalator up to my gate, just nine weeks after surgery, was a completely different experience! I chatted with my Uber driver instead of focusing my energy on not throwing up in his car, engaged with the Southwest attendant, walked to the escalator on solid ground, and the room wasn't spinning!*

*At the wedding, I sat with a friend, who twenty years ago was my high school homeroom advisor. During those difficult years, she listened and loved, while holding on to hope that light would break through my darkness. She's been following my story, and our chatter was contagious as we rejoiced in what God has done!*
*Healing is never linear. At best it's like a bull stock market—an upward trajectory, but with peaks and valleys along the axis. My body is amazingly resilient but has a lot of relearning to do. I am still in pain much of the time; the muscle spasms and swelling cause frequent headaches, and at times all my*

*symptoms are back in full force. But I've also had times when I feel pretty great, and I haven't been able to say those words in a very long time. Yesterday I spent the day making Christmas goodies for clients, friends, and family. It was always one of the holiday activities I looked forward to most, but one I haven't done in many years. Every day was such a painful challenge, I conserved my energy for only what was necessary. But yesterday I had a solid six hours when I felt like my old self! I blasted Christmas music and danced and sang in my kitchen as I created, and man did it feel good!!*

*Given that I am still pretty early on in my recovery, it's extremely encouraging to already see improvement. Just like remembering that moment on the escalator, when I focus on my victories, and I train my brain to say, "I feel great right now," even if it's a fleeting feeling, I'm creating a little trail of breadcrumbs to go back to so I know feeling great is possible. It helps form and cement new neural pathways so that one such moment turns into a few more, which suddenly turns into a whole day, a week, a month, a lifetime.*

The following January to March 2024 was the longest span of time in six years when I didn't travel to a doctor appointment, scan, procedure, or surgery, and I just let myself *be*. I had driven my body into the ground for so long, drowning out the heaviness in the constant hustle. My business partner and I had been transforming our practice into a full-service integrative health clinic, but when faced with some insurmountable roadblocks, we made the difficult decision to close. I used my extra time listening to talks about how unprocessed emotions can disrupt our body's energy flow,

*Christmas gift boxes*

contributing to physical symptoms, and how damaging and painful patterns can be passed down through generations. I wondered if I needed to address the emotional impact of all that had happened to me. In slowing down, and quieting the white noise of busyness, I could hear the whisper of my inner voice telling me that somehow, this was the missing piece.

In the past two and a half years, I'd had a stroke and had been uprooted from my home and life. I had spent a year relying on my parents' assistance, then I helped care for my dad in the last months of his life. I buried my father in between three major spine surgeries and several outpatient procedures. And I also launched and then closed an integrative health clinic. I'd put treating my laundry list of other chronic health conditions—Lyme disease, MCAS, EDS, mycotoxicosis, autoimmunity, and autonomic dysfunction—on the back burner, but those symptoms hadn't taken a hiatus. Additionally, right around my three-month follow-up, many of my neurological symptoms returned, including the all-too-familiar crushing spine pain and headaches. I kept trying to focus on what had improved since my fusion and ignore everything else, feeling desperate for my surgery to be a home run.

Kelly McCann, MD, hosted several enlightening MCAS summits and ended every talk by saying, "Don't lose hope." I'd never heard a doctor say those words and was drawn to the sentiment as it was how she approaches health—treating the *whole* person. She also brilliantly understood the complexities and interconnectedness of my conditions. I flew to Los Angeles and spent an idyllic day visiting my favorite haunts from years ago, as pieces of myself long forgotten came back to life. By the next morning, the tides had changed. Driving down the coast to Laguna Beach, rip currents of pain coursed through my body, but even worse, I was drowning in an ocean of grief. This was where my dad had gone for his cancer treatments four years earlier.

Marveling at the snowcapped Santa Anas, I thought of the birthday text my dad sent me while looking at the very same peaks.

Psalm 121:1–3 "I lift up my eyes toward the mountains. Where will my help come from? My help comes from the Lord, the Maker of heaven and earth. He will not allow Ashley's foot to slip; Ashley's Protector will not slumber or sleep." Thank you for encouraging me to be here, you led the way. Being here makes me appreciate what you go through, but yours is ten times harder, I can't imagine. I love you more for your hard work trying to heal yourself. Your quiet strength keeps me going on this path to healing. Ash, we don't know where we're going in life but knowing Jesus is, "the way and the truth and the life"—John 14:6. Well, I love you very much my *deer* girl. Happy Birthday.

My dad's one-of-a-kind sense of humor at its best—or his spelling at its worst.

One time, our California treatments overlapped, and he drove six hours each way up to San Jose just to spend a night with me. We had often talked about driving the Pacific Coast together. Nearly two years had passed since I'd last heard my dad's voice, but as I made this drive for the first time, my initial thought was to call him. I spent the rest of that day and the beginning of the next two in tears. I felt the overwhelming weight of all I'd endured and how hard I'd been fighting, for what felt like centuries. And I finally acknowledged that my tank had run dry. I no longer felt the need to prove that I was strong, but instead, admitted—if only to myself—that I was so weary. As I sobbed in my Airbnb, a Red Rocks Worship song came on my Apple Music, encouraging me not to give up, because breakthrough was coming. Then the next song again spoke directly to my situation—as Brandon Lake sang one of my favorites, "Don't You Give Up on Me."[16]

And I cried even harder, but this time out of being seen by my God, El Roi. I had no idea how true these words were about to become.

As part of her new-patient intake, Dr. McCann asked for a detailed health history, which took me about eight hours to write. I was blown away that she wanted to know my story and even more surprised at that first appointment when she had actually read it! With tears in her eyes she said, "I can't begin to imagine what you have gone through." I left that appointment with renewed hope, and a little more strength for the journey ahead. God proved he saw me and led me to a truly compassionate doctor who did the same.

The pain over the hunk of metal and twelve screws in my skull and neck started progressively getting worse, as did a bunch of other symptoms. I flew from California to DC, and left Dr. Henderson's office with the possibility of needing three more spine surgeries. My body was betraying me yet again and every day I reached a point when I wanted to give up. It was a physical battle for sure, but a spiritual one even more. I was losing hope and wrestling with why my health was regressing. I also didn't understand why suddenly I had lost my ability to cope with pain, especially when it had been the only constant during the past twenty years—at times much worse than this.

Finally, I figured out why it felt like the rug was being pulled out from under me: During those times after surgery when I felt well and like my old self, I started opening myself back up to possibility, and I let myself dream again. Which may not seem like a big deal, but for me it was huge.

The sicker I got with Lyme disease and then CCI, the more I let go, piece by piece, of my life, activities, dreams, goals, and aspirations.

## FROM SURGERY TO SAVASANA

For the longest time, my existence was putting one foot in front of the other each day. While, at first, those days were extremely difficult and dark, bit by bit, as I started to focus on how much beauty was woven through the pain and how much I still had to be grateful for, I actually found immense joy even while struggling to make it through each day. But part of the peace I had over my fusion surgery was the belief that God wanted me to live an abundant life—not simply exist. I believed that I couldn't get there by sitting on the sidelines or settling for mediocrity. I had to take steps—and sometimes leaps—of faith. I believed surgery was a jump off the deep end and that God was going to use it to give me back my health and my life.

The relatively good days that led me to start dreaming of the possibilities ahead set me up for crushing disappointment when the pain returned. Realizing this, my first thought was, *Why did I let myself start to dream again? What a colossal mistake! I've found so much joy and contentment in the small things. Why'd I have to go chasing rainbows?!* I thought the answer was going back to practicing gratitude for what each day holds and contentment for where I was, which are both important things to do! But not *all* the things. Shortly after, I read this verse from Lamentations. It was quite fitting as my own laments were swirling in my mind. "Yet I still dare to hope when I remember this: The faithful love of the Lord never ends! His mercies never cease. Great is his faithfulness; his mercies begin afresh each morning. I say to myself, 'The Lord is my inheritance; therefore, I will hope in him!'" (3:21–24).

Any time a verse starts with "yet," "but," "however," or the like, I know it's going to be good! There is so much packed into those few lines, and it spoke to my soul deeply. Daring to hope is essentially what it means to dream of possibilities—and this is a good thing!

## SPERANZA

But I realized I was basing those dreams for my future on my own strength and ability instead of on the strength God fills me with each new day. I had taken on the responsibility of my healing, despite knowing God holds the job title of "Healer."

My thirty-ninth birthday came, and birthdays are when I like to set an intention for the year ahead. My verse of the day was Ezekiel 36:26, "And I will give you a new heart, and I will put a new spirit in you. I will take out your stony, stubborn heart and give you a tender, responsive heart."

> April 9, 2024
> *My prayer this year is for newness in my healing and overall life. That I'll remember my past but live in expectancy of what's ahead.*

I had no idea how life-altering this prayer would be!

I returned to California for a week of appointments with Dr. McCann, and the first day she suggested I listen to a podcast she'd just recorded. It touched on the way adverse events in our childhood can actually cause gaps in the way our immune and nervous systems develop, affecting our ability to heal. I could definitely see this in myself and was intrigued. I mentioned it during our next appointment, and she asked me the most profound question: "Do you feel safe in your body?"

I stifled threatening sobs. *Safe?* My thoughts became a cyclone of all the ways I had felt unsafe in my environment, in my body's rebellion, in my deep-seated fears, in showing vulnerability and weakness, and in the isolation of illness. I'd spent so long trying to insulate myself from the brokenness and betrayal of my body with the perfect diet, supplement protocol, workout regimen, and overall clean lifestyle, as well as by avoiding the multitude of toxins that had made me sick. But I lived in constant fear of breaking the delicate bubble of control masquerading as security. Later in life, my dad provided safety in some ways, and now he was gone. Dr. McCann gently told me that finding safety in my body from myself—not from anyone else—was the first step I needed to take in order to truly heal.

That evening as I lay on the beach, I started to process this journey I'd been on and let my mind and soul feel whatever came up. What surfaced was how deeply lonely I had been. So many times I thanked God I was alone—that I only had to focus on myself each day—as that was already a monumental task. Yet in the same breath, I yearned to have someone beside me. I let myself grieve those lonely years through messy tears.

After my CCI fusion surgery, when I had a lot of time on my hands, I'd actually gone back on Match.com, and then immediately regretted it. I do a lot of grocery shopping—more than most—and at this point in my life had no interest in shopping for a man! But the idea of sharing life with a true partner and starting a family, were ways I'd let myself dream again. Now, I didn't know what to do with that dream—or any of them.

That week in California, I walked on the beach every morning and evening, and the intense wind made for huge waves and great surf. As a teenager, I thought I was supposed to have been born a West Coast surfer, and I caught a wave whenever I had the chance. I lived for adventure—alpine skiing in sub-zero temperatures, mastering new water ski tricks, and conquering the hardest inclines at the rock gym. I am fiercely competitive—with myself—in case you haven't

*Splashing waves at Laguna Beach*

figured that out by now! But in his all-knowing design, I think God gave me that extra drive because he knew I'd need every ounce of it. I'd long thought my days of thrill-seeking were over—surfing included. But in those moments of letting myself dream again, my spark, which had long been extinguished, reignited. I had sat on the sidelines for so long, and frankly, I was sick and tired of it! Every life-changing breakthrough had happened when I'd stepped into the ring. My soul needed a win.

Those beach walks were awesome in the truest sense of the word. There is something awe-inspiring about standing in the sand right in front of huge breaking waves. The thunderous crash, the sea spray hitting your skin, and the pull of the ocean as it recedes. Awe has the transcendent ability to shift us from being inwardly focused to being attentive to something even larger than ourselves. Similar to years ago, when the beauty of Italy drew my gaze to the beauty of God, my awe of those waves became awe of God himself.

As I walked, I slowly started picturing myself out there, bracing the cold water, ducking through the break, paddling out to the calm, and riding back in. Slowly, I realized I was letting myself dream again, and I was okay with it! Because this time my dreams weren't dependent on my own ability to live them out. The highs and lows in my life don't change who God is or his wisdom and ability to make anything happen.

On my way out to California, what should have taken seven hours ended up taking thirty-seven hours, with a cancelled flight, rebooked flight, delayed flight, and an unexpected overnight stay. Instead of it being a disaster, I befriended two of the nicest people in the American Airlines assistance line while waiting to get a hotel voucher: Carrie and Val. We stuck together through a late-night taxi ride to a hotel in the next state, then back to the airport the next day, only for more delays, and we laughed the whole time. Carrie happened to own a surf shop in Dana Point and offered to lend me a paddleboard. I had a free day before heading back home, and I had my usual pain, yes, but also a spring in my step and renewed hope in my heart. I said one of my favorite verses, Ephesians 3:20, as a prayer:

> Now to him who is able to do immeasurably more than all we ask or imagine, according to his great power that is at work within us. (NIV)

Then, I set out.

When I arrived at her shop, Carrie said if I took a paddleboard, someone would need to drive me down to the beach in their van, but a soft-top surfboard would fit onto my rental car. As I didn't want to be an inconvenience, I said I'd take the surfboard, then was immediately exhilarated and terrified! Just getting the surfboard strapped onto my car was an elaborate process and I didn't know if, once at the beach, I'd be able to get it off and back on by myself. But I kept thinking of a quote I have written on my office wall: "The first step towards getting somewhere is to decide that you are not going to stay where you are."

The wet suit fit like a glove, I got the surfboard off the car, and I did what I'd stood on the beach all those days dreaming of—plunging into the cold water, through the breaking waves, paddling out to the calm, and riding back in. There is nothing like catching a wave! I was cautious and careful, as it had been sixteen years since I'd been on a surfboard, and I was only seven months out from massive spine surgery. I mainly stayed on my belly and rode the waves cobra style. One time, I got into a low squat, but I got my sea legs back!

A few months later at the lake house, over the Fourth of July weekend, I slalom water-skied—something else I hadn't done in many years but I had made my goal that summer. When I

# FROM SURGERY TO SAVASANA

*My smile after surfing in Dana Point, California*

showed Dr. Henderson the video footage, he proudly showed his entire office, then advised that I not make it a habit. As I took these steps past fear into exuberance, like a pro surfer carving the waves, they etched deep new neural pathways and planted seeds of hope for more fulfilled dreams to come. Above all, though, they left me *sore*—ha! And again in awe of what healing God had done, of how far he had brought me, and of how faithful he is.

## SPERANZA

I wrote this when I got back on my yoga mat a few weeks after my CCI fusion:

October 13, 2023

*Every day we have a choice. We can let yesterday's struggles, limitations, and pain define us and determine the actions we take, or we can choose to start anew, noticing the way our body is speaking to us and what it's asking for. We can listen to the thoughts swirling in our mind, telling us what needs to be set free or reigned in. We can choose to focus on the good—to focus not on our limitations but on what we can do. Limitations will always be there, whether on my mat or in my day-to-day life. But I'm choosing to embrace each day for what it holds, knowing God will give me the strength I need for that day.*

When I opened up my Instagram the morning after surfing, there was a photo of ocean waves and this quote: "We must continue to jump into the water, make waves, and create ripples of hope and change. Nothing gets accomplished by standing on the shore and watching from a distance."[17]

I mean, c'mon! Yes. Absolutely. I need to acknowledge the enormity of all there is to be grateful for each day. To find beauty and contentment in the smallest of things and to joyfully live out my purpose. Finding purpose in suffering is what has kept me from sinking into darkness, depression, and despair, and the purpose I've found in the midst of even the deepest pain is that I can shine just by showing the strength God pours into my life.

And *yet*, I need to dare to hope! *Speranza!*

*Morning coffee and writing about hope, at home in St. Pete*

Twenty-Eight

# WASHING OFF THE WAR PAINT

I HAD A monumental task on my hands. *How do I begin to feel safe in my body?*

I'd had practitioners tell me that my body wanted to heal itself, that it held all the tools to do so, and that I merely needed to step out of the way and let it happen. My knee-jerk reaction was always, *How about you spend five minutes in my body? I don't think you'll tell me it wants to heal. My body is trying to take me down!*

Instead of taking that (highly ineffective) approach, Dr. Kelly—now a cherished friend—suggested a few tools and said, "Just see what resonates with you."

One such tool was the aforementioned book *How to Heal Yourself When No One Else Can*, in which the author, Amy B. Scher, describes how experiences from our early life can shape our subconscious mind to employ symptoms out of protection.[18] I saw this playing out most poignantly in how I equated strength with being worthy of love. Just like I'd researched endlessly with each new diagnosis, I went deep into healing places I had never thought needed healing, yielding many of the discoveries in this book.

Another revelation was how I had primed my nervous system to treat life like a fight. Think back to how many times in my story you've read the words *fight* or *battle*. I'm not alone. Our society promotes the use of such terms as "the fight against cancer," or "the battle of mental illness." It speaks of "kicking addiction," and "beating diseases." Amy experienced this sentiment while fueling her "war on Lyme" and wrote, "I was actually throwing the energy of a fight into my very own body. I was stuck in a process of fighting against everything, including *myself*."[19]

In addition to the "fight" mentality, my determination to fix myself was constantly sending my body a danger signal that something was wrong with it, becoming a self-fulfilling prophecy. I'd been the perpetual high scorer in the game of "Whatever You Give the Energy to Wins."

This understanding led me to accept the most profound shift of all: My body is not my enemy. My symptoms are not a show of rebellion. With its innate, inspired wisdom, my body has been doing everything in its power to keep me safe, and symptoms are its only way of communicating. I didn't listen to its whispers and when I wouldn't scream, it screamed for me. The deeper I let this fact sink in, the more it became almost comical that I'd ever thought otherwise. My body had been through hell—partly of my own doing, and partly not. But it had never let me down. In fact, quite the opposite—all the symptoms I'd looked at as betrayal were protection. My body had been shouting its pleas through a megaphone, and I was slowly removing my earplugs.

One concept kept popping up that I didn't understand at first: what it means to be authentically me. I'd found my identity and worth as God's beloved child. Wasn't that the end goal?

In her eye-opening book *The Highly Sensitive Person*, Elaine N. Aron, PhD, examines each stage of life through the lens of being an HSP. She explains how fear of change and failure in our earlier years can make us self-sabotage in ways such as drug abuse and holding on to pain. She describes HSPs as prone to being overly stimulated by the world, which can lead to apparent shyness that is really the inability to express ourselves due to this overstimulation. This can then make our minds go blank and cause social situations or public speaking, for example, to become traumatic, as our nervous system remembers a past failure and self-sabotages. These are just a few of the many manifestations of being an HSP.[20] I've often said that I always need to know the why, and apparently this also applies to the deep inner workings of what makes me, me.

With all this knowledge, I finally understood my entire life, and with that understanding came an acknowledgment of how harshly I had judged myself, compared myself, fallen short of my own expectations, and constantly put myself down. This recognition brought newfound acceptance and freedom to embrace all the parts of me, and to show up in the world as my authentic self! I also realized the physical toll of my ruminating thoughts. The energy expenditure of my constant analysis was exhausting my physical body!

As I embraced this nascent awareness and understanding, I began noticing less need to be in control; it was a slow surrender, but a surrender nonetheless. One morning, while out in California, I was in that sweet spot between being awake and asleep and I found myself praying. I gave the battle and victory over to God and spoke this over my body: *Life is not a fight; you are safe, and safe to heal.* When I fully awoke, I pictured what transpired as a conversation between my mind and my nervous system, and they're on the same page now.

I also found a willingness to dig up what I'd been burying. Several of the specialists I'd seen over the years offered the unsolicited advice to never get pregnant, saying that it would be detrimental to my fragile body. While I had no plans of pregnancy at the time, I still stuffed down my longing and the despair that their words were true. But now—well, I'd been letting my mind wander. I asked Dr. Kelly if she thought pregnancy was wise considering my body's challenges. She answered that I should sit with the question. She suggested that deep down I likely knew the answer, but pregnancy probably wasn't safe. Then she made another profound statement: "I think you were born for even more."

I fought back tears in her office, still with my defenses up. I was already in a tremendous amount of pain as some of the hardware in my skull felt like it was trying to force itself out, causing an egg-shaped lump and a pounding headache. By the time I reached my Airbnb, I was in agony. I employed all my tools—rest, ice, gentle massage, breath work, vagus nerve stimulation, and music. My nervous system settled a bit, and I got up to call my mom. No matter how old I get, she always wants to know how my appointments go. As soon as the word *mom* came into my mind, the floodgates opened, and I didn't stop them.

I curled up on the bed in the fetal position as sobs erupted from barren chambers of my soul that had long ached to bare children. In the depths, I did know the answer; my body was not fit for pregnancy, and it could jeopardize my life. More than that, as grateful as I am for the beauty born from my hard places, I'm not willing to risk my children inheriting EDS and spending a painful life inching toward the day their body fails them.

Black streaks of mascara stained my face like war paint, and as I got up to wash it off, tears still streaming down my cheeks, I remembered the John Piper quote I'd recently put in my journal: "Occasionally weep deeply over the life you hoped would be. Grieve the losses. Feel the pain. Then wash your face, trust God, and embrace the life he's given you."[21] It made even more sense now, and I sobbed some more. Just when I shed all the tears I thought I had, one of my sweet nieces texted me a photo of rice pudding she'd decorated with cinnamon, the way I had taught her. I cried all over again, but this time tears of joy and gratitude. It's just like God to make it known that he sees me, and he's given me these precious kids to love, even if they're not my own.

I went down to the beach, exhausted but in way less pain, and I sat with these thoughts a while longer. In this life of unexpected turns and detours, being a wife and mother was the only thing I thought would be a sure thing. I realized that in addition to the ache of loneliness, I'd been carrying shame for the unmet expectation that left me always alone. I greatly admire my siblings' marriages. They've set the bar quite high, as did my parents' commitment to their vows. And I was never willing to settle. Every time a relationship failed, I traveled the world. I left the Philippines acutely aware that God sees my every desire and loves to delight me but also has wisdom beyond my comprehension. Yes, I had hopes of fulfilled dreams, but was also so brimming with gratitude that I'd written in my journal:

## SPERANZA

February 2, 2015
*I am already blessed more than I can fathom for my whole lifetime. What I have already experienced—if nothing ever changes—is abundantly enough.*

As I let myself mourn the life I always thought would be, I spoke those words over myself once again. *"What I have is abundantly enough. I am enough."* I also decided that I don't need to figure out my future—and good thing! Nothing is impossible with God, and I trust his absolute best. I was reminded of quotes one of my truly inspiring friends posted on Instagram: "Faith is believing that God can. Trust is believing even if He doesn't." And, "The secret in my secret sauce is I don't believe God owes me anything."[22]

I then turned to another deeply healing practice—beach yoga—and by the time I got back to my Airbnb, I was a different person from when I'd walked through the door just a few hours before. This is the power of our emotions on our physical body. The next morning, I woke up in much less pain, and bursting with joy. I wanted to shout from the rooftop! I took a walk and began noticing a deep peace. Peace simply in being. Peace in the moment I was in, peace over my future, and peace in my body. And it occurred to me: This is safety.

Later I was thinking about these events, and the healing that happened when I honestly expressed my emotions. One rationale for keeping everything bottled up was that talking about my situation wasn't going to change it, thus emoting seemed a futile tease. No wonder I spent so long feeling unseen! But vulnerability—even if only between me and God, or in small ways such as admitting to a friend how much pain I'm in, how weary I'm feeling, or that I'd

# WASHING OFF THE WAR PAINT

*Downward dog on Newport Beach*

come to the difficult conclusion that I can't bear children—lightens the burden of carrying everything alone. When I keep my struggles hidden, I miss all the ways God wants to pour out his love, which is sometimes through whispers into my heart, and sometimes through the embrace and listening ear of a friend. Exposing my emotions to the light helps lift me out of darkness!

As I continue to welcome a dialog between my emotions and physical body, and I express instead of repress the hurt and the hard I've spent my life burying, it will no longer feel like one part of me is constantly fighting and betraying the other. Instead, I'll keep finding peace—and safety.

My friend Sean is a brilliant PT Fellow, and at my first appointment, he told me to be honest with him about my pain. He knew I was used to pushing through it, but he wisely said that going forward, when I heard his voice, my nervous system was either going to feel fear or safety, depending on whether I associated it with pain or the lack thereof. He further explained that my symptoms would follow accordingly. Another new concept that clicked with me.

Everything I'd learned about my inner landscape and nervous system gave me the foundation to heal. But transformation doesn't occur from understanding alone. Each time I have an experience that breaks an old pattern, it allows my body to reorient itself around a new norm, thus adding layers of safety to that solid ground beneath me.

They say practice makes perfect, and I was about to get more than I bargained for.

*Admiring the Capital after my neurosurgeon appointment in DC*

Twenty-Nine

# UNTETHERED HEART

MY FIRST PASS of this book didn't include this chapter. But once again, my scars gave rise to profound growth and healing, and this last chapter *had* to be written.

In between trips to California, I'd been working with Dr. Henderson to get answers about the onslaught of neurological symptoms that had returned. The day before the 2024 presidential election, I left DC with his recommendation that I have three more spine surgeries over the next nine months. My tenth surgery, to remove the hardware from my skull and neck, was scheduled for New Year's Eve. Three months after that, my fortieth-birthday present would be a surgery to repair a herniated disc in my thoracic spine, which was tethered to my spinal cord. The third surgery would clean up adhesions in my lumbar spine where I had the base of my spinal cord removed three years prior. After consulting with

Sean, my uber-knowledgeable PT, and Dr. Klinge, who performed that surgery, there was a chance that releasing the tethering in my thoracic spine would provide enough relief so that the third surgery might not be necessary. It was a wait-and-see situation.

The news of needing three more surgeries left me feeling broken beyond repair, a lemon that keeps going back into the auto body shop for more work until eventually the mechanic suggests it's time to trade it in for a properly functioning model. *Will these surgeries and this pain ever end? Or will this perpetuating cycle continue until the day my engine calls it quits?*

I spent several weeks wrestling with the spiraling thought, *What's the point?* In the midst of my angst, I was reminded of several truths. I am broken, because this world is broken. Nothing is as God intended when he created Adam and Eve in that perfect garden. But God sees my broken body, and hates my pain as much as I do, and he feels my agony just as acutely, because he experienced it tenfold. God didn't desert the world when it was fractured by sin—he stepped into it. Jesus walked this earth and endured every physical, spiritual, and emotional battle I will ever face, so that through my tears of affliction, I can look up to him and see my reflection in his tear-stained face.

December 8, 2024

*These times of crying out to God have proven to be healing in so many ways as I've come to see that sorrow and pain can coexist with healing, purpose, joy, and peace. I've written about peace more than anything else, as it has been a truly life-changing word. God's wisdom has guided every step of my journey, and through prayer and moments of stillness in his presence, God's peace has been my guiding light, my star of Bethlehem.*

*I used to think of peace as a lack of anxiety and a sense of calm, rest, and ease, but through an advent devotional I learned the Hebrew word for peace—*shalom*—means completeness or wholeness. What a revelation on so many levels! Thinking of this in terms of my health struggles, my body so often feels broken into pieces, but God steps in over and over again by giving me peace—giving me wholeness. It's in these seasons of adversity that I have a choice to make. I can bury my pain, refuse to admit how hard it's been, and pretend I am strong enough on my own, or I can sit with my brokenness, without allowing my spirit to be crushed, because Jesus gives me the strength to go on and not give up. My Jesus, who sees me, empathizes with me, weeps with me, wraps me in his loving embrace, and invites me into peace, wholeness, and completeness.*

It's no coincidence that as I opened myself up to vulnerability, I was forced into asking for help. My aging mom's health had continued to decline, and for the first time she was unable to be by my side during surgery. Maggie, whom I shared my culinary school adventures with, was happy to come to DC for an early morning at the hospital and a few nights with Spritz at my Airbnb. The night before surgery we had a mini reunion with another comrade, Gregg, and laughed over wild stories from our stages in Italy, as I felt wrapped in the caring arms of my friends.

*Maggie and Spritz exploring DC*

During my occipitocervical fusion, hardware to secure the bone graft was installed to allow my own bone to fuse properly. The New Year's Eve surgery removed the C2 and C3 nerves, along with the hardware that was no longer needed—and was causing systemic reactions in my body. The common denominator was the eight-inch incision that ripped through the muscles of my skull and neck once again. I had marched into every prior surgery, resolute and courageous, fearing that expressing my pain would expose my weakness

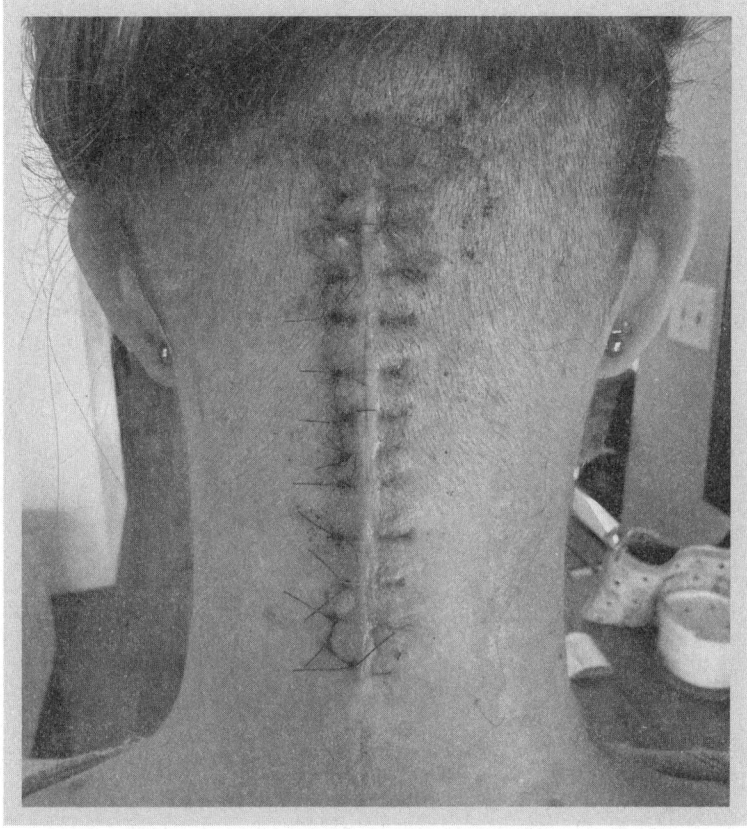

*The second incision, after hardware removal surgery on NYE*

and make me unworthy of love. This time, with my armor stripped off, I experienced, in full, the depths of exactly how much pain I had refused to acknowledge before. But even with this realization, I didn't let my body rest and recover.

Erinn, one of my closest friends from St. Pete, cheerfully came for a few days when Maggie left. She'd only been to DC as a kid, so a mere three days after surgery and hopped up on painkillers, I played tour guide as we explored Georgetown, the Lincoln Memorial, the

# SPERANZA

*With Erinn after the DC blizzard and surgery, my hat covering my 8" incision*

Capitol, and Washington Monument, racking up fourteen thousand steps a day.

A week after surgery, I woke up for my post-op appointment with my heart rate sky high, strained breathing, ice picks of pain raging beneath my bandage, and a headache as blinding as the unprecedented blizzard blanketing DC. It was January 6, 2025, and all available snowplows were ensuring the members of Congress could safely get to the Capitol. The rest of the city was left floundering, including my Tesla Uber whose system was malfunctioning from the weather conditions. We drove on unplowed highways for half an hour, with the windshield fogged up and the windows down!

Dr. Henderson and I reviewed the new MRI of my thoracic spine in preparation for my April surgery, and with one look at my imaging, he said the disc at T6/7 had gotten much worse. It was now pinning my spinal cord to the back side of my spine, and appeared to have herniated through the protective dura, causing a cerebrospinal fluid leak. Surgery could not wait three months. I asked what precautions I needed to take and what symptoms to watch for, and he answered not to bend my spine and to watch out for paralysis.

Suddenly, the words of the neurosurgeon from years before flooded my mind: "You have a herniation in your thoracic spine where only 1 percent of all herniations occur, and if you're unable to walk, come back and see me." Dr. Henderson explained the many risks of this surgery and that he didn't know of another surgeon who would dare perform it. Apparently, the surgeon from way back who spoke those words wanted me paralyzed first so he wasn't liable for paralyzing me during surgery.

In God's providence, Dr. Henderson was one of the few surgeons trained in an advanced method of repairing my spine, called a costotransversectomy approach. He would remove nine centimeters of my seventh rib and the piece of spine it attached to, giving him full visibility of my spinal canal. Then, he'd remove the embedded disc from my spinal cord, without severing the cord itself, and repair the hole in the dura. I also needed a spinal angiogram to map out the arteries in my thoracic spine, so he didn't inadvertently puncture one. Dr. Henderson dictated my visit notes, stating it was a life-threatening situation, while behind my poker face I came close to passing out.

The following hours and days were a flurry of frantic calls and emails lining up surgery, pre-ops, caregivers, travel, and another Airbnb—all from my current Airbnb and while struggling to recover from surgery a week prior.

I'd come so far the past months in understanding the deep workings of my mind and body, but when it came to putting it into practice, I was failing miserably. I was alone for the second week of recovery, and grateful no one was subjected to my hot mess. I had unrelenting headaches, uncontrollable pain, dizziness every time I stood up, and my heart was pounding out of my chest, because I'd just had major surgery! Yet, I was enormously frustrated at my body for not cooperating and was stuck in the mindset of needing to prove my worthiness through strength, yet again.

I had experienced God's beautiful, transformative love, which surpassed my striving. I'd been blessed to have my parents, family, and friends walk beside me through dark days of illness, even when I had nothing to offer them. That indeed was proof I didn't need to earn their love. Yet, I still couldn't grasp that in the middle of my mess, I could be found worthy of love. But whose love was I seeking? With no answer, I did what I'd always done best: I put my armor back on, and I marched into battle. It was me against the world, and if I wasn't strong, who was going to carry me? Two weeks after surgery, I flew home, met by the loving arms of my sister and niece, and I returned to work—and working out—careful not to bend my spine, but pushing through tremendous pain.

On a telehealth consult with the doctor who would perform the angiogram, he explained that the procedure was done under general anesthesia and would take up to five hours as he snaked a catheter through the left and right side of all thirty-two segments of my spine. He'd have to move extra cautiously, as my weakened connective tissue put me at higher risk of arterial puncture. He also planned to check on the small aneurysm in my brain, found during my angiogram a few years back. My surgery was scheduled for Valentine's Day, and the angiogram was to be three days before that. Surgery is a huge trauma to your body, and the effects of anesthesia alone can take six months to detox from your system. I was struggling to recover from one surgery and was about to have two more just days apart. Compounding my angst, I had no one to be there with me. I was alone.

My swirling thoughts put me back in the middle of the DC blizzard, snow pelting my face through the open windows. But for lack of a more fitting metaphor, God was in the driver's seat of that Tesla, navigating those snowy, unplowed roads. I gave up my steering wheel a long time ago, although I had too often taken it back. That week, my pastor preached on the promises of God. The essence was that because he always keeps his promises, I can claim them as done, even before seeing their fulfillment.

Shored up on a lifetime of God's faithfulness, I began thanking him for the many ways he was going to come through on his promise to use even this for my good. And that posture allowed me to see God's handprints everywhere. Gratitude actually changes neural pathways—it's impossible to experience anxiety and thankfulness at the same time! Anchored in God's steadfast love, I faced those most challenging weeks with the joyful assurance that he was right there beside me, weaving a breathtaking tapestry. I absolutely had moments of fear and panic. But instead of tiptoeing into an impossible situation, I marched in boldly, and with the eager expectation of how God was going to delight, surprise, and provide for me, like he always has.

When I arrived at the hospital for my angiogram, I discovered that I already knew my nurse, Ara, because heading into a prior surgery she redressed my PICC line when it wouldn't stop bleeding. This was the first assurance of many that I wasn't alone. The doctor gave me the good news that he only needed to map out the arteries in my thoracic spine and brain—not the entire spine like he'd thought—and when the anesthesia team didn't show up, he said I looked like someone who'd be good at staying still. He performed the angiogram while I was awake, which I wouldn't recommend, but I was grateful not to need anesthesia twice that week. A catheter went into the right femoral artery in my groin, and once it had carefully inched its way to my brain the doctor repeated, "Don't breathe, don't move, don't swallow." Then, he injected the hot lava and took X-rays. Behind my closed eyes, I could somehow see lightning bolts electrifying a dark night's sky.

Partway through the procedure, one of the sedatives made my whole body chatter uncontrollably and my heart rate spike so high I thought I was going to pass out, but I had to lie completely still. I started reciting over and over again, "You will keep in perfect peace all who trust in you, all whose thoughts are fixed on you" (Isaiah 26:3). That verse was my mantra through the rest of the procedure, as the catheter moved down to my thoracic spine, injecting fiery dye into each artery. After three more hours of lying flat, the arterial collagen plug held. I was given yet more encouraging news that my aneurism hadn't grown. Then, I was discharged to my Airbnb in the midst of another DC blizzard!

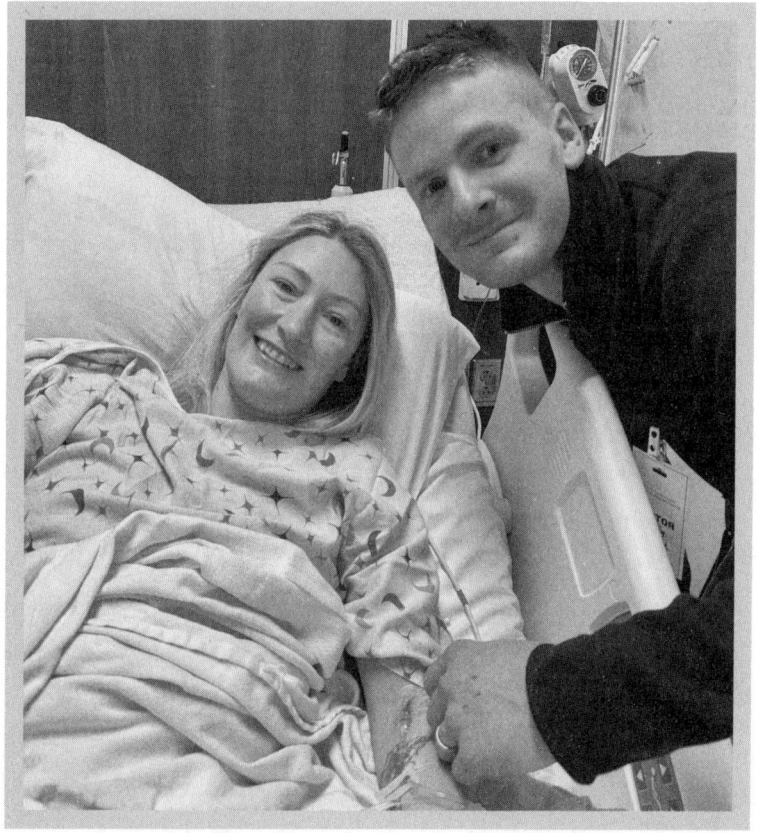

*A hug from my nephew, Tadju, after waking up from thoracic surgery*

In more last-minute provisions, my sweet little redheaded nephew Tadju, who is all grown up now, and his equally adorable wife, Katie, flew to DC the night before my surgery. Tadju cheerily drove me to the hospital at 5 a.m. the next morning. As I'd done so many times before, I told each new team my list of allergies: adhesive tape, the Dermabond used to seal incisions, famotidine for stabilizing mast cells during anesthesia, codeine to control pain, and cephalosporin antibiotics administered prophylactically. I also told them that I needed a scopolamine patch for post-anesthesia nausea, and that because I had EDS, I needed a glide scope for intubation; and that my occipitocervical fusion meant limited mobility and the need for extra caution with my neck. Additionally, I was only six weeks out from hardware removal, had pain and numbness in most of my head, and a tender and prominent MINX plug in my right femoral artery from an angiogram three days prior. Whew.

The assisting surgeon, Dr. Rosenbaum, informed me that between him and Dr. Henderson, they were bringing seventy years of experience to the operating room! He asked what surgery I was having done and without a blink, I answered, "a right T6/7 costo-transversectomy approach for a discectomy, intradural repair of disc, and duroplasty." His eyes grew wide as he exclaimed that no patient had ever recited a procedure so perfectly! Still the overachiever. Some things never change!

Before I was wheeled away to the OR, Dr. Henderson prayed that God would hold me in the palm of his hand, restore my health, and fill everyone in that operating room with his Holy Spirit.

As I came to through layers of consciousness, I realized I was still intubated and my eyes were taped shut. I heard a voice tell me to take a deep breath as the long tube was pulled from my airway. I gagged and coughed as pain exploded through my rib cage. I heard Dr. Rosenbaum's voice tell me there was no cerebrospinal fluid leak after all, that the catheter was coming out, and I'd be able to get up within a few hours. There was a flurry of activity around me. I was repeatedly asked to move my feet and squeeze my hands. Once I was in recovery, Dr. Henderson came in with wide eyes, revealing a mix of fear, shock, and awe under his furrowed brow. Then, he

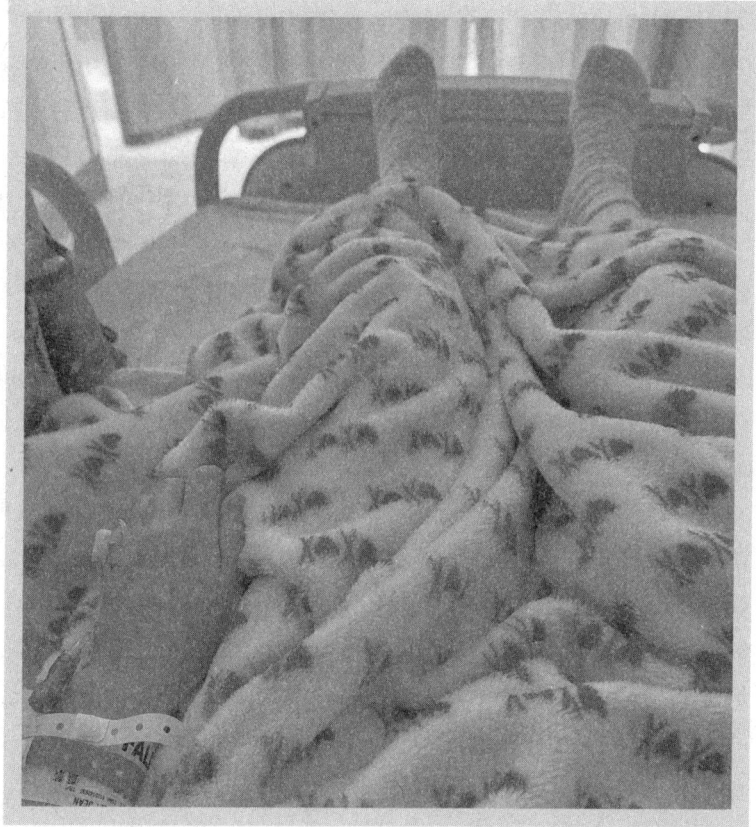

*Wiggling my toes in my hospital room after Valentine's surgery*

spoke words I will never forget: "It is only by God's grace you aren't paralyzed."

I didn't stop moving my feet and wiggling my toes for several hours, as I lay there overwhelmed by God's grace and hand of healing on my life, all the while praising my loving and merciful God. In the same breath, I had never felt so beat-up. As the grogginess wore off, I started taking inventory of my body and noticed over a dozen needle pricks and bruises on my arms and legs from neuromonitoring, as well as a few from blown veins. My scalp burned from being clamped in place and my lips were swollen from the breathing tube. My jaw, neck, and head ached from whatever position I'd been contorted into. The plug in my groin was throbbing, and bolts of pain struck my rib cage when I coughed, laughed, or breathed. Within a few hours, I got up and noticed dark red bruises on my eyelids. But all of this was overshadowed by awestruck gratitude, and I spent the afternoon periodically doing laps around the PACU—because I could. Beauty entwined with pain. That evening, as I was being wheeled to an MRI, my sweet nurse, Ara, came to visit. Another reminder I wasn't alone.

Every time I spoke with Dr. Henderson, the same look of disbelief washed over his face. In his nearly forty years as a surgeon, mine was the worst herniation he had ever seen, and one of the most challenging surgeries. The disc had been herniated for so long, it was as hard as a tooth, when it was supposed to have a jelly-like consistency. What's more, it had embedded itself in my spinal cord, rendering it unable to move within my spinal canal. There were miracles in each nuance. The hardened disc should have broken through the fragile sheath around my spinal cord, and the magnitude of the herniation alone could have paralyzed me. Neuromonitoring showed I had lost the spinal cord signal in my right leg. Each cut to free the disc from my spinal cord threatened to leave me unable to use my legs. And the major thoracic artery came into my spine at the same level as my herniation. If the artery was clipped, I would have been paralyzed from my waist up.

Dr. Henderson pointed out on my MRI where he had left a small amount of disc material. The remaining disc didn't pose a threat but was too close to the artery to be safely removed. God

# UNTETHERED HEART

*Recovering from Valentine's surgery at my Airbnb in DC*

had answered his prayer in abundance, filling him with his Spirit, guiding his skilled hands, and giving him wisdom and restraint.

For the first week after surgery, I was on the verge of throwing up, and standing brought on immediate orthostatic symptoms—a racing heart, dizziness, headache, and worsened nausea. The medication to control my pain was exacerbating these symptoms, so I stopped it. My rib cage stung like a rib had been ripped out, because one had been. It felt like my insides were trying to make their way out of the gaping hole in my spine, and razor blades of pain ripped through my scalp and neck from that surgery just weeks prior. But, it was a second chance—a redo.

Rather than being frustrated at my body for its rebellion, I listened. My symptoms screamed when I stood up, so I took it as a request to lie down. When the pain was almost too much to bear, I acknowledged how much my body had endured and thanked it for never failing me. Amidst the physical and emotional exhaustion, I rested without shame for not being productive. In actuality, I was doing the most important work. Honoring my body's requests sent a signal to my nervous system that the danger was over and I was safe to heal.

One afternoon a few weeks later, while lying in the sunshine with Spritz contently plopped on my chest, I was thinking about the enormous shift that had taken place. When tired or in pain, I'd been continuing to let myself unapologetically rest instead of chastising my symptoms and pushing through. To my surprise, I often felt drastically better after a short reprieve! My new softness was met with a responsiveness I'd never experienced before. I envisioned a helpless baby, who requires each one of its needs tended to before it feels safe enough to drift blissfully off to sleep, and I had a thought. *What would my life have looked like if I approached each one of my body's primal wants and needs in this same way? With this kind of love? It's not too late to start.*

A few months prior, I shared with my mom the misbeliefs I held since my childhood, their impact on my life, and the ways that unraveling them was helping me heal. This honest conversation was restorative for us both. The next time I visited her, a photo

# UNTETHERED HEART

*Me as a baby, on the beach with my beautiful mom*

of my beautiful mother lying on the beach and baby me snuggled close to her chest had been placed in my childhood bedroom. I am completely at peace in the photo, and my mom is adoringly smiling down at me. I had always felt wrapped in love. At the same time, I also perceived my environment as one of punishment, judgement, and fear. In believing I was unwanted, those traits became burdens strapped to my back—a penance of sorts.

Somewhere deep down, I never let go of the idea that I wasn't wanted, and I had spent my life punishing myself for existing. The love I was so afraid of losing by showing weakness and being deemed unworthy was my own.

## SPERANZA

Remember the verse I prayed on my thirty-ninth birthday, ten months prior? "And I will give you a new heart, and I will put a new spirit in you. I will take out your stony, stubborn heart and give you a tender, responsive heart" (Ezekiel 36:26). My herniated thoracic disc was hard, like stone, and the nerves coming out of my damaged spine went directly into my heart. Maybe all those years of not loving myself had literally hardened my heart, and my calcified thoracic disc was both the physical manifestation and the tool my body used to finally get my attention.

God had certainly drawn my focus to the ways he was at work, and how he had used this surgery on Valentine's Day—a day devoted to love—to do so much more than heal my body. He gently showed me that I needed love for myself. By blocking myself from love when I didn't think I was worthy of it, I was filtering all my experiences through that same lens, leaving me unable to receive the untainted love God was longing to sweep me away in. My love will always be a flawed version, but in keeping my eyes upward, I have the perfect model from whom to learn. As I let myself be washed in this unbounded love, I will find safety.

There is no fear *or lack of safety* in love, but perfect love casts out fear or *any feeling of being unsafe*. For fear *or lack of safety* has to do with punishment, and whoever fears *or feels unsafe* has not been perfected in love. (This is a paraphrase of 1 John 4:18.)

It amazes me how a verse I've read countless times can suddenly—like a veil being lifted—assume new and profound meaning. My trials refined me by fire, burning away the lies I believed as truth, and I can wholeheartedly proclaim, I am so grateful.

I can't say that writing a book like this has always been a dream of mine. I'd share accounts of my horrible/hysterical dates with my sister-in-law, and she always joked I should write a book one day. But airing my dirty laundry with the world? Never! In fact, I had a minor panic attack a few chapters into writing this! But let's go back to the question I grappled with: *What does it means to be authentically me?* Yes, my goal each day is to be a light. I am standing on two feet and cooking professionally because of God's grace over my life, his strength that gets me through the very hardest of days, and the healing he's done and is doing in this body that so often feels broken, yet in him is whole. So how could I not shine for him?! Being authentically me *doesn't* mean pretending life has always been so bright, or that it isn't still a struggle. And it doesn't mean covering up the parts I don't find worthy. In fact, it means just the opposite. Being my true self means being vulnerable, and it means letting the world see my victories—and, yes, also my mess, my brokenness, and my scars.

The more I experienced, the more compelled I felt to share those experiences, because in sharing my story—the highs and the lows—maybe I can help someone else heal.

Are you leaning into concepts that are new to you? Take the leap—your life will never be the same. At least that's my hope. *Speranza.*

*Dusk at il Ponte Vecchio in Florence, my 40th birthday trip to Italy*

# EPILOGUE

I'M STANDING UNDER the marble arches of Florence's Piazza della Repubblica, finally back in Italy twenty years after my life-changing semester here. The Vivaldi players have been replaced by the faint laughter of children on a carousel, and there's an Apple Store behind me as I write these words on my iPhone. Walking the familiar cobblestone streets, I was surprised to see third-wave coffee shops serving cold brew, and juice bars touting superfood smoothies. I wove through crowds waiting in line at an Insta-famous sandwich shop, next to Tuscan osterias frozen in time. Florence is wildly different and very much the same. A lot like me.

I was supposed to spend my fortieth birthday in DC, recovering from my eleventh surgery, but in January, when the timeline was moved up, I had an idea: *Go to Italy instead!* Four months after my Valentine's Day operation, I returned to the place that had been patiently holding some of my most cherished moments. Fittingly, this city that birthed the Renaissance had also breathed new life into my listless soul, awakening my heart to the splendor of my Creator and igniting the spark which fueled my culinary career. I'd always

# EPILOGUE

felt most at ease, most at peace, most at home, most myself in this land that pulses at a slower beat, and I was so ready to embrace it once again.

As I settled into the familiar rhythm, walked the winding streets, marveled at the massive Duomo, stumbled upon favorite shops, photographed Insta-worthy vignettes, sipped a spritz near my former school, and dunked the saltless bread into peppery Tuscan olive oil, I felt a shift. My nervous system recognized this voice of safety and responded. Suddenly a door appeared in that thick pane of glass, and as I stepped over the threshold, the innermost parts of me let out an exhale, unraveling the tight, tense, fist of protection I'd been coiled into. I looked down in awestruck wonder and gratitude at the word tattooed onto my wrist: *Speranza*. And my whole body let out one giant sigh.

# ACKNOWLEDGMENTS

YOU'VE HEARD THE saying, "It takes a village to raise a child," but to truly flourish, we need a tribe for our entire life. I would like to pour out my gratitude to the multitudes who each played a distinct role, yet together have carried me to this place where writing my story was possible.

Mom and Dad, thank you for your unwavering belief in the omniscience of God, and for your faith that he indeed is my true healer and the architect of my life. Thank you for being my loudest cheerleaders and most supportive fans. I forever love you both. To my siblings and your spouses, thank you for the many ways you model excellence to me and for your encouragement and love. To my nephews and nieces, I love you all more than words can say, and thank you for being beacons of light in my life. And to my extended family—my favorite memories are the one's we've made while enjoying great food and investing in each other's lives. Thank you for the many ways you have shaped my story. I love you all.

Kelly T. thanks for getting me through high school with a smile on my face, and for being a phone call away, no matter how much

## ACKNOWLEDGMENTS

time has passed. Mrs. Moz—A.P. American Lit laid the foundation for a life of writing, yet more profoundly, thank you for your love and investment in my life. And to all my PVCA family, thank you for teaching me to seek truth, think rationally, and always persevere to reach the prize.

Elissa, my BFF—you changed my life with that first text, and whether we're cooking, traveling, laughing, or crying, it feels like I've come home whenever we're together. Thank you for your unwavering love, support, and encouragement. I love you to Cambodia, Vietnam, and the Philippines and back. To my Filipino single ladies, thank you for embracing me, your very own Elsa, and for showing me the depths of God's love through how you love me and others. Erinn and Nicole—you've made St. Pete home. Thank you for beach walks, long talks, wine nights, and for your enduring friendship even when I've struggled to always show up.

My nurses-turned-cherished-friends, Lisa and Heather, I am immensely grateful for the love, care, and friendship you've poured into my life. Thank you for loving me, no matter how difficult my veins were, or how hopeless my situation sometimes felt. And to the entire team at BRM— thank you for holding my hand through what often seemed like unending days of pain. Thank you for never losing hope in my healing, even on the darkest of nights. To Dr. Klinge, thank you for your caring spirit and skilled hands, and for your encouragement to share my story. Dr. Henderson, I am beyond grateful for the mighty ways God has used you to restore my health. Thank you for your prayers over me before each and every surgery, and for inviting God to lead and guide you. Sean, thank you for so cheerfully and faithfully keeping me standing tall each week (and Spritzie thanks you for the noggin scratch). Kelly M., thank you for

## ACKNOWLEDGMENTS

truly seeing me, for wanting to know my story, and for your message of hope. You showed me that vulnerability was safe, and set me on a path of profound healing, for which I am eternally grateful. This is only the beginning of so many more chapters to come!

To the entire team at Forefront Books, including Justin, Kia, Lauren, and Landry, thank you for diligently and joyfully bringing my book to life. To my developmental editor, Hope, you are a divinely orchestrated gift. Thank you for making my book shine, and for your beautiful heart toward my story. Topher, my writing guide, thank you for helping me chip away everything that wasn't the angel. Mariana, thank you for your exquisite photography, and thank you even more for so honestly sharing your soul. Thank you to my marketing and PR teams, for helping bring my book to many!

To my army of prayer warriors from all corners of the world, I am so grateful for you. Thank you for holding me up in the grasp of your intercession when I had no strength left. Thank you for your endless cards and notes of encouragement. And thank you for the enduring reminders to keep my eyes fixed above, because in Him, there is always hope.

# NOTES

1. Jill Carnahan, *Unexpected: Finding Resilience Through Functional Medicine, Science, and Faith* (Broadleaf Books, 2023).
2. Savannah Guthrie, *Mostly What God Does: Reflections on Seeking and Finding His Love Everywhere* (Thomas Nelson, 2024).
3. Jill Carnahan, *Unexpected*, 61.
4. Carnahan, *Unexpected*, 61.
5. Timothy Keller, *Jesus the King: Understanding the Life and Death of the Son of God*.
6. Amy B. Scher, *How to Heal Yourself When No One Else Can: A Total Self-Healing Approach for Mind, Body, and Spirit* (Llewellyn Publications, 2016).
7. Don Piper with Cecil Murphey, *90 Minutes in Heaven* (Fleming H. Revell, 2004).
8. Henry Sweets, "Craft: Tom Colicchio's Restaurant Experiment in Understatement Still Proves Less Is Indeed More," *Edible Manhattan*, October 2011, https://edibleman-hattan.com/uncategorized/craft-at-10-tom-colicchios-experiment-in-understatement-still-proves-that-on-the-plate-less-is-indeed-more/.
9. Carnahan, *Unexpected*, 139.
10. Guthrie, *Mostly What God Does*.
11. "Oceans," track 12 on Hillsong, *Zion*, Hillsong Music Australia, 2013.
12. C. S. Lewis, *The Problem of Pain* (HarperOne, 2001), 91.
13. Carnahan, *Unexpected*.
14. *Get Smart*, directed by Peter Segal (Warner Bros., 2008), DVD.

# NOTES

15. Jim Denison, "Lauren Daigle Urges Christians to Pray for Courage," Denison Forum, April 17, 2024, https://www.denisonforum.org/daily-article/lauren-daigle-urges-christians-to-pray-for-courage/.

16. "Don't You Give Up on Me," track 11 on Brandon Lake, *House of Miracles*, Bethel Music, 2020.

17. Maria Shriver, (@mariashriver), "How are you creating change?" Instagram, April 24, 2024, https://www.instagram.com/p/C6JmsM9x_9N.

18. Scher, *How to Heal Yourself When No One Else Can*.

19. Scher, *How to Heal Yourself When No One Else Can*, 50.

20. Elaine N. Aron, *The Highly Sensitive Person: How to Thrive When the World Overwhelms You* (Broadway Books, 1996).

21. John Piper, "Embrace the Life God Has Given You," *Desiring God*, audio transcript, March 10, 2007, https://www.desiringgod.org/embrace-the-life-god-has-given-you.

22. Michele Struss, (@hispaintbrush_michele), "I was so humbled to be asked..." Instagram, June 11, 2024, https://www.instagram.com/p/C8GE16cP1Gz/.

# ABOUT THE AUTHOR

ASHLEY ONDRICK is a personal chef, health coach, and storyteller whose journey through pain, healing, and resilience has shaped every aspect of her life and work.

While studying economics and finance, a semester abroad forever altered her path, awakening her to the beauty of her Creator and igniting her culinary aspirations. After refining her craft in kitchens from Italy to New York City to Singapore, Ashley spent years executing farm-to-table events in the greater Boston area. She later founded A (Mostly) Healthy Chef in Tampa Bay, where she helps clients use food as both medicine and celebration—teaching them to eat with intention, gain confidence in the kitchen, and reclaim ownership of their health.

A longtime advocate for the transformative power of microfinance, Ashley spent a year living in the Philippines and traveling throughout Southeast Asia. Her volunteer work in this field has continued for nearly two decades.

Remarkably, Ashley has also faced immense physical challenges, including a connective tissue disorder, anorexia, Lyme disease, and

## ABOUT THE AUTHOR

chronic pain. In writing Speranza, she felt called to share her arduous yet faith-filled journey to give her suffering purpose and invite others to do the same. Through years of healing—and the tension between control and surrender—she has dismantled false beliefs about her worth and God's love, ultimately discovering the wholeness she had been seeking all along.